parks of the 21st century

parks of the 21st century

reinvented landscapes, reclaimed territories

Victoria Newhouse

with Alex Pisha

New York · Paris · London · Milan

contents

why now?

The stone which the builders rejected has become the cornerstone.
—Psalm 118

Following pages: Brooklyn Bridge Park, Brooklyn, New York (page 138); Renaissance Park, Chattanooga, Tennessee (page 96); Parque Bicentenario, Mexico City, Mexico (page 204); Parc Dräi Eechelen, Luxembourg City, Grand Duchy of Luxembourg (page 280)

Many of the abundant new parks the world over have a curious resonance with this verse from Psalm 118, which is rendered in similar terms elsewhere in the New Testament. These new green spaces occupy terrain that has long been considered worthless—industrial riverfronts saturated with chemical residue, airport expanses ironed smooth and stripped of vegetation, and, ironically, waterlogged quarries. For indeed, just as the rejected stone became the essential centerpiece, this spurned land has been transformed into public open areas that in their turn reinvigorate underused or undervalued urban areas.

So what has precipitated this worldwide burst of park building, especially parks on reclaimed land? And why have parks become more important to our well-being than ever before?

The confluence of three conditions worldwide has provided the impetus for today's new parks. The first was the launch of the environmental movement. Two scholars—the marine biologist and conservationist Rachel Carson (*Silent Spring*, 1962) and the landscape architect and regional planner Ian L. McHarg (*Design with Nature*, 1969)—brought public awareness to the ubiquitous fragility of the natural world. McHarg in particular revolutionized thinking about the relationship between nature and the built environment. In the United States, he inspired the creation of the Environmental Protection Agency (EPA) and the enactment of the Clean Air Act in 1970, which was followed by the Clean Water Act in 1972, the Safe Drinking Water Act in 1974, and a slew of related legislation. The myriad issues McHarg raised are even more pressing today as the effects of climate change become more widely known.

Since the 1970s, environmental awareness has increased, in particular as regards the planet's warming as a result of burning fossil fuels. Alterations to the climate system have produced extreme weather: floods, storms, heat waves, wildfires, droughts. Of these, flooding is most relevant to the subject of this book. In addition to causing serious economic repercussions, floods claim human lives; contaminate air and water, undermining public health; and endanger animals and insects, threatening ecological balance.

The second factor is the advent of the post-industrial age. This term, too, was popularized by two eminent scholars, in this case the sociologists Alain Touraine (*The Post-Industrial Society,* 1971) and Daniel Bell (*The Coming of Post-Industrial Society*, 1973),

who used the word to describe the conversion into a service society of what for over two hundred years had been a worldwide manufacturing society. Overnight, countless factories, together with the associated storage, moving, and shipping facilities, became obsolete, leaving once-beautiful natural shorelines scarred and contaminated and major urban sites empty and inaccessible to the public. Already by the 1960s, Boston had begun to transform old wharves along the southern and eastern edges of the city's peninsula for other uses. Baltimore began a similar transition at the same time, and innumerable riversides would follow suit. These spots are known as brownfields—land contaminated by a previous use—which is a description that could be applied to most of the parks here.

Inland areas had also been given over to industry. In the United States, the Rust Belt extends west from central New York State to southeast Wisconsin. In Germany, the Ruhr Valley was home to numerous industries, including three hundred coal mines. In France, the mines of Nord-pas-de-Calais, the country's northernmost region, provide a further example. Ohio's highly publicized fire of 1969, caused by industrial pollution on the Cuyahoga River in Cleveland, was another occurrence that fueled passions about the environment.

By the mid-1990s, Charles Waldheim, professor of landscape architecture at the Harvard Graduate School of Design and director of the Office for Urbanization, was advocating an approach he called "landscape urbanism," that is, making landscape rather than architecture the stimulus for contemporary urbanism. Waldheim considers landscape relevant because so much of the built environment has been rendered obsolete or inadequate as a result of social, technological, and environmental change. His concepts have been embraced by leading landscape architects like James Corner, Michael Van Valkenburgh, and Walter Hood in the United States; Kathryn Gustafson in the United Kingdom; Michel Desvigne in France; and Kongjian Yu in China. The parks described in *Parks of the 21st Century* illustrate the landscape urbanism strategy.

The third consideration behind new parks is the rapid erosion of public space, which began with mid-twentieth century suburbanization; now, in the early 2020s, public space is increasingly replaced by commercial initiatives, such as malls, that are policed to bolster private property and personal security. Social media may be today's public space, posits Beatriz Colomina, an architectural historian, theorist, and curator at Princeton University.

The decrease in size and availability of public space means that in addition to streets, inundated in 2020 by protests of racial injustice, parks endure as one of the few remaining physical places where people can come together to debate, demonstrate, and demand change. Well-known protest sites include the People's Park in Berkeley, California; the Speakers' Corner in Hyde Park in London; and, more recently, Tiananmen Square in Beijing and Taksim Square in Istanbul. President Donald Trump's June 4, 2020, imposition of eight-foot-high fences around what have been for 220 years the public areas of Lafayette Square and the Ellipse in Washington, DC, is one of the most egregious recent removals of public space.

For my own part, I came to recognize new and unfamiliar applications of landscape architecture in the course of writing my last book, *Chaos and Culture*. As part of an in-depth examination of the design and construction of Renzo Piano's Stavros Niarchos Foundation Cultural Center in Athens, Greece, I studied the landscape component of the complex. The landscape architect, Deborah Nevins, developed the concept in conjunction with Piano; their ideas pointed to the developments in landscape design that inspired me to write about the subject.

As I began my research, I became intrigued by public parks built on top of existing infrastructure, whether a Texas freeway or a thousand-year-old abbey. To locate recent (mostly post-2010) parks that fit these parameters, Alex Pisha, a landscape designer and writer, and I traveled as widely as time and practicality allowed. We were not able to showcase beautiful new landscapes in many parts of the world, including Japan, Australia, the Middle East, and Russia. And certain practitioners we admire greatly—Martha Schwartz and Walter Hood to name but two—have not yet created landscapes that meet our specific criteria. I am grateful for Alex's collaboration in choosing and describing the landscapes here.

The High Line in Manhattan is a well-known example of the sort of park we looked for. In terms of attendance, public awareness of landscape architecture, and would-be imitators, it is probably the most successful park of the twenty-first century. The converted railway opened to the public in 2009; by 2015, its designers, James Corner Field Operations and Diller Scofidio + Renfro, were able to document sixty similar projects around the world. And by 2019, the park, which had been expanded to 1.45 miles, was receiving 8 million visitors each year—more than the Metropolitan Museum of Art (7.4 million in 2018), the Museum of Modern Art (3 million in 2018), and the Statue of Liberty (4.3 million in 2018). Even the reduced spaces of the High Line have not deterred the hordes of visitors who in good weather can make the park feel like the subway at rush hour. That a repurposed rail line can outpace storied cultural and historic destinations is a strong signal of today's heightened interest in landscape architecture.

The new green spaces demonstrate the adaptive reuse of obsolete railroads and airports; they cap highways and revitalize abandoned industrial and shipping sites; they transform former quarries and military facilities. The sites for these new parks were usually contaminated, sometimes dangerously so, by their previous uses, which left behind conditions that required complete removal, or at least specialized cleaning, of polluted soil. The designers of these projects have gone beyond the rehabilitation procedures required by the High Line in presenting parks with varied ecologies using sustainable construction and maintenance procedures.

The Sumerian *Epic of Gilgamesh* (c. 2000 BCE) contains the first known literary description of a park-like landscape, and Sumerian parks became the prototypes for Persian *pairidiza* (paradises)—walled hunting parks. In China, and later in Europe, carefully guarded royal animal preserves or hunting parks in the countryside originated in the Shang dynasty (1600–1050 BCE). In China, these also symbolized an earthly paradise. The third century BCE saw the beginning of megaparks, which often featured elaborate constructions; these vast, open areas were used in part for agriculture and pasturage. Throughout Chinese history, the custom of allowing commoners to enter these royal preserves to gather fuel and catch game came and went.

Both relatively small gardens and large hunting parks were important status symbols for the rulers and elite members of European and Asian society. Only sacred groves in Europe and Asia, trees and springs associated with the worship of a deity, were not off limits to the public. However, in Rome in 55 BCE, Pompey the Great opened the first public park, and this amenity soon spread to cities throughout the empire, forecasting the democratization of parks in the nineteenth century. In the seventeenth century, several of London's royal hunting grounds, such as St. James and Hyde Park, were opened to the public on a limited basis.

Contemporary parks, unlike walled gardens of old—the Garden of Eden, the medieval *hortus conclusus*, and, more recently, the Jardin du Luxembourg in Paris and Central and Prospect Parks in New York City—almost always contain seamless transitions to the surrounding city, meshing with their environments. Paths frequently align with adjacent streets, and boundaries are blurred. For example, at the Parc aux Angéliques in Bordeaux, it is unclear just where the green space begins: development is planned within the park, which is set apart by a simple incline. At Lorsch in Germany, too, the park and town blend together. While some parks in this discussion have definite edges, all share an effort to connect with the larger context. Even elevated parks such as the High Line and the 606 relate visually to their surroundings.

Nor are today's landscapes always the peaceful oases parks used to be. They are often located in noisy places—under traffic-clogged bridges or beside highways or train tracks—and programming is also at odds with quiet serenity. Among the events that take place in contemporary parks are endless numbers of staged performances, including concerts of popular and classical music, theater productions, and film screenings; sports tournaments; classes, from yoga to nature walks; and numerous ethnic and seasonal festivals.

An interest in remediating brownfield sites arose in tandem with an interest in addressing abandoned structures. The 1970s saw both New York City artists taking over empty loft buildings for studios and landscape architect Richard Haag creating Gas Works Park (1975) in Seattle, Washington, on the site of a former coal gasification plant. Derelict industrial properties suitable for adaptive reuse vary dramatically in size and shape, and designers regularly have to reconcile their visions with eccentric footprints.

With open land growing increasingly scarce, these new green spaces reclaim territory and activate interstitial areas. My discovery of one such park, the Dequindre Cut in Detroit, was an additional inspiration. That one of the nation's poorest cities would look to a landscape to improve the state of its finances fired my interest in the role of nature in reviving abandoned sites worldwide. The Dequindre Cut (part of the Joe Louis Greenway) has expanded the possibilities of repurposed railroads. It introduces green space to areas of the city where it was lacking, and, like other linear parks, it connects widely disparate neighborhoods. For a fairly modest project, it has had a powerful local influence in its creation of public space, its embrace of public art, and its demonstration of options for increased green space.

Alex and I began our selection with areas that had provided or still provide means of transport—rail, car, and airplane. We noted that landscapes with similar histories, such as abandoned rail yards and rail lines, could be repurposed in a

variety of different ways that would result in a variety of different parks. The Coulée Verte René-Dumont (Promenade Plantée), built on an obsolete railroad in Paris, is planted following a gardenesque strategy; the Natur-Park Schöneberger Südgelände in Berlin uses an approach of planting waste areas to make a successional forest on a site with vestiges of rail lines, turntables, and repair yards. The tremendous variety available in repurposing single-use sites encouraged us to organize the parks according to previous use rather than chronologically or geographically.

Highway caps must be considered invented sites. Capping major highways is an increasingly common procedure as noisy, carbon monoxide–choked superhighways proliferate around the world. While these caps do not remediate land in the traditional sense, they help to reconnect neighborhoods cut off from one another by highways and add to public space. Both Klyde Warren Park in Dallas, Texas, and Park Over-Bos in the Netherlands cap generous segments of major highways. OLIN and Gehry Partners have developed a proposal to build landscaped, bridge-like covers over segments of the sadly mistreated Los Angeles River.

Former airports offer one of the most extreme examples of interference with nature. Not only was vegetation removed, but any semblance of their original topography was obliterated. At Alter Flugplatz in the suburbs of Frankfurt, a carefully devised framework initiated a process of reclamation. The famous Tempelhof Airport in Berlin is an exaggerated version of this phenomenon. After the airfield was decommissioned, the public commandeered the site and refused to allow any constructed intervention whatsoever, including a thoughtful scheme by GROSS.MAX. The rejected project is one of the great missed opportunities in adaptive reuse of landscapes.

After our study of former places of transportation, we turned to industrial premises, quarries, and military locales. Historically, factories have been installed on riverfronts, which provided water power and connection to shipping and rail networks. But several factors combined in the transition to the post-industrial era to eliminate the usefulness of most of these facilities: increased use of trucking and the introduction of container ships in the 1950s; the globalization of world trade in the 1970s. The "before" circumstances of New York City's East River and Shanghai's waterfront are examples of the appalling state of such sites. These conditions, along with riverfront highway construction, deterred public access to waterways.

More parks have been built on derelict industrial sites on the waterfront than in any other type of location, in part because the beauty of the settings and the attraction of water activities have advocated using these locations. In some cases, notably Shanghai and New York, which I discuss in detail, park systems run for miles beside a river. These large-scale interventions have the capacity to rehabilitate key parts of a city.

Inland parks on industrial sites, too, present distinct solutions to the wounds inflicted by industry. The stunning revival of a Japanese water purification plant in Changchun, China (the former capital of Japan-occupied Manchuria), does just this. The same can be said of Mexico City's Parque Bicentenario and Bordeaux's Jardin Botanique. They present two very different visions of instructional parks, the former an assembly of five small parks designed around specific ecologies and the latter a venue for investigating local natural resource management and biodiversity.

Material extraction, such as quarrying, is one of the oldest and most destructive of human activities. Former quarries are characterized by polluted wastewater, degraded soil, even contaminated air. Most disused quarries were considered uninhabitable: too expensive to develop or remediate, too large or small, too isolated. More recently, abandoned extraction sites have attracted the attention of local governments and landscape architects, particularly in China. Among these refurbished quarries are the Quarry Garden in Shanghai and the extensive Huadu Lake Park in Guangzhou.

What we call strongholds are buildings or areas that have suffered intense armed strife, as in the case of the Carolingian Abbey of Lorsch in Germany, or served a military purpose, like the forts in Luxembourg City and Utrecht, and the training areas in Tianjin and Fuzhou. Like quarries, these facilities have outlived their initial purposes and have been transformed into stunning parklands.

We have also included four of the innumerable landscape projects in development around the world. Each one addresses a different problem. The small Graffiti Pier Park in Philadelphia by Studio Zewde is a rehabilitation of an obsolete pier. Sanlin Eco Valley in Shanghai by Tom Leader Studio is a medium-sized illustration of President Xi Jinping's goal of beautifying China and improving the country's environmental quality: over 80 percent of that country's cities suffer air pollution that kills 1.2 million people each year. The attempts to upgrade the Los Angeles River and the former Fresh Kills landfill in Staten

Island are two of the largest landscape projects progressing anywhere in the world in 2021.

As the most manipulated natural waterway of its size in the world, the Los Angeles River is a prime example of the troubled history of water management in modern times. Many professionals have studied the river; currently, landscape architect Studio-MLA (Mia Lehrer) and, separately, a team consisting of landscape architect OLIN, architect Gehry Partners, and hydrology consultant Geosyntec, together with the nonprofit River LA, are designing solutions to improve the river's ecology and decrease the likelihood of catastrophic flooding.

Freshkills Park is a remediation of the biggest garbage dump in the Western world. It is one of many of the increasingly frequent attempts to reclaim landfills. The most pressing concern occupying James Corner Field Operations and city officials is how to accomplish a rehabilitation that will allow public access and also restore the ecosystem in a way that will sustain wildlife. With 80 percent of the site given over to renewed habitat, wildlife has precedence over humankind.

While organizing our discussion according to site history allows easy comparison between parks that share a previous use, there are also correspondences across typologies. A prime theme is environmental performance; also critical are aesthetics, cultural identity, the way in which materiality plays a part in telling a story, and how and by whom the parks are being used. One park attribute that reappears with regularity is the incorporation of surviving remnants from the site's previous life, including massive infrastructure components and huge, industrial machinery.

Among such relics, which lend scale and an awareness of history to the landscape, are the large sedimentation tanks at the Culture of Water Ecology Park in Changchun and the big gas tanks at the Cultuurpark Westergasfabriek in Amsterdam. Many practitioners use recycled materials in unusual ways—like the repurposed concrete at Hinge Park in Vancouver, which structures a wetland. Natural mediums serve too: remnants of oak trees felled in a major storm create an enclosure for the Jardin Botanique in Bordeaux.

Another correlation across parks with varied previous uses is the landscape architects' adoption or development of distinctive processes to generate the design. In Bordeaux, two landscape architects working side by side, Catherine Mosbach and Michel Desvigne, were worlds apart in their approach. Mosbach proceeds abstractly, working instinctively, and in the face of political correctness, she dares to reject the value of community participation. Desvigne's technique is different: he builds mock-ups, meets with potential users, and specifies every last detail in what he considers test sites.

Undoubtedly, the most significant discovery is the many extraordinarily beautiful new parks in the People's Republic of China. Alex and I were particularly struck by the similarity between efforts at ecological improvement being made in those parks and in current parks in the West. While post-industrialization in the West can be traced to the mid-twentieth century, in China industry has simply been relocated, leaving behind empty spaces that inspired the creation of parks. Relatively few of these noteworthy landscapes have been published in English, and little attention has been directed at the vastly dissimilar context.

Western and Asian parks have very different antecedents, and this is reflected in the alternative means by which they take shape. In the United States and Europe, democratic ideals were the linchpin of the nineteenth-century park movement. Green spaces were intended to be areas for public gathering and moral uplift. Equally important, they provided a healthful respite from the miserable living conditions of the urban poor and new immigrants.

By contrast, China has no tradition of public space. Late in the nineteenth century, only a handful of privately owned European-style gardens in Shanghai—the Zhangyuan Garden (1860s), for one—provided green space where the wealthy could regularly enjoy entertainment and social interaction. City-built parks were adapted from these precedents or from existing public spaces, such as markets, plazas, and Buddhist temples. Green areas were also created around landscape features, such as lakes and rivers. The great majority of early twentieth-century parks in Shanghai were built within the American and English concessions (merged to form the Shanghai International Settlement in 1863) and the French concession, and they were used almost exclusively by international residents.

Like their historical backgrounds, the processes of park building in the West and in China diverge notably. In the United States, new public parks nearly always come about through private/public endeavors, with the cost of construction and occasionally of maintenance shared between the city and donations from the public, including corporations and nonprofits. The elaborate programming of contemporary parks in the United States has become essential to allow open areas to remain financially viable in the absence of city funding.

estate in the vicinity. The High Line attracted $2 billion in new investment to New York, producing a spike in land values that forced longtime residents to leave the neighborhood. High Line imitations have been built or are being planned in Chicago, Philadelphia, Atlanta, Miami, Austin, and St. Louis.

Frequently, locations so contaminated that they cannot be developed are selected for parks (the abandoned brownfield sites we present are prominent examples); surrounding neighborhoods are inhabited by low-income families, typically people of color. This confluence of circumstances almost always leads to gentrification, which together with the inevitable displacement of original residents, is not a new problem. In 1857, New York City forcibly removed a middle-class Black community to make way for Central Park. Roughly 350 people in Seneca Village, founded in 1825 by free Blacks, lost their homes when the city used eminent domain to take the land.

Seeking to address this ongoing problem, the Atlanta Beltline Partnership (2005) has included an affordable housing plan and an anti-displacement tax fund in the project for a greenbelt around Atlanta. But housing has been slow to materialize. This "green gentrification," which all too often brings about racial and class inequality, is a downside to park building.

While such drawbacks are few, they have the potential to be quite serious. Other problems are limited amenities and inadequate security, which discourage visitors. The handsome design of Freeway Park (1976) in Seattle wasn't sufficient to save that highway cap from a lack of attendance, and in 2021, these issues are still being addressed.

Improper upkeep is another problem. With the exception of a small number of recent hardscape parks, such as the Bentway in Toronto and the Topography of Terror in Berlin, almost all open spaces include living material that needs continuous attention. Michael Van Valkenburgh has written eloquently about plant growth and death as well as the drastic effects of water, soil, insects, and weather on the survival of greenery. He points out, "People put their energy into the good deed of creating public parks; keeping them in good shape is much less sexy, requiring patient, routine, never-ending labor." The annual maintenance cost of Van Valkenburgh's Brooklyn Bridge Park is about $4.32 per square foot, double the average cost of park maintenance in Shanghai.

The Allegheny Riverfront Park in Pittsburgh (1994–98), a luscious river edge designed by Van Valkenburgh, has not been able to fulfill its potential because of deferred care. It "is in bad shape," he says, "falling apart, overgrown with weeds, painted with graffiti." In 2019, Pittsburgh was reported to be short $400 million for park repairs and $13 million for park maintenance.

Upkeep of Bryant Park in midtown Manhattan was grossly neglected in the 1960s and 1970s; its visitors included drug dealers and those experiencing homelessness. Only in 1980 did Daniel Biederman, a systems consultant, and Andrew Heiskell, chairman of Time, Inc., implement a thorough renovation. Landscape architect Hanna/Olin (today OLIN) with architect Hardy Holzman Pfeiffer formulated improvements to the original design and plantings and added two restaurants and four concession kiosks. Currently, it is an enticing destination that draws thousands of people every day.

The critical importance of parks has been forcefully brought home by the coronavirus pandemic. My long walks in New York City's Central Park during the worldwide shutdown in 2020 have been a powerful incentive to consider the role of landscape within a changed world. In late April, the park had returned to life: trees in bloom and masses of delicate young flowers helped me come to terms with the crisis.

The city was quiet, but the park was even quieter, as it always is compared with the congested streets (though by then vehicular traffic had declined tremendously). Walking through areas restricted to pedestrians—cycling is limited to specific roadways—never fails to be calming. The annual rebirth of vegetation and revival of wildlife in Central Park provided a glimmer of hope as little else did during the dark days. The many joggers and couples, both old and young, that I passed appeared to share my feelings. So many of the park goers smiled, despite their masks, in a conspiratorial sharing.

I am not alone in finding solace in nature during this crisis. Parks around the United States are more crowded than usual: from Seattle in the Pacific Northwest to Houston in the South, Columbus and Cincinnati in the Midwest, and New York City and New Haven, Connecticut, in the Northeast, parks are full of people walking, hiking, exercising, strolling with pets, picnicking, working on laptops, or just relaxing. Many cities in the United States have closed vehicular streets so as to provide more space for pedestrians. The phenomenon validates one of my convictions: that today's parks fulfill the need for more public space.

Previous twenty-first-century crises—in New York City, for example, Hurricane Sandy in 2012 and the September 11, 2001, terrorist attack—affected architectural and landscape design, and it is likely that the coronavirus pandemic will do so

Dequindre Cut

Detroit, Michigan
2009–2016

SmithGroupJJR

1.4 miles
cost: $8.8 million

Public meetings to discuss the transformation of an abandoned railroad corridor on Detroit's east side into the Dequindre Cut greenway began in the early 2000s, at about the same time as plans were being laid for Manhattan's High Line. The Cut, however, didn't aspire to be the paradigm of sophisticated design achieved by the $250 million, 6.7-acre High Line, the costliest adaptive reuse of a rail line. Nor does it attempt the kind of custom-made design of Chicago's elevated 606. Rather, the Dequindre Cut sought to create a unifying identity for disparate neighborhoods, provide much-needed green space to underserved communities, and act as an outdoor gallery for the display of urban art.

The Dequindre Cut, a nearly two-mile-long trail, begins a loop known since 2019 as the Joe Louis Greenway; an additional three miles of the planned thirty-two will start construction in 2021. The greenway was the idea of the charismatic Maurice Cox, director of the city's Planning Department from 2015 to 2019. Cox has taught at a number of universities and also served as mayor (2002–4) of Charlottesville, Virginia, where he presided over the southern city's new zoning code and presented a vision for its future. His plan for Detroit was to transform the formerly thriving metropolis into a "symbol of landscape design." Indeed, Detroit is the first American metropolis to be named a UNESCO City of Design.

However, since the 1970s, Detroit has been known as a city in drastic decline, due to struggles in its main industry, automobile manufacturing, as well as middle-class flight to the suburbs. The associated drop in population, from a prosperous metropolis of two million in the 1950s to 673,000 in 2019, left the city the poorest in the United States. By 2010, it was estimated that twenty-four square miles of the city were vacant, due in large part to wholesale removal of deteriorated structures. Within a few years, Cox and his team set out to turn the liability of vacant land into the asset of open green space. In addition to bringing neglected parks back to life and creating greenways, the Detroit planners have added nearly 300 miles of bicycle paths to city roads since 2007.

Cox's commitment to landscape as a means of reviving an entire city goes far beyond the usual piecemeal interventions. The use of landscape architecture for urban renewal owes a debt to architect and urbanist Charles Waldheim, who believes that landscape architecture can supplant architecture, urban design, and planning in remediating post-industrial urban sites in the process of economic restructuring. Indeed, each of the parks discussed in this book illustrates the implementation of this theory.

For more than a hundred years, many distinguished architects and designers have contributed to Detroit's built environment. Ludwig Hilberseimer (1885–1967) and Alfred Caldwell (1903–98) made an early attempt to implement urban renewal in their plan for seventy-eight-acre Lafayette Park (1955–63). The German, Bauhaus-trained architect and planner and the American Prairie school landscape architect used landscape as the primary ordering element for the district, a mixed-income, multicultural community on Detroit's Lower East Side, for which Ludwig Mies van der Rohe (1886–1969) designed the architecture (1953–63). Other architects and planners in Detroit included Albert Kahn (1869–1942), a master of industrial design; Paul Philippe Cret (1876–1945), the architect of the handsome Beaux-Arts Detroit Institute of Arts; and Daniel Burnham (1846–1912), with four office buildings to his credit. Among the additional noted designers who worked in Detroit during this time was Frederick Law Olmsted (1822–1903); his partially realized 1880s project for Belle Isle (a small island in the Detroit River; Piet Oudolf is currently designing a garden there) contributed to its popularity as a gathering spot.

Lafayette Park's captivating natural setting and elegant residential enclave contrasts brusquely with the declining neighborhoods around it. Mies alternated high rises and two-story townhouses; later, a school and shopping plaza were added by others. Like Olmsted, Mies, Hilberseimer, and Caldwell saw the urban park as an antidote to the unhealthy conditions of industrial cities and positioned the buildings within a park-like setting interspersed with a rich unifying tree canopy. But while this parkland is an asset for those who live in Lafayette Park, it segregates the middle-class community

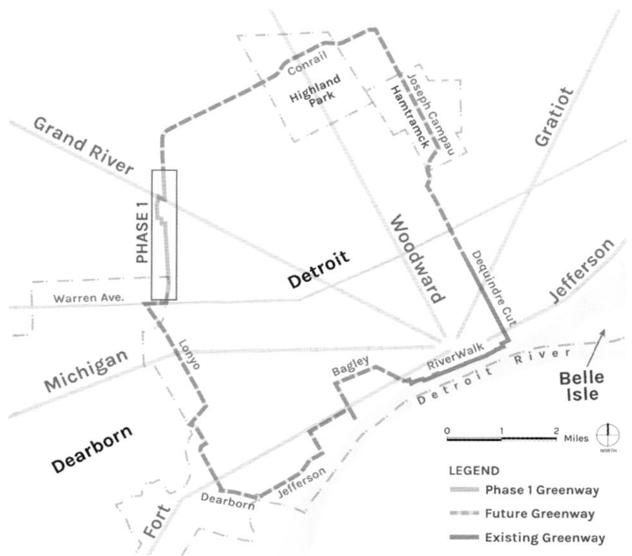

Joe Louis Greenway, schematic map

Dequindre Cut, preremediation

High Line, New York, James Corner Field Operations and Diller Scofidio + Renfro

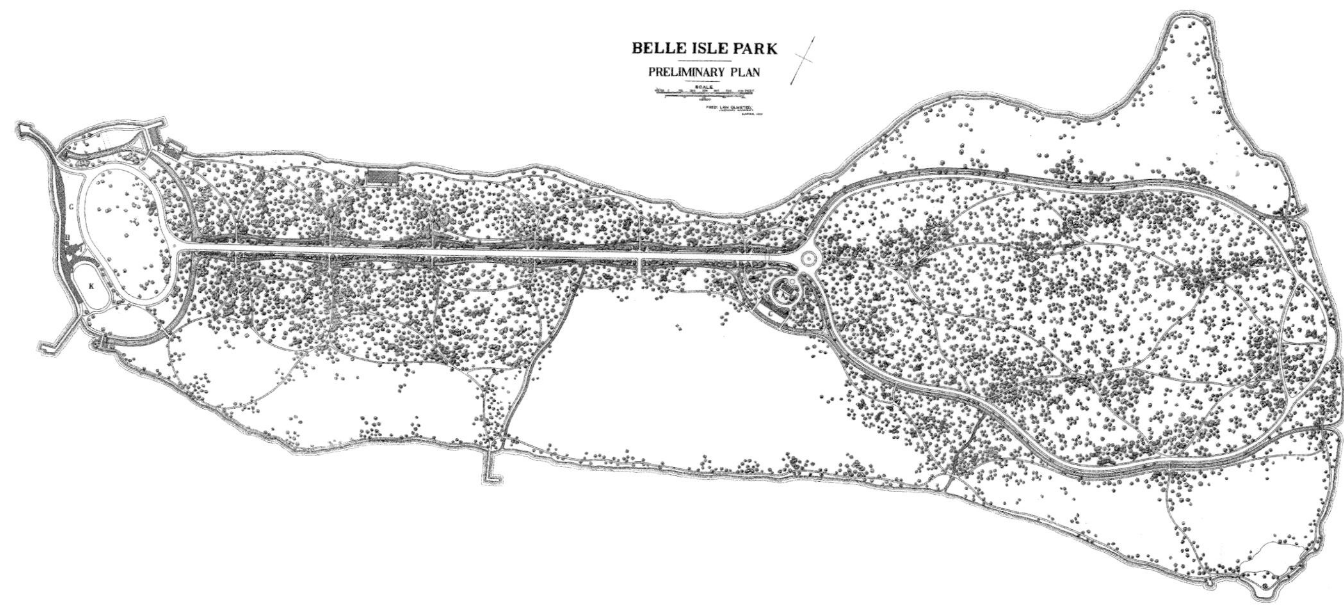

Lafayette Park, Detroit, 1953–63, Ludwig Mies van der Rohe, Ludwig Hilberseimer, Alfred Caldwell

Belle Isle Park, Detroit, preliminary plan, 1880s, Frederick Law Olmsted

from the city's urban core, which includes the nearby neighborhoods traversed by the Dequindre Cut.

The Cut begins at the shore of the Detroit River, the only river to be designated both an American Heritage River and a Canadian Heritage River. The river was the source of the city's development—it attracted French colonizers (many of whose descendants left the legacy of their names, like Dequindre), opened the region to trade, powered the rise of industry, and to this day serves shipping needs—but the once scenic shoreline, like many around the world, was made inaccessible by warehouses, cement silos, pot-holed roads, and vast expanses of surface parking. It was badly in need of attention.

In 1970, Henry Ford II, already thinking of ways to stimulate the city's economy, partnered with the city and with Detroit Renaissance, a private non-profit, to build what was then the tallest hotel skyscraper in the Western Hemisphere. The expanded Renaissance Center (1977), designed by John Portman, now contains commercial space and the headquarters of the General Motors Company, which owns the complex, in addition to the hotel.

In 2003, the city's civic leaders founded the Detroit Riverfront Conservancy to ensure access to 5.5 miles of the shoreline and contribute to Detroit's revitalization. As part of this ongoing mission, the city's Planning and Development Department in 2014 created a fifteen-year vision for redevelopment of the riverfront. A framework for the plan was completed in 2017 by Michel Desvigne and Inessa Hansch with Skidmore, Owings & Merrill, but it has not yet been realized. Desvigne's proposed transformation of the riverfront would include an educational wetland and would increase access to the Detroit River.

Detroit's Grand Trunk Line, which provided the route for the Dequindre Cut, was built in the 1830s by its predecessor, the Pontiac and Detroit Railroad Co. Unlike the High Line in New York City (1933), elevated above street level and used for food delivery, the Dequindre Cut, which was used to transport heavier cargo as well as passengers, was sunk below street level in the 1930s to relieve road congestion. In New York, truck transport replaced train delivery, making rail lines, including the High Line, obsolete. In Detroit, by contrast, it was the failure of industry and the city's waning population in midcentury that rendered trains unnecessary. Consequently, the Dequindre Cut fell victim to urban decline.

The idea of creating a series of linear parks in Detroit has been around since at least 2000, but it was due to Cox that they are being assembled into a greenway loop. Cox's inspiration came from the Grand Rounds Scenic Byway in Minneapolis, which has fifty miles of parkway and over one hundred miles of trails. He was also influenced by Superkilen, a half-mile-long linear park in Copenhagen designed by BIG, Topotek 1, and Superflex. In addition to the usual amenities, Superkilen exhibits meaningful found objects from the sixty nationalities of people living near it.

North of Gratiot Avenue, a major thoroughfare, the Cut runs to the east beside a deteriorating neighborhood; to the west it follows the edge of the flourishing Eastern Market District. The many markets here act as a vast gathering place half a mile from the city's downtown business center, one that has been popular with residents and visitors since the late nineteenth century. Here, the former railroad corridor is at grade, then gradually drops twenty-five feet as it advances south to the riverfront. The intersection between the Cut and the river was immediately eyed by a developer as a prime location for housing, though the Planning Department discouraged such overtures in an attempt to avoid the costly gentrification that has taken place around the High Line. As it happens, Detroit's riverfront is one of the few such watersides in the United States that is relatively free of luxury condos.

The Cut was funded by a combination of public, non-profit, and private partnerships involving the federal government, the State of Michigan, the City of Detroit, and other entities. The Detroit Riverfront Conservancy raised $163 million for the adaptation of the railroad and is working toward a $60 million endowment.

Alex and I visited the Cut on a warm, sunny day in September 2017. We arrived from the river, where a short trail leads to the beginning of the Cut proper, and strolled along the first and second phases, occasionally hopping onto a golf cart provided by the Conservancy. We admired the dense, natural vegetation and trees on either side of the twenty-foot-wide asphalt path that has replaced the rail lines. The first phase of the low-budget greenway, 1.8 miles long, was designed without irrigation, limiting plantings to easy-to-maintain, drought-tolerant species. Security concerns, stemming from the areas that are below street level, required clear and open visibility, and so clean-cut lawns, chosen for low maintenance and the need to keep sightlines unobstructed, border each side of the pathway. Additionally, staggered clusters of canopy trees provide shade without compromising safety along these open strips. The steep embankments of the rail corridor were

Detroit River, waterfront park and greenways, plan

Dequindre Cut, pedestrian and bicycle lanes

stabilized by means of erosion control blankets, naturalized plantings with deeper root systems, and the replacement/addition of retaining walls.

The most visually arresting aspect of the Cut is the profusion of graffiti—often of remarkable artistic merit—that covers every inch of the overpasses and abutments that support the street-level bridges above. The artwork was carefully preserved during construction—although some bridges were unstable and had to be removed—and is regularly augmented by commissioned murals. In view of the keen interest in the graffiti, the Conservancy envisions a program of art and culture comparable to the city's Heidelberg Project (1986). This installation was created by the artist Tyree Guyton next to the site of Black Bottom, a predominately Black neighborhood named for the marshes and Savoyard River that once occupied the area. As was typical of many urban renewal programs during the mid-twentieth century, Detroit labeled the neighborhood as an example of urban decay and razed it, eliminating a Black community. Guyton's installation includes an accumulation of discarded household artifacts set in place around the artist's family house, which he adorned in brightly painted polka dots of various dimensions as a protest against the city's devastation after the Uprising of 1967. Two hundred seventy-five thousand people visit Guyton's project each year, and certainly it is tempting to think of it as a model for programming that might include music groups like the one we encountered on our visit—young people providing a lively performance within a recess of the Cut's overhead structure.

Within ten years of the Dequindre's opening to the public in 2009, visitors averaged 34,000 a month in the spring, summer, and fall. This adaptation resembles linear parks elsewhere in the United States. The cities of Atlanta, St. Louis, Portland (Oregon), and Houston are creating extensive pedestrian and cycling trails within or around their city limits. Like the Joe Louis Greenway, these trails link various communities and provide public open space.

Detroit's aspirations for diversifying its landscapes extend beyond the Dequindre Cut. In 2018, Michael Van Valkenburgh and David Adjaye won the competition to expand the West Riverfront Park. Approximately 250 people attended presentations by the four competition finalists, providing an opportunity to observe the intense community engagement that has marked every step of Detroit's renewal. By May 2019, design of the westward extension of the park, renamed the Ralph C. Wilson, Jr. Centennial Park, was well underway. A cove featuring a sandy beach half the size of a football field, with fresh water as deep as ten feet, promises to be one of the park's most popular attractions. When it opens late in 2022, at an estimated cost of $55–60 million, three and a half miles of riverfront—of a planned five and a half miles—will be newly accessible. The park will augment aquatic and wildlife habitation areas and will include abatement and mitigation of contaminated sediments in the river.

Cox hasn't always had a smooth ride. There has been strong resistance to an ambitious tree planting program for city streets due to the cost and time needed by homeowners for maintenance. Projects like the revitalization of the Fitzgerald neighborhood by landscape architect Spackman Mossop Michaels fell seriously behind schedule due to problems including a loss of government funding. Nevertheless, the plan for a central park and axial greenway through the underserved Fitzgerald neighborhood is proceeding as part of the larger Landscape Stewardship Plan for open space improvement, led by the Spackman firm. Hood Design Studio, landscape architects based in Oakland, California, is renovating the 160-acre Detroit State Fairgrounds and the 350-acre Rosa Parks neighborhood, where the 1967 Uprising originated. The firm's hybrid landscape institutes a new pattern based on the site's evolving history. Nearby, Hood's proposed mile-long sculptural installation Street Trees would be composed of pine and oak logs; it is intended to encourage new plant life and provide shade.

Stunted lending, predatory schemes, and tax foreclosures remain serious handicaps for the city's residents. On the positive side, Detroit was released in 2018 from the state oversight that had been in place since the city declared bankruptcy in 2013, attesting to its improved financial status, and late in 2017 the city's credit ratings were upgraded. The Dequindre Cut, alone among the examples of adaptive reuse we studied, stands as the recognizable symbol of a city's transformation, leading the way for others to follow.

Dequindre Cut, graffiti art

Heidelberg Project, Detroit, Tyree Guyton

Ralph C. Wilson, Jr. Centennial Park, Detroit, rendering, Michael Van Valkenburgh Associates

Evening revelry on the 606

The 606 (Bloomingdale Trail)

Chicago, Illinois
2015

Michael Van Valkenburgh Associates

13 acres (2.7 miles)
cost: $95 million

Richard M. Daley began his twenty-two-year term as mayor of Chicago (1989–2011) by stating his intention to give the city more parks than any other in America. One of his first moves toward this goal was to replace the thousands of trees that had died of Dutch Elm disease; he continued with signature projects along the lakefront, including Navy Pier, the Museum Campus, and Northerly Island (an airstrip made into a park). However, the 24.5-acre, $490 million Millennium Park (2004) is by far the most famous and most successful of his beautification efforts.

The park is a jaw-dropping repurposing of an industrial wasteland that had occupied the site from the 1850s to 1997. It is hard to understand how the city could for so long have neglected this prime lakefront property, which extends from the Art Institute of Chicago at the south to East Randolph Street at the north. Two huge art objects are on display in the park: Anish Kapoor's *Cloud Gate* (popularly known as "the Bean") and Jaume Plensa's Crown Fountain, which in warm weather is always filled with gleeful, splashing children. Along with the Frank Gehry–designed, four-thousand-seat Jay Pritzker Pavilion; an ice-skating rink; and the Lurie Garden, a naturalistic and ecologically sensitive landscape created by Gustafson Guthrie Nichol with garden authority Piet Oudolf and lighting expert Robert Israel, these public artworks have transformed the park into a gathering place for Chicagoans and a draw for tourists. Constructed on a four-foot layer of new soil spread over the roof of subsurface parking—under which the tracks of the Canadian National Railway still operate—the park's unexpected combination of landscape, architecture, and art have made it the number one tourist attraction in the midwestern United States, with 25 million visitors in 2016.

Equally impressive was Daley's inauguration of a project to improve the city's riverside promenade. Rehabilitation of the Chicago River in the 1980s led to the mayor's 2001 call for studies of what has become the 1.25-mile Riverwalk in the downtown Loop. Stretching from Lake Shore Drive to Franklin Street, the project recalls Daniel Burnham's famous 1909 Plan for Chicago, which included just such a pedestrian path between the two-tiered roadway he designed for Wacker Drive and the river. Alex and I went to Chicago to walk the 606, a new railroad park. But on that clear fall day, the Riverwalk's promenade—handsomely designed by Sasaki and flanked by thriving cafés and restaurants—presented an irresistible attraction.

By the time Daley left office, the first phase of the Riverwalk had been completed, and the second phase had begun construction. When Rahm Emanuel succeeded Daley in 2011, he lost no time in initiating further improvements. One of these was the 606, a trail that has recently replaced the Bloomingdale Line, a branch of the Canadian Pacific Railway. Industrial traffic on the Bloomingdale Line began to decline in the 1980s and came completely to an end in the 1990s. Emanuel wanted to make the new public ground "his own: a park that would be more out in the neighborhoods." This unifying concept is reflected in the park's name, the first three numbers in most Chicago zip codes. Emanuel turned to Michael Van Valkenburgh Associates, along with the local firm Ross Barney Architects, for the design framework plan for the linear park.

The former railroad line, running beside West Bloomingdale Avenue in northwest Chicago, fulfilled Emanuel's objectives. The route defines the southern extent of the Logan Square community, an area well outside the downtown Loop. In the 1998 Cityspace Plan, a project to develop public spaces, the district was designated as having the highest need for new open lands. The stretch of former rail line runs for 2.7 miles, from Humboldt Park to the north branch of the Chicago River, and encompasses thirteen acres; twenty-two schools are within a ten-minute walk. The public/private project benefits the four neighborhoods (Logan Square, Humboldt Park, Wicker Park, and Bucktown) crossed by the Bloomingdale Line. Funds were raised through a partnership between Chicago, Cook County, the city's park manager, and the Trust for Public Land in addition to federal and state contributions and private donations.

The original at-grade Bloomingdale Line had by 1913 been elevated sixteen feet above street level on a thirty-foot-wide right of way to avoid endangering pedestrians. The structure, traversed by thirty-seven overpasses, owes its solid appearance

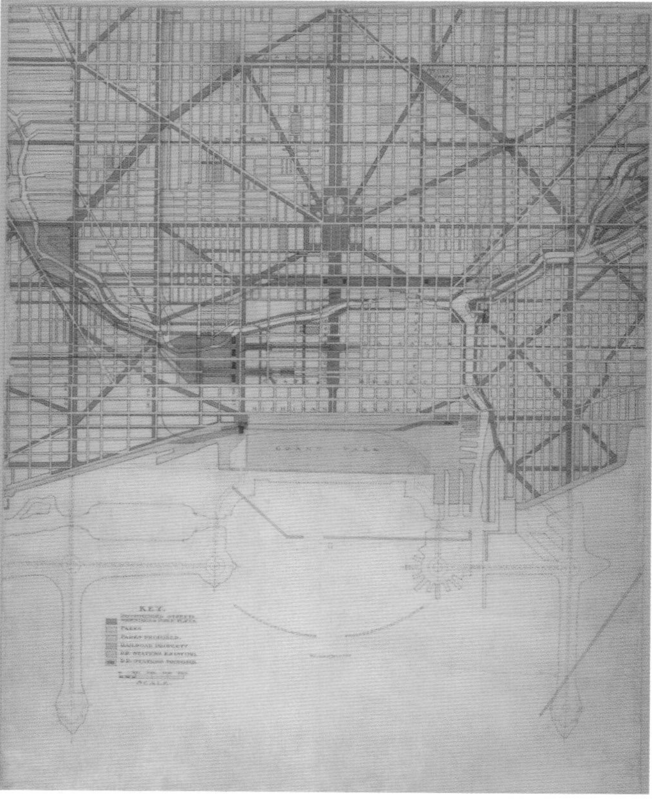

Northerly Island, Chicago

Crown Fountain, Chicago, Jaume Plensa and Krueck + Sexton Architects

Riverwalk, Chicago, Sasaki and Ross Barney Architects

Plan of Chicago (street system), showing Chicago River and Wacker Drive (below center), 1909, Daniel Burnham Jr. and Edward Bennett

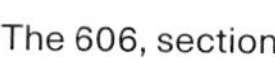

The 606, section

Northwest Chicago, neighborhood parks and bike routes, context plan

to the massive, poured-in-place-concrete, soil- and crushed-rock-filled retaining walls that support it. Tapering toward the top, the battered concrete walls make a robust base for the park, one that contrasts with the High Line in New York, where a metal framework gives rise to empty, forbidding spaces underneath.

In 2003, Ben Helphand, executive director of NeighborSpace, created a "friends" advocacy group for the Bloomingdale Trail, the only non-profit urban land trust in Chicago that preserves and sustains gardens on behalf of dedicated community groups. Helphand and six of his friends played a role similar to that of Joshua David and Robert Hammond, the New Yorkers who spearheaded the effort to convert the High Line into a park. Helphand admits that he trespassed on the disused railroad just as locals in Manhattan had visited, admired, and even encouraged professional photography of the abandoned rail line. "It was an exciting view," he says, "and it was easy to get up and down, but just hard enough to keep most people away." As at the High Line, a ruderal ecology had emerged. Helphand notes, "Bikers and joggers were already using the area, and there were homeless people living on it, using electricity they pulled illegally from adjacent buildings."

Guided by Vivian Garcia, the Chicago Parks District's manager for the 606, we climbed a ramp, one of twelve accessible entries. Tall evergreens often signal approaches to the 606, while grasses such as prairie dropseed (*Sporobolis heterolepis*) and ivory sedge (*Carex eburnea*) embellish bordering areas. As we walked along the trail, we were at times startled by speeding cyclists. Their presence, along with that of dogs and other pets, is one of several differences between the Chicago and Manhattan parks. Another is the extensive grading along the 606, which provides topographical variety throughout and whose western limit climaxes at the spiraling Exelon Observatory. This ziggurat-like landform, which recalls the swirling shape of Michael Van Valkenburgh Associates' Connecticut Water Treatment Facility in New Haven (2005), offers a venue for winter and summer solstice observances as well as for active rail lines. We walked by one of a series of changing artworks, a massive sculpture by Chakaia Booker, a New York artist who makes abstract works from salvaged rubber tires. Continuing on, we enjoyed an overview of the small Park No. 567 (2013) and its spire garden, also by Michael Van Valkenburgh Associates, at North Leavitt Street—even though the tranquility was shattered by the nearby rail, a reminder of the park's not-so-distant past.

The ten-foot-wide, concrete, mixed-use pathway of the 606 is bordered on both sides by two-foot-wide rubber-surfaced running lanes. Galvanized steel fences, like those used by New Zealand sheep farmers, enclose the trail's edges, which are lined by well-designed but infrequent wood and concrete benches. Unobtrusive modern lighting stanchions occasionally extend into overhead arches. The Transportation Department regards the trail as a "transit landscape for bikers and commuters," which explains much of the continuous movement on the path. The ramped entrances make the park accessible to all users, but a visitor we encountered complained that limited seating and lack of toilets were problems for her elderly grandfather.

Planting on the 606, inspired by prairie landscapes, is organized according to a "rolling bloom" concept devised by the artist Frances Whitehead: species in adjoining sections bloom over the course of five days. Whitehead viewed the progression as a way to raise awareness of climate change. The sequence begins toward the west in early spring and continues east. The arrangement is determined to a certain extent by Lake Michigan, which is so large that its waters prolong the retention of summer heat and winter cold in what is referred to as the "lake effect."

Tracking the blooms establishes a phenology, or life cycle, that reveals the influence of seasonal and yearly variations in climate. A predecessor in tracking horticultural life cycles, Tokyo's Cherry Blossom Festival has been around since 720 CE. The 606's stainless-steel markers every tenth of a mile—initially installed at the request of runners—identify the species chosen for the sequence by Michael Van Valkenburgh Associates: apple serviceberry (*Amelanchier × grandiflora* 'Autumn Brilliance'), Chinese lilac (*Syringa × chinensis* 'Red Rothomagensis'), and weeping forsythia (*Forsythia suspensa*). Whitehead likes to think of the whole as a giant sculpture.

In addition to the numerous well-attended community meetings that informed the project, residents adjacent to the park were given a voice in how the privacy fences and vine selections would be planned for their properties. This input created an edge that varies in plant material but does not affect the species chosen for the walkway itself: ferns, sumac, inkberry, yellow buckeye, and quaking aspen. Programming of the 606, attuned to the community's interests, has helped to draw over 1.5 million annual visitors. With an event planned for every day of the week, this entertainment factor might be considered excessive. One of the more surprising, and most popular, attractions is campouts for scouting groups.

Despite the efforts to include park users in creating and putting to use the 606, Juanita Irizarry, currently executive director of Friends of the Parks (distinct from Friends of the 606), feels that the Mexican and Puerto Rican communities (47 percent of the local population) were not adequately represented. She would also like to ameliorate neighborhood connections: "Most people at the poorer west end never see the middle-class east end," she says. "There is no real engagement." An equally important criticism Irizarry makes is the tremendous (50 percent) spike in house prices brought about by the new park. Gentrification is also an issue for critics of the High Line, which has increased real estate values by as much as 103 percent.

In addition to the trail itself, the 606 links six pocket parks, including four new ones. The Julia de Burgos Park, a half-acre open space that predates the 606, has been retrofitted. A giant, spider-like climbing device on a rubber surface dominates a small playground. The intimacy of the area seemed appealing and well-adapted to the two moms and their children who were using it at the time of our visit.

These modest parks follow a Chicago tradition that dates to the turn of the twentieth century, when fourteen such neighborhood green spaces were built to relieve overcrowded tenement conditions on the city's South Side. The South Park Commissioners entrusted the creation of the approximately ten-acre parks to the Olmsted Brothers, Daniel Burnham, and Edward H. Bennett. When the green spaces began to open to the public in 1905, they enjoyed such tremendous success that they became a model for the nation.

The 606 pocket parks, Riverwalk, and parts of the thirty-mile lakefront follow plans introduced by Burnham early in the twentieth century. Burnham achieved extraordinary success as the designer, with his partner John Wellborn Root, together with Frederick Law Olmsted and Charles B. Atwood, of the World's Columbian Exposition (1893). But even before that triumph, the firm was renowned for its architecture and urban plans. Burnham was an early environmentalist, and undeniably he would have been happy to see some of his more-than-century-old plans realized.

Klyde Warren Park

Dallas, Texas
2012

OJB Landscape Architecture

5.2 acres
cost: $110 million

The year 2019, the *Dallas Business Journal* reported, was the fifteenth in a row in which CEOs ranked Texas the best state in the country for business. Dallas and Houston were already among the leaders of US economic growth in 2015, according to *Site Selection* magazine. Both Dallas and Houston are well-known for friendly business climates, helped by the fact that Texas has no state income tax, a low state tax, low labor costs, and light regulations. Furthermore, both cities have a rich cultural life, boasting art museums, a symphony orchestra, and opera companies.

Unlike Houston, however, Dallas lacked any true sense of place within its urban core; as Gertrude Stein famously said of Oakland, California, there was "no there there." At the time of the Winspear Opera's completion (2009), the Arts District promised to be a vibrant cultural area. I visited the Winspear at that time and was impressed by the open spaces planned by the district's board members to accommodate food trucks and other attractions. But as more and more commercial towers filled the spaces between the arts venues, it lost any semblance of being a site for culture as the Menil Collection campus in Houston is, for example. Sheila Grant, the wife of Jody Grant (chairman emeritus of Texas Capital Bank), identified the problem as the absence of a "town square." She yearned for a Dallas equivalent to New York City's Rockefeller Center or London's Royal Hospital Chelsea, setting for the annual Chelsea Flower Show, and she set out to make a comparable public space with a centrally located park.

Jody Grant, who has been called the "glue and leader" of the project, identified the eight-lane Woodall Rodgers Freeway as a promising site for a 5.2-acre park. The idea of capping part of the highway had been around since the 1960s, but the kind of enthusiasm that would have facilitated fundraising was lacking. In 2004, Grant; TREC, the local real estate council; and Texas Capital Bank teamed up to relaunch the project with an initial donation of $1 million each. By 2012, this seed money kickstarted city, state, and federal funding of $58 million and private donations of $52 million. Also fueling interest in seeing the success of the public/private park partnership was a 2001 decision by aircraft manufacturer Boeing to select Chicago over Dallas or Denver (the third finalist) for its headquarters because of the midwestern city's more vibrant downtown.

There was also an important practical reason for covering over the Woodall Rodgers. As landscape architect Jim Burnett of OJB Landscape Architecture tells it, he tried to take the architect Robert A. M. Stern and a group of developers from the Ritz-Carlton Hotel to the Nasher Sculpture Garden, a distance of four-tenths mile. The uncomfortably hot walk showed him that the connection between the Arts District, Uptown, and the downtown residential and commercial district needed to improve.

On a glorious, sunny day in May, Alex and I visited Klyde Warren Park, which was named after the young son of billionaire energy magnate Kelcy Warren, a major donor to the project. We approached from the east, entering into a broad allée of Shumard's red oak (*Quercus shumardii*). This magnificent space is paved with gravel that surrounds the bases of the trees, reminiscent of the arrangement we saw in many historic French parks. And indeed, there is a Gallic aesthetic at play here, with metal chairs and tables similar to those often found in French parks provided by Fermob and clustered beneath slender white metal archways with suspended lighting. At midday, every one of the chairs was occupied by people having lunch. It was a happy scene, inviting comparison with Manhattan's Bryant Park, one of the models for the Dallas green. We learned later that popular food trucks parked on the nearby roadside are a major factor in Klyde Warren's success as a luncheon venue: the vendors are under contract to the Woodall Rodgers Park Foundation (created in 2004 to manage and maintain the park), and each one contributes to its operating costs.

The broad lawn with its tree-lined border can accommodate as many as 6,500 people and is heavily programmed, sometimes with as many as four or five events a day. We walked across the lawn to a children's playground in the southwest corner of the park. It is neatly surrounded by a metal fence composed only of vertical pickets, on which admiring parents were leaning to watch their progeny. Astroturf-covered mounds built up with geofoam and a winding water feature

Spectators in front of Muse Family Performance Pavilion

View to southwest

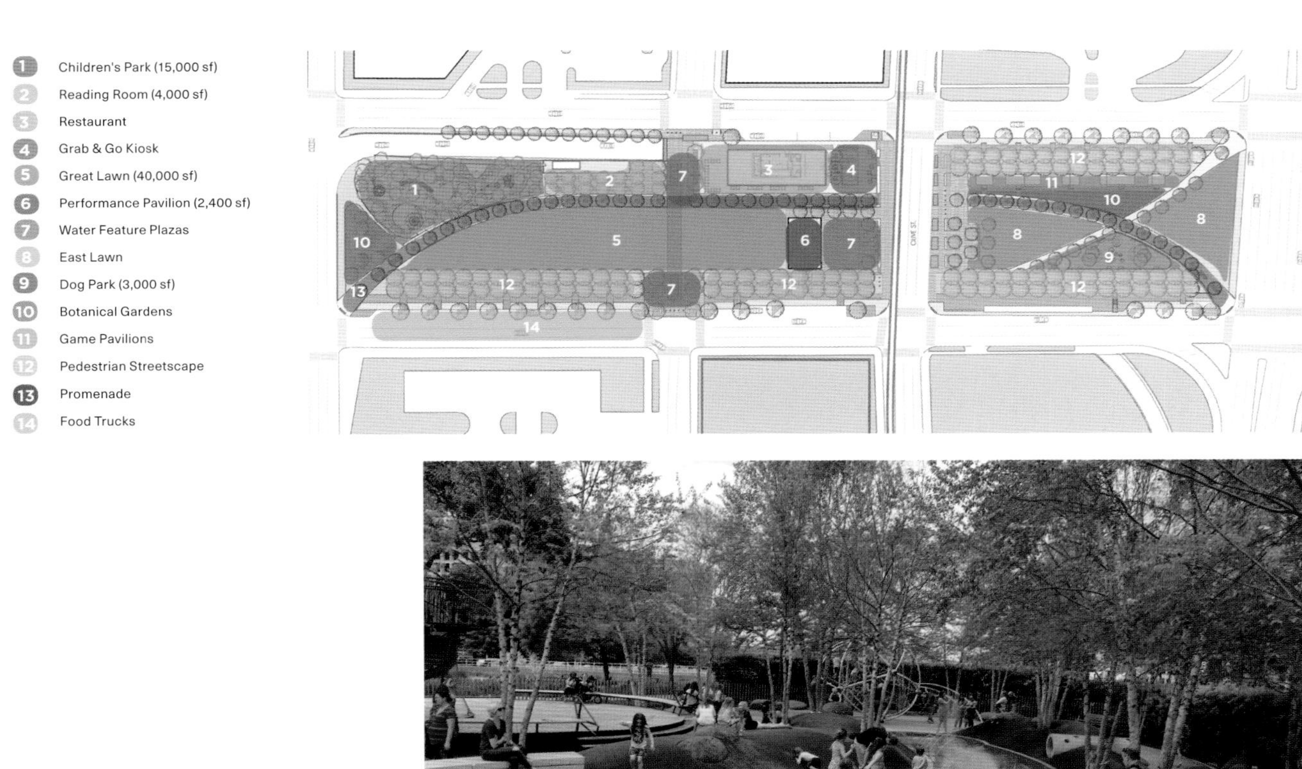

Plan

Interactive fountains in Children's Park

occupy part of the space; a large oak—a "learning tree"—and clusters of river birches (*Betula nigra* Dura-Heat) provide dappled shade.

As we made our way to the restaurant, an elegant glass box, we passed a reading area that offers books and magazines for use in the park. Both the restaurant and a performance space in front of it were designed by Thomas Phifer and Partners. Another dining option, Relish, offers fast food takeaway. Near the café, however, we discovered the park's single drawback: its northeastern third is cut off from the main area by Olive Street. The Woodall Rodgers Park Foundation, which maintains the park, has tried repeatedly to reroute this street, but its direct access to the freeway from Uptown has defeated the effort. The break is particularly regrettable because it shortchanges the project's densest floral plantings while also separating the dog park and gaming pavilions (such as foosball and table tennis) from the rest of the park.

The structure that made the park possible is as noteworthy as the park itself. A 6.5-foot-deep deck was braced on concrete walls built along the sides and in the median of the highway; this assembly brings the park to the same level as the surrounding streets and also meets the state highway clearance requirement of 16.5 feet. The deck consists of three hundred-foot-long prestressed concrete box beams alternating with 4.5-foot-deep concrete trenches. These trenches are deep enough to plant trees and also accommodate plumbing and electrical equipment. Geofoam fill lightens the load. Atop the cover is a layer of topsoil, typically 12 inches deep. The innovative cap structure is the world's largest suspended infrastructure to contain a park, and it has become a model for other projects.

Klyde Warren receives over a million visitors each year and has had an economic impact of $2.5 billion. Within two years, rents in neighboring Uptown had risen between 30 and 60 percent, with the buildings adjacent to the park enjoying the largest increases. Because these are office buildings, they avoid the problems associated with gentrification. In addition, the residential population in Uptown rose more than 50 percent between 2010 and 2016.

From every point of view, success has been such that as of 2021 an expansion was being planned. The $100 million project will add another 1.65 acres, containing a second large lawn and an event building, and will end near the Perot Museum of Nature and Science.

View over highway with north (top) and south caps

Park Over-Bos

Breda, Netherlands
2008

Complex Urban Landscape Design

32 acres
cost: $10.02 million

The city of Breda was first settled in the eleventh century, when its fortifications were built at the confluence of the Mark and Aa Rivers. The center of this charming town of almost 185,000 inhabitants is filled with historic palaces that are staunchly protected by historians and town planners. The twenty-first century brought to the outskirts of Breda, first, the broad A16 highway (2006), which continues north to Rotterdam and south to the Belgian border and Antwerp, and, second, the high-speed railroad line from Amsterdam to Antwerp, which runs almost directly alongside the highway. The rail line raised concerns in Prinsenbeek, a bucolic suburb of Breda, about safety and especially about noise—already a problem with the roadway.

To address local opposition to the rail line, Ed Nijpels, the mayor of Breda, proposed sinking both railway and highway below grade and building a park over them. However, in contrast to the city planning process for historic districts, in which there is limited participation by residents, urban planning in the Netherlands generally cannot proceed without agreement from local inhabitants. In this case, the villagers of Prinsenbeek firmly nixed the mayor's idea and demanded a voice in the design for what they described as a "village forest" on top of the highway. Complex Urban Landscape Design was one of three firms invited to submit proposals for Park Over-Bos, winning the commission as a result of their extensive meetings with the public.

Cor Geluk, a founding principal of Complex Urban Landscape Design, and his wife, Beatrice Pialoux, the firm's business manager, together with their two teenage children, met Alex and me early one Saturday morning in June at an entrance to Park Over-Bos. Geluk and Pialoux explained that the concept was to bridge the highway twice, toward the north and toward the south, to create a circuit that would tie seamlessly into the surroundings. Plantings were designed in an orderly grid to set off the winding paths and varied topographies found throughout the park.

Among the precedents the CULD office used for this project were the Bois de Boulogne (1852–56) and the Parc des Buttes-Chaumont (1864–67), both in Paris. The latter is on the site of a former limestone quarry and, like the Bois de Boulogne, was designed by horticulturist Jean-Pierre Barillet-Deschamps (1824–73) and engineer Adolphe Alphand (1817–91). Buttes-Chaumont incorporates whimsical features like concrete site furniture that imitates logs and leaves, an example of how the artifice of its design is masked by an apparent naturalness. However, it is the section of this park that reveals a complex understanding of below-grade infrastructure. These components include a partially buried rail line and a network of irrigation, drainage, and sewage systems. Similarly, Park Over-Bos is a wonderful marriage between engineering and landscape architecture.

The park extends over half a mile on each side of the highway and is far more than two highway coverings. Between the north and south caps, the eastern flank of the park (beside the railroad) benefits from a dense edge of mature canopy trees belonging to the private properties beyond. This borrowed landscape makes the park feel larger than it is.

At the northern cover, we were greeted by a broad platform constructed of oak. The platform seemingly hovers over a narrow stream and presents a space for visitors to gather, fish, and relax. As we moved farther along, a mixed grove of oaks, pines, and birches and a softly undulating topography screened us from the fact that we were directly over the highway. Crossing over the highway and rail line, we found the park's highest promontory, a man-made mound that provides astonishingly expansive views across the park.

As we climbed the mound via steps of Violetta granite quarried in Norway, Geluk and Pialoux explained the two biggest challenges: water management and the creation of topography. Water is directed away from the highway and partly captured for irrigation purposes. Excess water is pumped underneath the roadway. Gabions crossing the stream act as weirs, slowing water movement and increasing oxygen levels in the water.

More complicated was the design team's wish to create a varied topography, which requires a thick soil profile in some places and a thinner one in others, which led to an irregular distribution of weight on the cap structure. CULD had originally specified a soil depth of 6.5 feet, but due to weight concerns, the depth had to be reduced to approximately three feet.

At the top of the mound, one of the oak benches that line the walkways was occupied by an older couple. The two immediately recognized Geluk and Pialoux and complimented the park, which they visit every day, enthusiastically. The spot is popular with a wide range of people: children enjoy climbing the hill, teenagers socialize with their friends, young parents stroll to the top of the mound, and seniors rest on the benches to absorb the view.

The pine, oak, and birch of the little woodland on the northern cap were chosen for their shallow root systems and also to provide contrast with the more typical canopy trees in the nearby private park. As we walked south toward the second cap, parallel to the highway and rail line, Geluk explained that the trees were placed to help guide one of the park's maintenance strategies. Roughly aligned, the trees inform the workers where to mow and where not to. The result is two zones: one of cut lawn adjacent to the path and the other of soft meadow with tall grasses. Grass surrounding the trees is left uncut to protect the trunk and roots, but the definition of the spaces between each tree was purposely left to the crew. They can decide to mow a straight line or a more curvilinear line. This free choice has fostered a sense of ownership of the park among the workers, and the result is a space that is dynamic and constantly changing. The dirt paths here, Geluk explained, were based on the informal pathways, or "desire paths," people usually follow. "I like to design on the flow of people, not according to a concept."

As for the highway, the CULD team wanted drivers to feel as if they were passing underneath a forest. And indeed, in this flat country, the sight of the park's terrain and trees rising over the highway and slowly descending beside it offers a reprieve from the monotonous horizontal viewshed.

We continued across to the second cap, where lawns are generously scattered with wildflowers, traversed by paths, and appear to have an organic topography. A bifurcated reinforced-concrete bridge led down to ground level: one branch goes south, the other north at a gradual slope that allows for bicycles, which have their own clearly designated path. To the south of the bridge is a deer preserve consisting of a tree-surrounded lawn and a small pavilion inspired by De Stijl designer Gerrit Rietveld. The preserve is located on an island, which keeps the deer from roaming about the park and reduces the amount of fencing required.

For all the merits of what we had already seen, the last portion of our walk—beside a stream—was the most delightful. A profusion of native plants bordered our path, each identified by a small, elegant label. A merry birthday party in an adjacent house humanized a landscape in which ducks and other wildlife are equally at home as humans. This was our second party of the day: the first celebrated a newly planted tree. It was a touching illustration of the interest this community takes in its natural surroundings. And as happy with the park as the couple we had encountered earlier were a father and his young son, who were absorbed by fishing in the stream. Given that Geluk and Pialoux wanted to make the park a place to linger, rather than to simply traverse, they seemed gratified by their success.

Plan

Gabion weir in stream

South cap, small woodland

View from highway, rendering

Overleaf: North cap, fishing platform

RICHTING
BREDA
RICHTING
ANTWERPEN
A16
RICHTING
ROTTERDAM
A16
HSL
STADSDUCT
VALDIJK
STADSDUCT
MIDDENWEG
heuvel
brug
vlonder
station
prinsenbeek
bibliotheek
kerk
markt
beekse straat
meester bierensweg
middenweg
valdijk
lunetstraat
0m
100m
200m

airports

As early as the 1860s, when railroad travel started to expand, transportation planners were concerned about what passengers would see as they traveled through the countryside. Concurrently, suburbs were starting to grow; one of the first, Riverside, Illinois, was planned by Calvert Vaux and Frederick Law Olmsted beginning in 1868 as a rejection of the tight quarters typical of urban areas, as well as the lack of hygiene and fresh air. Olmsted was interested in how the body moves through space and tried to create within the community a scenic experience that felt integrated with the environment.

Increased automobile traffic in the 1910s and the advent of commercial aviation in the 1920s raised similar questions about driving and flying. For air travel, the subject was complicated by the new popularity of aerial views adopted for the design of urban and landscape plans. The first aeronauts discovered landscapes previously unseen; Le Corbusier and Alvar Aalto were among the many architects and planners who used bird's-eye views as a different way of seeing landscapes and creating urban design.

In 1966, Robert Smithson's preliminary studies for the Dallas Fort Worth Airport led to a series of experiments with large sites, earth masses, and aerial perspective. Land Art created by Smithson and other artists was an important moment in landscape architecture's history. With aerial imagination a continuing interest in design discourse, landscape architects welcomed the opportunity to create airports that would be seen from the sky as well as the ground. In fact, airport exteriors and landscapes are almost always more inventive than airport interiors, which have become giant shopping malls.

West 8's introduction of mass plantings and landscape elements transformed Schiphol Airport in Amsterdam in 1992, while Shlomo Aronson Architects abstracted characteristics from surrounding agricultural lands for his contribution to the renovation of Ben Gurion International Airport in Tel Aviv in 2004. But surely the top prize for recent airport landscape must go to the one developed by Peter Walker and Partners for Moshe Safdie's Jewel Changi Airport in Singapore (2018). Eight acres of lush vegetation within a climate-controlled glass dome—like precious gems displayed in a jewel box—offer a thrilling welcome to arriving travelers.

Abandoned airports likewise offer opportunities for expressive landscape design on their large, flat expanses. While airports are far from obsolete, different times and changing needs have led many to close down. Already in 1959, Croydon Airport in London, one of the first commercial airline terminals, was superseded by Heathrow. Reasons an airport ceases to operate may include the decision to move it farther away from the city it serves, its inability to meet current technical and security demands, and the decommissioning of military bases. With the help of innovative ideas, the large spaces of defunct airports have been made into beautiful parks.

Former runway parallel to Yunjin Road

Xuhui Runway Park

Shanghai, China
2018–2020

Sasaki

36 acres
cost: $25.7 million

The Xuhui and Huangpu districts of Shanghai, near the Huangpu River, were historically upscale residential neighborhoods in what was known as the French Concession. They are now commercial areas, filled with department stores and shopping malls. The government-controlled West Bund Group is in the process of revitalizing many of the post-industrial sites within this neighborhood, including the obsolete Longhua Airport, with new high-priced residential towers and cultural facilities intended to make Xuhui the future city center. The American firm Sasaki won the commission to design and build Runway Park by means of a bidding process that took place in 2012. Construction of the surrounding high-rise buildings and of a subway line allowed Sasaki to divide work on the project into three phases: the first (2018) is between Fenggu and Longlan Roads, the second (2018) is between Longyao and South Longshui Roads, and the third (2020) is between Longlan and Longyao Roads.

The name Runway Park, which commemorates the site's previous life, clearly sets forth the landscape's theme. It is a measure of Shanghai's tremendous expansion that the small Longhua Airport, the only civilian airstrip until 1949, has been replaced by two huge airports at either side of the city, one by Paul Andreu and one by Foster + Partners. Both the park and the adjacent Yunjin Road were designed by Sasaki, and were intended to evoke the motion of an airplane, with vehicles, bicycles, and pedestrians moving along an integrated system. Several components in the park visually evoke air travel: lobed leaves of trident maples (*Acer buergerianum*), which suggest airplanes, say the designers; benches with underseat lighting; even the runway graphics reproduced on the pavement of the children's playground. However, the calm beauty of this linear park speaks more of landscape than of flight.

A major feature of the park is its rain garden, which accommodates storm water from the park and the street; a richly vegetated constructed wetland in the southern area of the park performs a similar function. Because the rain garden was the first system of its kind in Shanghai, it at first encountered skepticism and stiff opposition from the government. In fact, the installation was approved only after Kongjian Yu's Sponge City initiative came into being. Yet it is precisely this sponge system of water management that makes the park unique: runoff from the street feeds into the rain garden, where plants such as purple loosestrife (*Lythrum salicaria*), soft rush (*Juncus effusus*), lizard's tail (*Saururus chinensis*), and a variety of daylily and iris begin to filter it and remove contaminants. The cleaned water is stored in cisterns on site and used to irrigate some of the trees and gardens.

The long central spine running through the park was formerly the airport's runway. Sasaki chose to soften the edges of the path by breaking the three-foot-thick concrete slabs, manipulating them to appear almost like flagstone pavers set in a lawn. Farther south, where the park runs parallel to a canal, a beautifully detailed fused bamboo deck hovers over the water. Meanwhile, within the Four Season Garden, the path becomes a gentle ribbon of concrete that rises and falls, offering a rich experience highlighted by the diversity and amplitude of the plants. All plantings are species native to the Yangtze River Delta, with some varieties selected specifically to attract butterflies and other insects in the effort to reestablish land and marine habitats. Thanks to the length of the green space and its variety of plants and materials, the relatively narrow thirty-six-acre park appears wider than it is.

Alex and I visited sections 1 and 3 in 2018 and returned to see the whole park in fall 2019. Our second visit benefited from a riot of autumn colors on the Chinese flame trees (*Koelreuteria bipinnata* var. *integrifolia*). The elevated boardwalk that joins the planted, raised terraces of the strip has the same textural roughness as the earlier parts to the north; grade variations are addressed by short stairways alternating with ramps. Sasaki

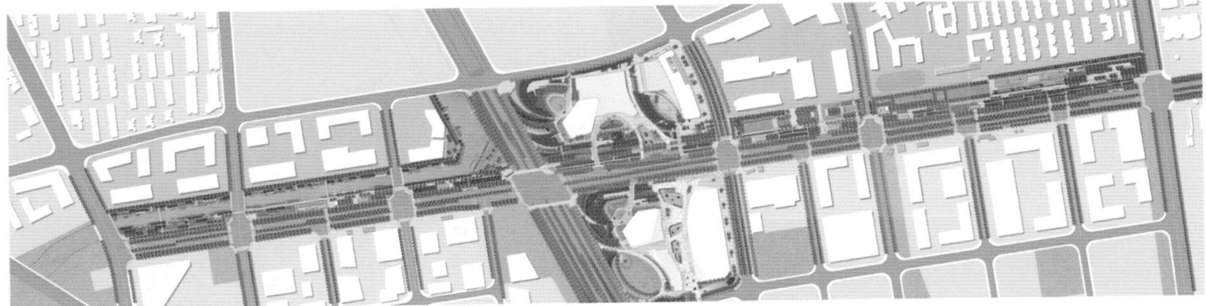

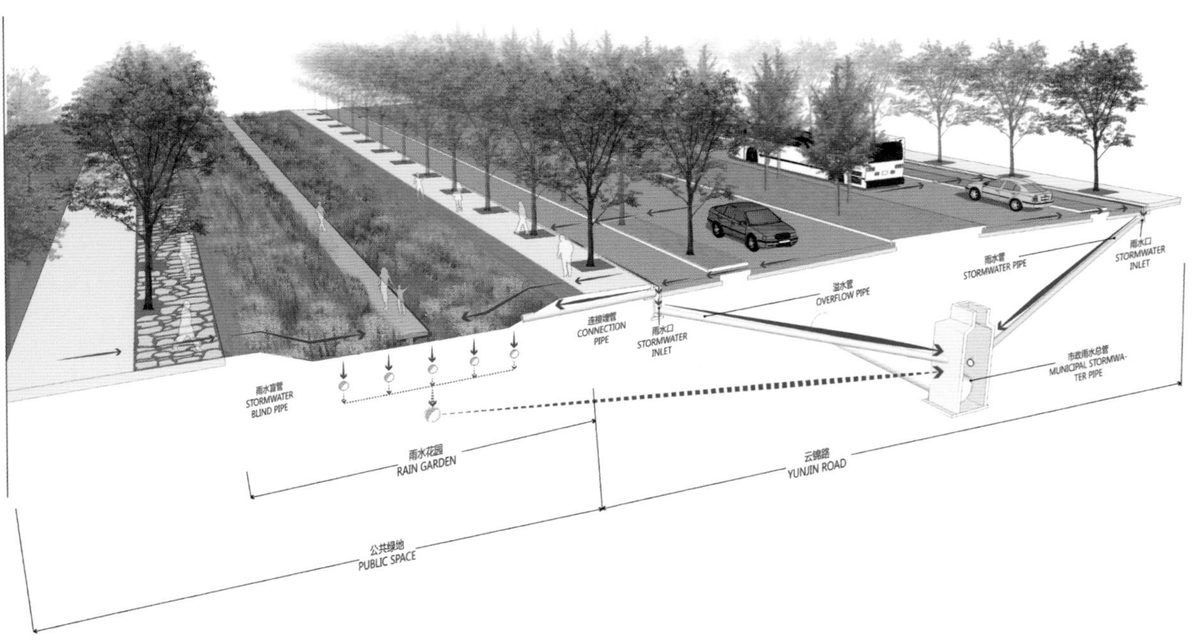
雨水管
STORMWATER PIPE
雨水口
STORMWATER INLET
溢水管
OVERFLOW PIPE
连接管
CONNECTION PIPE
雨水口
STORMWATER INLET
市政雨水总管
MUNICIPAL STORMWA-TER PIPE
雨水盲管
STORMWATER BLIND PIPE
雨水花园
RAIN GARDEN
云锦路
YUNJIN ROAD
公共绿地
PUBLIC SPACE

Friedrich's masterpiece *Das Eismeer (Sea of Ice,* 1823–24). Like Friedrich's depiction of humanity confronted by nature, vegetation's takeover of these huge concrete slabs evokes a palpable sense of humankind's diminutive role within the physical world.

Moving through the park we discovered a narrow strip of tarmac that acts as a path through what is now a series of woodland rooms. Once used to land helicopters, this area has been reclaimed as a dense successional forest. Within this forest, stacked concrete slabs rise to create one of several "lookouts" over the surrounding countryside, a reference to similar structures built in Germany in the late nineteenth century. Here, the foot path had become so narrow that we instinctively looked down to keep our footing. The reduced scale makes a sharp contrast with the broad runway and allowed us to notice the delicate flowers emerging from the concrete in this hybrid nature.

Elsewhere we saw children absorbed in games of their own devising and middle-aged men playing cards in the shade as well as dog walkers, cyclists, joggers, and rollerbladers. The absence of spaces or equipment devoted to these activities doesn't deter the Flugplatz's hundred thousand annual visitors. Michael Triebswetter, founder of GTL, says:

> What we see in Bonames is that the way people use the park is changing with an ever-developing ruderal vegetation, creating new paths when wildness takes over the old ones, playing new games. No playground is needed at all, and no so-called playground was ever intended.

It was atypical in Germany in the late 1990s for the public to participate in the design process of this kind of civic project, but Alter Flugplatz struck a responsive chord: numerous meetings and guided tours, both conveying information about the repurposing, were well-attended. Fifteen to twenty guides still lead visitors through the park regularly, providing information about the biodiversity and ecological value of the former airfield. Individual donations of two hundred trees include a mix of fruit, ornamental understory, and canopy, some of which are planted in a grove running parallel to the former runway. The donations indicate enthusiasm for the airport transformation even though the grove is out of character with the designers' ruderal concept. Near the donated trees, long gabions filled with concrete rubble act as retaining walls and host a variety of plant species. Along the former

Large broken slabs

Ruderal vegetation

runway, the gabions reappear as benches for the many rollerbladers.

Alter Flugplatz offers interesting comparisons to other parks on rehabilitated land. Parc du Peuple de l'Herbe, which occupies a former quarry in the northwestern suburbs of Paris, has a similar goal of renaturation (page 234). There, the landscape architecture firm Agence Ter was asked to restore 280 acres; that is, to return the site to its pre-quarry condition and attempt to erase signs of human interference. The idea of "renaturation" parallels the international "rewilding" movement, which works toward replacing unused or underused buildings with meadows, urban wildlands, or even vegetable gardens as a means to reduce maintenance and improve the ecology.

The initial construction expenditure for Alter Flugplatz was minimal, and costs for upkeep (mowing, minor repairs, etc.), paid for by the city, are negligible thanks to the ruderal concept. The landscape is continuously changing, in a state of simultaneous decay and regeneration, as it is taken over by flora and fauna first and enjoyed by people second. Unlike Xuhui Runway Park, which is highly engineered, manicured, and artificial in its ecologies, Alter Flugplatz doesn't require human activity (i.e., maintenance) to thrive.

Narrow opening to forest

Goldenrod in meadow

Path through successional forest

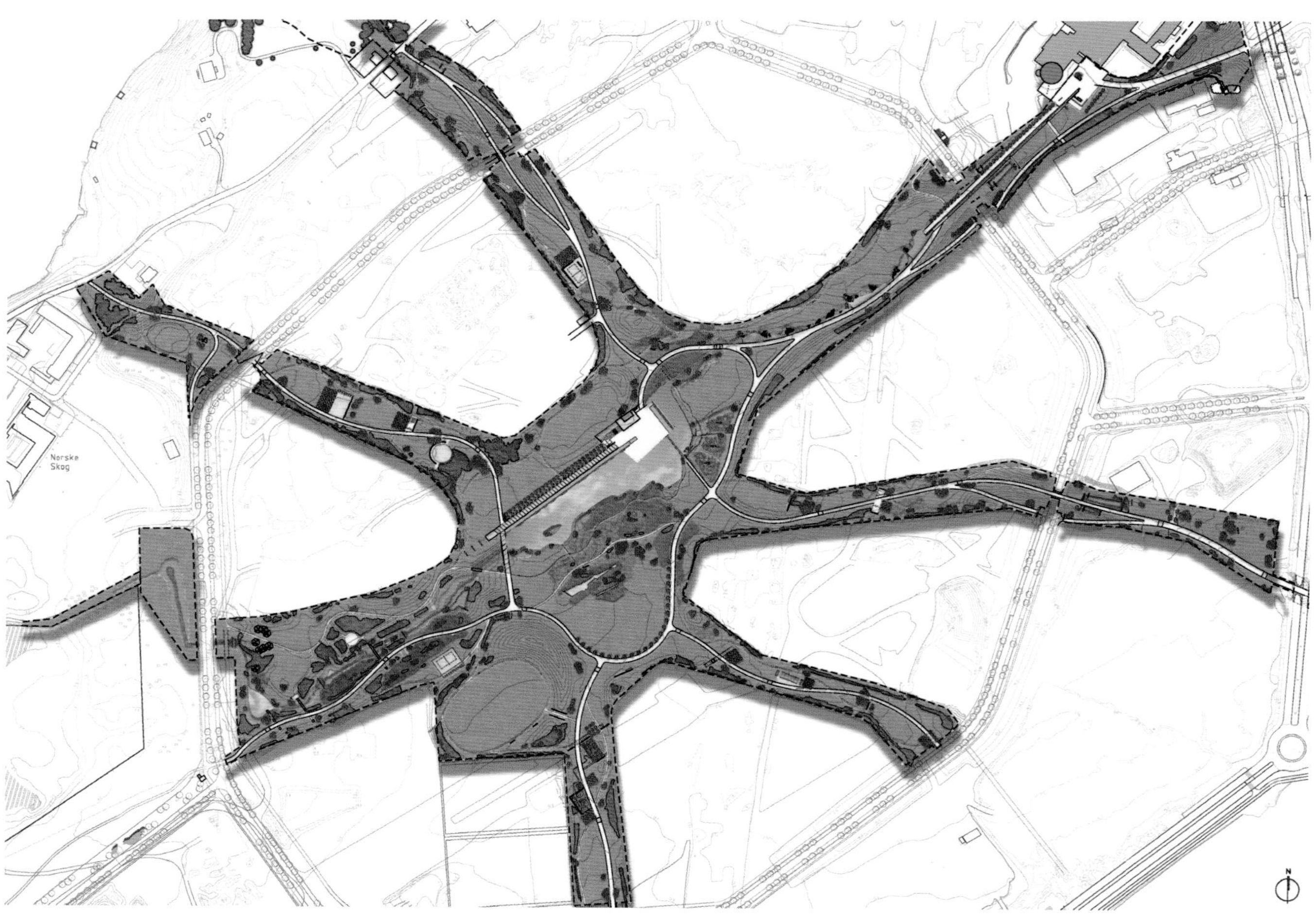

Plan

Nansen Park

Oslo, Norway
2008

Bjørbekk & Lindheim

116 acres
cost: $13.25 million

In the 1940s, to prepare for the construction of Oslo Airport on the Fornebu peninsula site on the inner Oslo Fjord, bulldozers began what became the complete flattening of the rocky terrain; even the shoreline was altered to become more regular. For the 840-acre wasteland that remained after the airport was moved in 1998 to Gardermoen, twenty-three miles from the city center, landscape architect Bjørbekk & Lindheim sought to replace the airport's flat linearity with the organic forms and topography of the area and its coastline, to recapture the former natural setting.

Underlying this largest land reclamation in Norway was a practical consideration. To accommodate the rapid growth of Oslo—the fastest growing city in Europe (between 1990 and 1999, the population increased 12 percent; by 2018, the population had reached one million)—the Ministry of Local Government and Modernization planned a number of local developments, among them Fornebu, just five miles from downtown. Here, the city of Oslo built roads, infrastructure, and utilities. In 1999, the nearby Bærum Municipality (two miles away) and the Finnish studio Helin & Siitoner designed a master plan for the residential and commercial development. Envisioned for the center of Fornebu was 116-acre Nansen Park, named after the explorer and Nobel Peace Prize laureate Fridtjof Nansen. The remediation of the heavily polluted area (done almost entirely on site) was funded by the government's sale of the land to developers.

The master plan proposed 6,300 residences by 2000 (increased in 2016 to 11,000) and workplaces to accommodate 20,000. Sustainability was a high priority in numerous discussions of the project with the area's potential inhabitants. There is no dense urban tradition in Norway, and while the government and the developers pushed for more height and density, future locals succeeded in requiring the community to conform to the national development form known as "building in landscape." Even though the city's five-story limit was occasionally breached, the buildings at Fornebu produce a pleasant, mid-to-high-income suburban environment that owes its success more to Nansen Park than to the architecture.

Alex and I met Simen Gylseth, a landscape architect with Bjørbekk & Lindheim, on a sunny July morning outside the former airport's late-1930s air traffic control tower and adjacent terminal buildings. The buildings, now used mostly for cultural purposes, mark one of many ways to enter the park. The plan takes the form of a large octopus, with each arm containing park entrances, bike paths, and various programs. As we looked over the landscape before us, parts of which are a constructed nature preserve, Gylseth explained that a major inspiration for the design was the separateness and spaciousness of the vast green tract. To recapture the former rolling hills and expansive views of distant rises to the north and west of the city, the designers adopted a cut-and-fill approach: polluted soil was removed, treated, and returned to the site together with paving taken from the runways. A little more than three feet of topsoil was distributed on top. All of this was completed in two years.

The park's seven tentacles (100 to 330 feet in width) separate seven topographical areas. In our half-day visit, we had time to experience only two of the arms. We strolled through the restored landscape on one of the multiple narrow paths covered in crushed local stone and admired the large lake and plaza; in the remaining tentacles are a dog park, playground, sports fields, amphitheater, beach, and other facilities.

Water is a major theme of Nansen Park and a key component in the site's remediation strategy. The site is almost completely bounded by the inner Oslo Fjord, and views to this body of water are at times present. Within the park, the designers have created a formalized and technically sophisticated sequence of fountains, runnels, weirs, and pools that are often both poetic and playful. A thin waterway stretches the length of the park from north to south, starting as a narrow trough fountain made of weathered steel. The fountain spills into a channel with sides also constructed from weathered steel and a bottom of concrete cast with wave patterns. The channel widens to nearly five feet and is crossed by small bridges of steel plate that are laser-cut with patterns. As the runnel transitions to a more naturalized state, still reflecting pools alternate with oxygen-infusing streams and weirs, which emit a pleasant burbling sound. Runoff from the adjacent roadways is collected

and cleaned by passing through biological and mechanical filters before running through open green swales to the 65,000-square-foot, two-foot-deep Central Lake. From here the water is pumped back up to the initial fountain. Surplus water passes through an overflow and infiltration area and into the fjord.

The large Central Lake and Festival Plaza in which it is located are the serene high point of the park. At the plaza (which will eventually include a WC and a café), a mother and child occupied one of several benches; park furniture is placed at regular intervals on the Festival Plaza's pavement of large slabs of cut granite, which borders the lake. Young couples lounged on several of the other benches.

Wide granite steps lead down to the lake on the northwest side of the plaza, while three unique bands define the north edge of the lake: a wide platform of Kebony, a paved area of in situ–polished concrete, and an allée of silver willow trees (*Salix alba* var. *sericea*). Together they are a study in hard and soft edges. Large stone slabs (imported from China for reasons of economy) are partially submerged in the shallow water at the north end. Occupying a sloping plane of the same stone, an artwork by Herman Dreisetl of Atelier Dreisetl, which designed the park's water elements and treatment, consists of rotating steel elements that children can manipulate to direct the flow of water.

Strollers, joggers, and dog walkers, as well as numerous crossbladers using ski poles to propel themselves at breakneck speeds, availed themselves of the narrow paths throughout the park. But these park patrons were outnumbered by the crowds we encountered near the southern end of the park: men, women, and children laden with beach equipment. All were heading down a steep hill beyond the park's far end to the seashore. We were told that the park is just as popular in winter, when people visit to admire the beauty of freshly fallen snow. Like the cherry blossom festival in Tokyo, these winter outings glorify a specific moment in nature.

Near the beach, a large constructed mound acts as an overlook. The summit contains a ring of Swedish whitebeam (*Sorbus intermedia*) planted in a gathering circle. From this vantage point, we saw a small meadow that contains part of the only remnant of the airport—the original runway. On the hillside, the designers created a woodland with hazelnut, pine, and aspen; completed in 2017, it is itself a test site for naturally growing species. Along the park's northern edge, a pine forest was restored. Stands of birches in front of the pines provide a unique contrast between the ground plane and the canopy; vertical strips of white birches' bark foreground the horizontal band of dark, shadowy pines. A shrub layer is noticeably absent. Instead, a simple mossy groundcover blankets the forest floor, presenting a space of restrained beauty.

To assure the environmental friendliness of the water treatment process, no fertilizers or other chemicals are allowed

on the site. Together with the poor quality of the soil, this directive posed a challenge for the vegetation. Nevertheless, most of the hundred thousand plants installed over a two-month period have survived. These include several willow species such as purple osier, brittle, and bay, and also lady's mantle, sedges, geraniums, lilacs, and roses. The wild roses grow among rocks scattered throughout the landscape, while the lilacs provide purple accents.

Gylseth told us that one of the project's biggest challenges was to satisfy the community's insistence on the preservation of nature, despite the fact that there was nothing natural left to preserve. Inherent in Norwegian culture is an admiration for untouched nature and landscape, and many families take camping trips to remote parts of the country where hotels are not allowed because of the threat they pose to the beauty of the site. Any perceived danger to nature at Nansen Park—the laying of wooden planks to prevent invasive plants from spreading where trees were being planted, for example—was vigorously opposed. A "nature center" along the coastline, which serves as a critical habitat for native animal species, was created at the behest of the citizenry, as was a similar "preserve" within the park.

Indeed, the renaturation of Nansen Park is completely artificial. Unlike the process at Alter Flugplatz in Bonames, where vegetation self-propagated once the airport was decommissioned, at Nansen, every hill, stream, and plant had to be re-created because the topography had been altered so radically. In this context, the designers' greatest accomplishment is that their restoration of nature feels authentic, and that the clearly constructed components—streams and some planting designs—harmonize with that restoration.

Aerial view of restored coastline

Granite outcroppings and stream

View to southwest

Fountain and water channel

Central Lake and Festival Plaza

Central Lake water feature

750-acre void

Former Tempelhof Airport, 1936–41, Ernst Sagebiel

Proposed park, plan, 2011, GROSS.MAX.

Proposed park, aerial view, rendering, 2011, GROSS.MAX.

took matters even further and passed a law in 2014 that forbids indefinitely any development on the site. Despite the fact that Berlin is classified as 45 percent green, and considering GROSS. MAX.'s anticipation that a park at Tempelhof could easily accommodate multiple uses in accordance with the extensive citizen participation during the design process, every amenity currently on the site—toilets, barbecues, biergarten, food carts, scruffy community gardens, signs explaining the history of the site, and eleven entranceways—is temporary. Also located there is the organization Taschengeldfirma, which offers learning programs, such as bicycle repair, for the socially disadvantaged. To ensure security, Grün-Berlin, the city's park management department, restricts specific activities, such as kite-flying, windsurfing (the expansive area is conducive to wind sports), and soccer, to certain areas and has also fenced off sixty-four acres to be used exclusively for wildlife preservation. The last fulfills a nationwide objective that originated with the early twentieth-century German conservation movement.

Shortly after the law against development was passed, local citizens formed a board to oversee the park's maintenance (approximately $3.38 million per year) and security. As we visited Tempelhofer Feld with Dr. Michael Krebs, then director of Grün-Berlin, an elderly woman interrogated us suspiciously about the reason for our visit. The skepticism with which members of this group regard any outside interest in the park is exemplified by the three years—*three years*—of discussion that were necessary to reach an agreement to plant twenty apple trees.

The huge void of Tempelhofer Feld is quite different from the rich natural landscape found at Alter Flugplatz in Bonames and numerous other parks on reclaimed land. But it is important to emphasize that the starkness of the Berlin space is what the inhabitants of the city wanted: every year, there are 400 requests for special events (typically, 80 are accepted) and 2,000,000 visitors (with as many as 30,000 to 50,000 a week in the spring).

A similarly natural green area in the southeast Adlershof suburb of Berlin suggests an alternative to the strictly hands-off approach that Tempelhofer Feld has taken. Designated in 1993 to replace an obsolete airfield in Johannisthal, the park, subtly designed by the local firm Büro Kiefer, tempered the preservation of nature with visitor needs and recreation. As at Tempelhofer Feld, sixty-four acres were set aside for wildlife, again to meet national preservation goals. But the emptiness of Landscape Park Johannisthal is moderated by dense groves of trees at the entrances, open meadows, a children's playground, and an elevated timber promenade around the reserve. The park, devised in an effort to attract a new residential community, may one day offer an instructive case study in how to balance intervention and non-interference.

Landscape Park Johannisthal, Berlin, Büro Kiefer

Overleaf: Some of the two million annual visitors

waterside industry: parks

The post-industrial era has seen the demolition or relocation of factories around the world, many on riverfronts and almost all leaving behind heavily polluted sites. Even with the need to remove ground contamination, these transformations have provided rich opportunities to introduce green spaces into relentlessly overbuilt areas. Such rehabilitations typically make beautiful natural riversides accessible to the public for the first time in what could be more than a hundred years.

Many of these newly created landscapes retain and repurpose massive industrial buildings or other artifacts as giant sculptures. Gas Works Park in Seattle, Washington (1975), designed by Richard Haag, was one of the first such experiments. The German landscape architect Latz + Partner adopted a similar approach at Duisburg Nord (1997) in the Ruhr Valley, once known for its unique concentration of steel factories. These two parks have become popular recreational and cultural areas.

Almost every former industrial site must be remediated before it can be used for a park. But once these areas are cleaned up, cities, other governmental entities, technology giants, and private developers turn them into new outdoor spaces as centerpieces in large-scale planning efforts, amenities to draw residents to new housing, or design must-sees to stimulate tourism and investment in a city in decline.

Environmentalists, too, see benefits in parks on damaged land. Green spaces built on former industrial areas are engineered to address particular types of restoration, from cleaning polluted soil to counteracting extreme weather, especially the more frequent floods brought on by a changing climate. Widely ranging solutions address coastal edges and often incorporate means for mitigating pollution before it can contaminate waterways.

Race Street Pier in Philadelphia adapts a late nineteenth-century two-level pier into an unusual park. The green space is the first part of a plan to improve six miles of Delaware River shores. The project's largest component is Penn's Landing, a mixed-use development that accommodates water guidelines and green roofs; it includes a highway cap.

Like Race Street Pier, Waterloo Greenway is part of a much larger rehabilitation project, in this case, a continuous landscape along Waller Creek, a waterway misused for over a century because of its devastating floods. The endeavor will link a series of small parks, both old and new; reconnect downtown Austin to the less affluent eastern part of the city; and put into effect new flood containment measures. The stream's revival has opened up the possibility of millions of square feet of development in this fast-growing city.

Both Waterloo Greenway and Renaissance Park in Chattanooga, Tennessee, built on the site of a former factory, associated green space with economic considerations. The Chattanooga open space was intended to buttress residential construction in a city suffering from a sharp economic decline. At the same time, it captures and cleans runoff, filtering it through a series of planted armatures in a wetland. Long Dock Park in Beacon, New York, was planned as part of a mixed-use development project including a hotel; the recession of 2007–9 put an end to the hotel project but not to the corresponding green space. The designers spent years managing meadows and berms that will slowly rectify soil contaminated by years of rail and other uses. Additionally, new and existing wetlands filter storm water and control floods.

The Parc aux Angéliques in Bordeaux reverses the typical sequence of development: landscape first, buildings second. The green space, a test site for a landscape with indeterminate futures, consists of a gridded forest that alternates with clearings to inform the positioning of further development. Hinge Park in Vancouver conforms to the city's EcoDensity plan, implemented in 2006 to encourage sustainability and affordability in the world's fourth most expensive real estate market.

The Expedia Group is one of a number of technology and internet enterprises that have updated the sleek corporate headquarters of the mid-twentieth century into expansive corporate complexes set amid stunning new open areas. Landscape architects, architects, and other contributors from the design professions are selected not only for expertise but for public recognition. The Beach, part of Seattle's new Expedia campus, extends a greenway along the edge of the property to continue a bicycle trail and expand an existing park to the south. A stepped dune that acts as an amphitheater and gathering space dominates the site.

Many of these parks feature an educational component, a welcome inclusion at a time of widespread alarm over environmental degradation. Long Dock provides art and environmental classes in a historic structure. Hands-on lessons in water management at Hinge Park allow young visitors to pump the water that sustains the park's wetland in dry weather. A colony of busy beavers that have made their home at the park can be observed in person or via social media. And the Beach demonstrates the dynamics and diversity of aquatic ecologies in the Puget lowlands.

Master plan for the Central Delaware River, 2011, OLIN

Race Street Pier

Philadelphia, Pennsylvania
2011

James Corner Field Operations

1 acre
cost: $6 million

Inspired by William Penn's definition of Philadelphia as a "Greene Countrie Towne," in 2011 the Delaware River Waterfront Corporation, founded in 2009, released a master plan for the Pennsylvania side of the Delaware River from design firms Cooper Robertson, OLIN, and Kieran Timberlake, among others. Numerous community stakeholders served as consultants in the effort to provide places and activities that would draw people to the edge of the water. Massing of the development and optimal solar orientation also comply with this goal. At that time, the cost of improving nearly six miles of riverfront, including thirteen green spaces (one every half mile), was estimated to be $770 million over thirty years.

The largest component of the plan is Penn's Landing, a forty-five-acre project by landscape architect Hargreaves Jones that will include a mix of business, commercial, and low-rise residential. The area, named in honor of the place where William Penn first touched shore, will also contain gardens, a play area, interactive water feature, ice rink, café, river esplanade, and terraces, together with an informal amphitheater. Storm water guidelines address the capture, reuse, and infiltration of water and how to accommodate green roofs.

In addition to creating more than sixty-four acres of riverside parks and nearly five miles of multiuse trails, the Waterfront Corporation's ambitious project called for upgrading all the connector streets to the riverside parks in order to improve pedestrian and bicycle passage under the elevated eight-lane I-95 highway. As it has in so many US cities, the interstate severed the relationship between the city and the river's broad course. In fact, so objectionable is I-95 to the community that a twelve-acre highway cap (which will incorporate an older, smaller cap) estimated to cost at least $90 million is planned between Chestnut and Walnut Streets. This green space will slope down to the river and Penn's Landing, creating a site. Including the cost to cap, the project is estimated at $225 million.

Structurally, the deck over the freeway is a steel trough system (as opposed to a conventional concrete slab) thin enough to tilt toward the waterway, in line with the overall objective of featuring river views. An economic and engineering study for the undertaking, commissioned in 2014 by the Waterfront Corporation and prepared by a team headed by Hargreaves Jones, confirmed that a park framed by development would be able to support the associated public space. Full funding will be provided by city, state, and foundation support.

Race Street Pier is the first of the thirteen riverside parks. The two-level pier was originally planned in 1896, with the lower level for cargo unloading and shipping and the top level for recreation; it was completed in 1901. In 1919, the second level became structurally unsound and was closed, and the whole pier was condemned in 1928. The city rebuilt Race Street Pier, reopening it in 1931. But by the time James Corner Field Operations received the commission in 2009, the pier had once again completely deteriorated.

The November Saturday that Alex and I visited fell on the weekend of the Philly Bike Expo. Although the Expo focuses on bicycles, it had attracted a Harley-Davidson rally. The motorcycles turned the downtown into a deafening mayhem of traffic jams; fortunately for us, Race Street Pier provided a welcome relief.

The Benjamin Franklin Bridge dominated the view, but even with this behemoth of a neighbor, Race Street Pier captured our attention. We gazed at the huge cables of the bridge and its stone towers with a pocket of dense green foliage at the base, which marks the beginning of the park. Unlike other bridge-adjacent parks (such as Brooklyn Bridge Park, where the overhang can be intrusive), Race Street Pier has turned the Benjamin Franklin into an asset. The massive footings provide a spectacular contrast in scale with the relatively small park and its exquisite detailing. Furthermore, the structure's tremendous height dissipates traffic noise, except for the trains that pass by every ten minutes on weekdays.

The park presents itself to the public realm of the street in unique ways. Two rows of pin oak trees, which line the sidewalk along North Christopher Columbus Boulevard, prepared us for the dynamic and varied green space projecting into the river. On the pier are swamp white oaks (*Quercus bicolor*) that were left over from the contract-grown trees for the National September 11 Memorial in New York City. Along with the swamp white oaks are clusters of serviceberries, multistemmed river birches, and red maple trees lifted above the ground plane by weathered steel planters.

Field Operations retained the two-level concept of the original pier. A ramped, stone-paved walkway—one leg ascending to the upper level and the other descending toward the river's surface—organizes the park in a scissor configuration. We started our loop around the park on the upper leg, the Sky Promenade. Favored by joggers, this area is characterized by a single line of the swamp white oaks and by guardrails canted inward to draw attention to views of the bridge. The line of oaks parallels a line of light standards, strengthening a one-point perspective. Decking of Trex, a sustainable synthetic product with the texture of wood, clads this level.

The lower level encourages more passive activities: even on the chilly day of our visit, people were sprawled on the Sun Lawn, picnicking, playing with their dogs, or enjoying other activities. The grass is bordered by a narrow path of gray concrete pavers, and the size of the pavers is matched by the dimensions of the two hundred LED lights embedded in the path. The lighting is irregularly spaced and provides interest at night. The upper level of the pier ends in amphitheater seating that cascades toward the river, while the lower level terminates in a generous river terrace, popular for music and other kinds of performance, for community activities such as yoga classes, and, predictably, for wedding pictures.

We noticed that most of the wood benches scattered around the plaza were occupied by people of all ages who socialized and at the same time enjoyed the arresting views up and down the Delaware River. Part of the paving near the entrance was retrofitted with metal grating; like the original wharf drops used to load and unload cargo, glimpses of the water below permit more intimate contact with the river.

Although Race Street Park was one of the smallest parks we visited, we found the diverse spatial experiences particularly memorable. Many of the park's trees, which provide ample shade and a feeling of enclosed space beneath the canopies and between the raised steel planters, were donated privately. The varied landscapes of the more formal rows of trees and tiny lawns contrast with the delicate woodland garden. This open space is an elegant beginning for the series of parks planned for the riverside.

View from Benjamin Franklin Bridge to Race Street Pier

Penn's Landing, rendering, Hargreaves Jones

BENJAMIN FRANKLIN BRIDGE

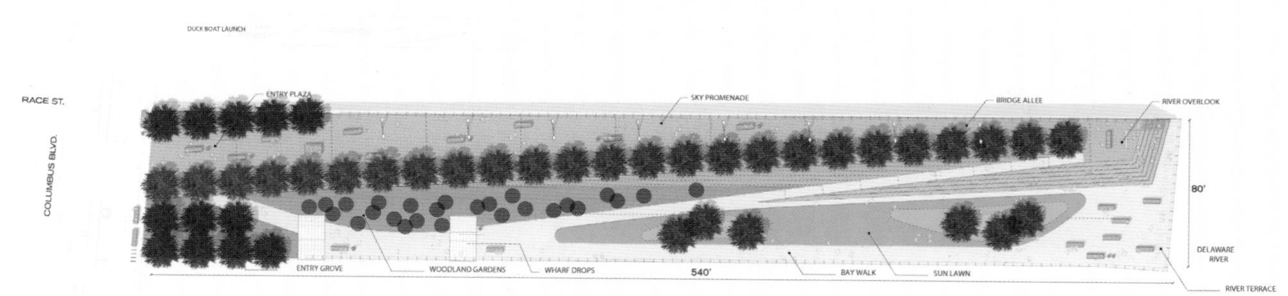

Sky Promenade

Site plan

River Overlook

Sun Lawn

View to west past Waterloo Park with Moody Amphitheater (right) and Texas Capitol (background)

Waterloo Greenway

Austin, Texas
2021

Michael Van Valkenburgh Associates

11 acres
cost: $250 million

Residents of Austin have long had a love/hate relationship with Waller Creek, the seven-mile urban riparian ecosystem that extends from the northern part of the city southward through the University of Texas campus to Lady Bird Lake, a popular recreation area. Like most of the countless creeks near the city, Waller has been subject to dangerous overflows—in 1981, for example, eleven inches of rain caused a flood that led to the deaths of thirteen people and $36 million in damages.

Efforts to combat flooding for more than a century, including decades of street improvements carried out by the city, have produced a stream that in many areas is defined by stone and concrete retaining walls and rapidly eroding vegetated slopes. The creek, already subject to some interventions, lacks much of its natural bank and runs in what is essentially an urban canyon cut off from the streets around it.

In recent years, however, support has grown for rehabilitating the stream and implementing flood control; that is, turning Waller Creek into an asset rather than a deficiency. A decisive factor in the change in public opinion must have been the lure of 10–12 million square feet of potential development in one of the fastest-growing cities in the United States.

Also influencing public awareness may have been promotion by environmentalists of the importance of rivers and streams. In talks, publications, and websites, various ecological groups have explained the role of streams in absorbing rainwater, runoff, and snowmelt; preventing pollutants from contaminating water downstream; and providing food and habitat for plants, fish, birds, and other animals. Streams are also instrumental for recreational activities, like fishing and hunting, and for agriculture, though the goals of commercial interests and of preservationists can often be at odds.

In 2011, the Waller Creek Conservancy and the City of Austin held a competition for a thirty-seven-acre site consisting of a one-and-a-half-mile segment of Waller Creek between 15th Street and Lady Bird Lake. City residents were involved in developing the brief, which included "remaking a currently fragmented and undervalued section of Austin into a vibrant, livable, and workable district." The winning proposal, by Michael Van Valkenburgh Associates, provides a continuous landscape along the creek, one of the largest transformations of any urban creek in the United States. Like the Dequindre Cut in Detroit (page 26), the 606 in Chicago (page 34), and the waterfront in Shanghai (page 144), the scheme will link a band of small parks, each one with its own attraction, and connect with Austin's city center. While the whole project, renamed Waterloo Greenway (supported by the renamed Waterloo Greenway Conservancy), is scheduled for completion in 2026, the first phase, a renovation of Waterloo Park and three-tenths of a mile of Waller Creek, is due to open in 2021.

The greenway centers on the lower section of Waller Creek. Among the historic, new, and refurbished parks included in the plan, besides Waterloo Park, are Symphony Square, Palm Park, and new areas named the Refuge, the Narrows, and the Lattice. Along the creek, a diverse collection of native plant communities—dry and wet riparian, midgrass prairie, juniper oak savanna, and bottomland hardwood forests—will replace the invasive species that have proliferated.

In addition to these waterside areas, the Waterloo Greenway will begin to reconnect downtown Austin to the less affluent eastern part of the city. Already in the 1920s, the city used the physical interruption of Waller Creek to divide the two areas; since the 1960s, the roughly adjacent I-35 interstate highway has further separated the city. At the same time, the greenway establishes a singular precedent for waterway restoration within an urban context. In contrast to earlier attempts to control Waller Creek, which opted for walls and revetments to hold back slopes, the landscape architects have proposed a combination of reestablishing the creek banks when possible and creating a series of terraces and restored stone retaining walls where riparian slopes are not feasible. The steeply pitched inclines will first be regraded, allowing for a shallower angle, then stabilized using a combination of geotextiles and intensive planting. At the water's edge, the toe of the slope will be structured with locally quarried or salvaged stone.

The greatest change to the hydrology of the creek was the construction of a massive tunnel to redirect flood waters out of the small waterway and directly into Lady Bird Lake. The municipality built the mile-long, roughly twenty-four-foot-

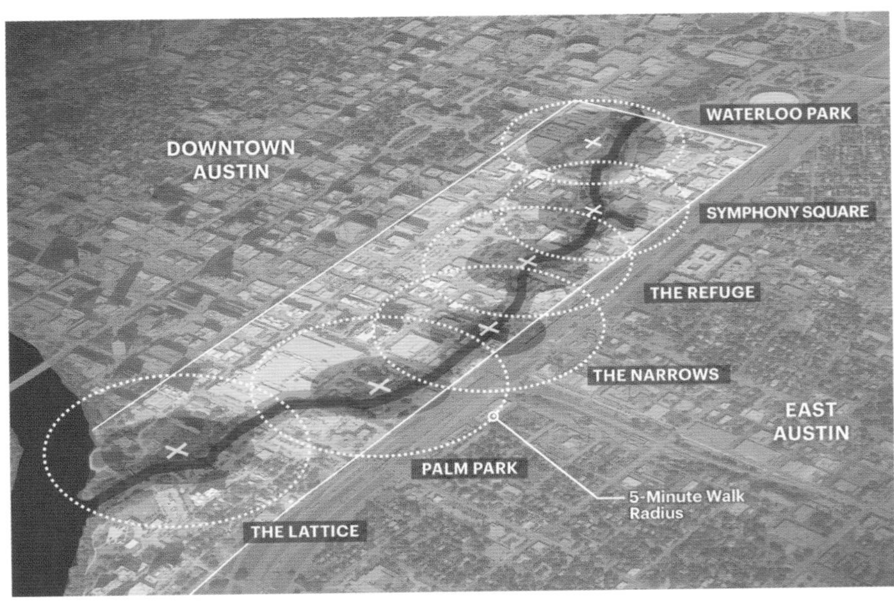

Waller Creek, preremediation

Existing and proposed parks along the Waterloo Greenway, diagram

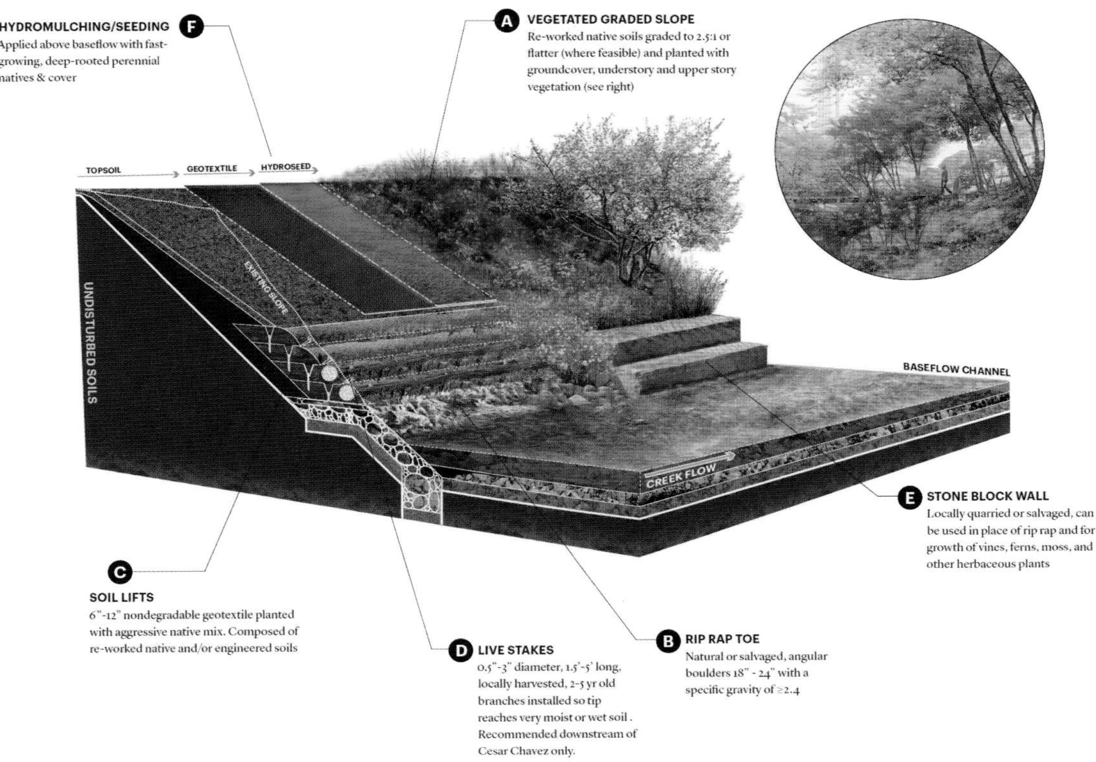

Riparian slope restoration, diagram

Heritage live oak near Moody Amphitheater

diameter underpass (2015) beneath downtown Austin at a cost of $146.5 million. During a severe storm, water enters the passage near Waterloo Park, drops seventy feet, and then flows toward the lake, where it is discharged. This highly engineered intervention almost guarantees that Waller Creek will not flood and also removes twenty-eight acres of land from the hundred-year floodplain. The creek retains its role as urban infrastructure, but as a much-needed piece of green infrastructure instead of as a large drainage canal. Waller Creek will also encourage nearby redevelopment, particularly important since the city plans to use this income to pay back the bonds that were needed to construct the tunnel.

When Alex and I visited Austin in the spring of 2019, we easily looked past the shortcomings of the open space, including trash left by people who are homeless, and focused instead on the vegetation, which sparkled in the bright sunlight. Majestic cypress trees rise on the riverbank, as do Mexican palmettos (*Sabal mexicana*), which spread their profuse fronds amid various shrubs and bushes, including many invasive species. The greenway's hybrid quality—nature and engineering, nature and the city—is immediately apparent.

The renovation of Waterloo Park includes the stunning new Moody Amphitheater by Thomas Phifer and Partners. The facility, with a capacity of close to three thousand, has a roof, known as the "canopy," featuring hundreds of thin steel members that recall the delicate grid of an Agnes Martin painting. The roof appears to float over the sidewalk of Trinity Street. On the lawn beside the new pavilion, several "heritage trees" (with trunk diameters greater than twenty-four inches) have been saved and transplanted. A second outdoor venue, the renovated Symphony Square amphitheater (2019), is one block southeast of Waterloo Park. Dedicated to classical music, the amphitheater seats 350 on stone and lawn risers.

John Rigdon, the director of planning and design for the Waterloo Greenway Conservancy, noted, "The project is a pushback against development and technology; it is trying to create public space in the face of an increasing loss of free, democratic spaces." The naturalistic Waterloo Greenway contrasts with the artificiality of another Texas waterway, San Antonio's famous Riverwalk. Instead, Austin's new landscape initiative will see the little-publicized rehabilitation of a degraded and channelized stream evolve into the creation of an exciting cultural and recreational hub for the city.

Trail along Waller Creek, rendering

Tennessee River, view to south of Renaissance Park (foreground) with Ross's Landing and 21st Century Waterfront Park (across river)

Renaissance Park

Chattanooga, Tennessee
2006

Hargreaves Associates (now Hargreaves Jones)

23.5 acres
cost: $8 million

A set of new parks in Chattanooga stands out in two singular ways. The open areas not only play an ambitious role in the city's renewal but also draw attention to Tennessee's Native American heritage.

In 1985, in response to the city's dire economic failure and its consequent decline in population, a group of residents in collaboration with the River City Company developed a master plan called Tennessee Riverpark: Chattanooga. The group proposed that twenty miles along the shore of the Tennessee River, starting at the Chickamauga Dam and ending at Moccasin Bend, be converted into an urban cultural park. In the three months after the unveiling of the private/public scheme, private donors pledged $42 million toward its implementation; the overall cost was estimated to be $120 million. While much of the project has not been realized, the Riverfront Parkway, a state-owned road that cut off part of the city's downtown from the river's south shore, was rerouted. The year 2000 saw a second revitalization effort: creation of the 21st Century Waterfront Plan.

As is true for many industrial waterfronts, the goal of both of these plans was to reconnect the city with the river, which had always been considered Chattanooga's backbone. Cleaning up the loading docks and other obsolete facilities would open previously obscured views to this scenic waterway, encourage real estate development, and support the creation of cultural institutions and recreational facilities. The linchpin of the 2000 plan was three public parks: the 12.5-acre Ross's Landing, which folds into the 39-acre 21st Century Waterfront Park (2005) on the southern shore of the river, and the 23.5-acre Renaissance Park (2006) on the northern shore. For then-mayor Bob Corker, the owner of a construction company (and US senator from 2007 to 2019), it was clear that Hargreaves Associates (now Hargreaves Jones), the only competitor to promote development along with the parks, should receive the commission.

In the early nineteenth century, John Ross (who would become principal chief of the Cherokee Nation) used a spot on the south shore of the Tennessee River as a ferry landing and trading post. In 1835, with the Treaty of New Echota, the Cherokee ceded their land to the United States, setting in motion the government's forcible relocation to Indian Territory (present-day Oklahoma) of the Cherokee, the Creek, and hundreds of Black slaves. So arduous was the three-month-plus journey that it became known as the Trail of Tears. Ross's plot, which had become the boundary between the Cherokee Nation and the United States, served as a starting point for the march. In 1974, it was listed on the National Register of Historic Places as Ross's Landing.

A series of seven ceramic medallions created for the 21st Century Park by Team Gadugi, five Cherokee artists working together in Oklahoma, commemorates the Trail of Tears. In these large carved and glazed clay disks, Alex and I observed representations of Cherokee history, religious beliefs, and struggles with white settlers. They are located in what is known as the Passage, a space that connects downtown Chattanooga to the riverfront and features cascading water that is a favorite among children in hot weather.

Emerging from the Passage, we found ourselves at the monumental stair-like structure Hargreaves Associates built above the river in an area made unsuitable for development by frequent flooding. The concrete steps with grass treads, along with a performance lawn, were designed to absorb and retain storm and flood waters while providing an inviting seating area overlooking the fast-flowing river. Protective railings lining the park's riverside path are noticeably absent. This is in part because the harbor front is still active, mostly with tour boats offering river cruises that moor along the edge of the park. A more practical reason is that railings would likely be damaged by large debris coursing through the river during a flood. That this concern is germane was demonstrated during our visit to SWA's Buffalo Bayou Park in Houston: robust metal guardrails installed along some of the paths proved no match for the large fallen trees racing through the bayou after Hurricane Harvey.

A quick drive across Chief John Ross Bridge took us to Renaissance Park, on the Tennessee River's northern shore opposite the 21st Century Waterfront Park. The two green spaces are quite different from one another: the 21st Century Park is urban and sharp; Renaissance Park is wilder, more of a riparian landscape. Two pedestrian bridges carving through Renaissance Park recall a military bridge built on the site in 1864 (Chattanooga's first bridge) and also the numerous rail, pedestrian, and vehicular bridges that span

21st Century Waterfront Plan, plan

21st Century Waterfront Park, ceramic medallions of Cherokee history in Passage, Team Gadugi

21st Century Waterfront Park, stepped seating

Renaissance Park, view of wetland and landforms

the Tennessee River. Both bridges culminate in dramatic views of the river and downtown Chattanooga.

Lawn-covered landforms at the northern, inland entrance to the park contain the heavily contaminated soil left after the demolition of an appliance factory and enameling facility. Mary Margaret Jones of Hargreaves says that this "nasty soil"—34,000 yards of it—was dug up together with similarly contaminated soil from the flood plain; the earth was reused in a series of sculptural wedges covered on three sides with native grasses and on the fourth with lawn. The land, rich in wildflowers, slopes down to a meandering stream that was redirected from its natural coursing to the north.

Renaissance Park provides a succession through three environments. The first is open and urban with lawns and artificial landforms. The second is more enclosed and intimate, with wetlands and meadows. The third is looser and more informal and acts as a transition between park and river.

Water enters the site at the north through a culvert and then passes through gabions before wandering through the wetland and entering the river. The gabions are filled with riverine plant species that help clean the water. These armatures act as filters, slowing the water flow to allow carried particles to drop to the bottom and build up soil and plant life.

Penetrating deeper into the park, we found a mixed forest that includes oaks, sweetgum, white redbud, and sassafras together with other adapted and native plants. The forest opens to reveal a riverside edge of switch cane (*Arundinaria gigantea*), Solomon's seal (*Polygonatum biflorum*), and Virginia sweetspire (*Itea virginica*). Three hundred feet of the eroded riverbank have been newly stabilized by means of a bioengineered system, and a boat ramp under Market Street Bridge provides river access for kayaks and canoes.

The pleasantly natural feeling of the different environments is somewhat compromised by the wide concrete emergency access paths mandated by the city administration. Additionally, the 490-seat amphitheater and randomly placed sculptures seem irrelevant to this bucolic setting. The park hosts public events, art exhibitions, and commemorations of historic episodes that took place on the site. However, a family we encountered on our visit told us that one of the green space's most popular activities is watching its rich wildlife. Indeed, on this beautiful day in June, we saw that the stream was filled with large turtles.

The renewal of the riverfront effectively spurred the city's revival. By the time the 21st Century Park was completed in 2005, the Tennessee Aquarium had been expanded (at the time, the largest such freshwater facility in the United States), a visitors' center for the city constructed, and a considerable amount of housing added on both sides of the river. Repeating findings for other American park projects, 41 percent of those interviewed at five residential buildings in Chattanooga said they were willing to pay a premium to live close to Renaissance Park. Furthermore, the city's neglected downtown, renamed the Innovation District in 2015, has experienced a tremendous increase in private investment ($480 million). Collaborations between the city's civic institutions and the leaders of its other renovation projects, such as the master plan for the waterfront, together with successful speculation in a high-speed internet network, have made an important contribution to the revival's success.

Aerial view

Gabions with wetland plantings

Stabilized riverbank at kayak launch

Intertidal wetland

Long Dock Park

Beacon, New York
2004–2019

Reed Hilderbrand

23 acres
cost: $9.9 million

The town of Beacon, New York, with a population of 14,000, is located on the east bank of the Hudson River sixty miles north of New York City. It is here that the waterway widens, and consequently views of the river and of the majestic highlands beyond are particularly stunning. A small peninsula, which extends into the waterway close to the town, was taken over by industrial and waste functions for more than 150 years. Only after those uses ceased did preservationists awake to the site's potential as a destination for recreation and relaxation.

Remnants of historic long docks are still visible in the water, evidencing the land's history as a shipping port (1815–90) and then a ferry port between Newburgh and Beacon (1890–1904). Subsequently, it would serve as a railroad siding, fuel storage facility, salvage yard, and informal garbage dump. The ecology of the peninsula was harmed by these activities and further damaged by a partial overlay of asphalt-coated concrete paving slabs. Retrieved from a repaving of the Newburgh-Beacon Bridge, the slabs were intended to stabilize the terrain, which was infilled with basalt; instead, they prevented water from draining properly, creating a constructed wetland. Despite these abuses, Scenic Hudson, a non-profit environmental organization, bought the twenty-three-acre site in the late 1990s with plans to create a public/private enterprise for building a park and hotel.

The town vetoed the proposal for an urban development, and the recession of 2008 led to Scenic Hudson abandoning plans for the hotel, leaving only the park. Commissioned to design the park, Gary Hilderbrand of landscape architecture firm Reed Hilderbrand, who grew up in nearby Wappingers Falls, was inspired by the conditions he found in this tidal area, which is prone to huge seasonal storm surges and, in winter, massive floating ice sheets. Inundation comes primarily from upwelling (from the ground) to the site's porous basalt. In fact, the site flooded four times during construction. The park, which Hilderbrand describes as "rugged," is designed to accommodate these natural occurrences. Even the kayak pavilion, which is constructed of corrugated steel and panels of aluminum grating, is designed to withstand floods. In addition, the design team wanted to give the feeling that the park had always been there. As a result, Hilderbrand retained many of the mature black locusts, willows, alders, and cottonwood trees already growing on the site.

The landscape architects drew formal inspiration from the existing man-made topography: bars (linear mounds formerly containing gas tanks, which were used to buttress water flow) and arcs (the crescent shapes of the peninsula). Hilderbrand added new wetland areas, which filter storm water, manage floods, and resist erosion, to the preexisting wetland. Materials were found mostly on the property; even the dozens of soil-masked abandoned concrete slabs were repurposed for parking lots and terraces.

To facilitate financing and to adjust to the stages of remediation and construction, the project was planned in phases over a period of ten years. Hilderbrand notes that the incremental process was both liberating (to have something to build on) and limiting (not being able to complete the undertaking immediately).

The first phase saw the restoration of the shoreline by a team of scientists helped by the environmental sculptor George Trakas and in collaboration with the Dia Art Foundation and Minetta Brook, a non-profit public arts organization. It was mid-August when Alex and I walked to Trakas's *Beacon Point,* a pier that extends 250 feet into the river. The installation attracts fishermen as well as those seeking a lookout over the Hudson. Recycled oak benches run past the kayak pavilion and alongside the pier in the adjoining surcharge meadow, giving the site an interlocking quality. Protected by the shade of the existing black locust and balsam poplar trees, the seating encourages visitors to explore the paths that lead to the water's edge.

A meandering, narrow path running inland from the river, and each walkway that curves from it, invite exploration; indeed, exploration and discovery are what the vastly different environments of Long Dock Park are about. Some routes lead to the Hudson's rocky beach, where visitors may be surprised by glimpses of the majestic waterscape; others lead away from

Photograph of site, early twentieth century

View to south from Long Dock Park to Dennings Point and Hudson River

Ice floes at Beacon Point

Plan

the coast, winding their way through masses of blue flag iris (*Iris versicolor*), broadleaf cattail (*Typha latifolia*), arrowwood viburnum (*Viburnum dentatum*), and many more species. The longest paths are arcs that sweep through the wetlands and meadows, which seem more extensive than they actually are.

Following one of the arcing paths, we passed through tall grasses and flowers to a small clearing where a stepped concrete seating area offers space for education sessions. Part of the second phase, the arching concrete shape is nestled within a crescent landform that acts as a barrier against flooding and affords views over a wetland and the river. Just beyond is the original wetland Hilderbrand used as a model for those he added to the site.

The intertidal zone was the focus of subsequent phases, which produced the River Center, an arts and environmental education facility housed in a restored 1860s barn; parking; meadows; and constructed wetlands. Hilderbrand had intended originally for the meadow grasses to be kept relatively low by means of an annual mowing. However, taller species have self-propagated and taken over, changing the effect. Although the landscape architect is disappointed by this unanticipated alteration to his design, the meadow is a successful bird habitat and, precisely because of its wildness, one of the most beautiful areas at Long Dock. A kayak pavilion developed by Architecture Research Office, based in New York City, is tucked into the head of Quiet Harbor next to *Beacon Point*.

The civic plaza/market completed as part of the final phase of construction contrasts with the natural setting of the rest of the park. Rough lawns surround a neat area overlooking the river that is furnished with two pavilions and long metal benches. This resource can be used for weekly markets as well as for picnicking and, on occasion, for firefighters who bring their vehicles onto the wide plaza to flush and fill their tanks with water from the Hudson.

The constantly changing exhibitions at the magnificent Dia Beacon (2003), housed in a former Nabisco printing plant, draw me frequently to the waterside town, and I always conclude with a visit to Long Dock Park. The park is just as enchanting in a bleached landscape of snow and ice as it is in other seasons, when the place is a riot of color. Amtrak and Metro North trains, a reminder of the site's history, pass regularly—the only disturbance in this haven of tranquility.

Arcing path beside meadow

Overleaf: Natural and constructed wetlands

Garonne River, view to south
with Parc aux Angéliques
(foreground) and left bank
rehabilitation, Michel Corajoud

Parc aux Angéliques

Bordeaux, France
2012, ongoing

Michel Desvigne Paysagiste

185 acres
cost: $1.33 million

For centuries, Bordeaux was a sleepy provincial city on the banks of the Garonne River, known for its wine (introduced by the ancient Romans) and its historic architecture. From the late 1940s on, during the long mayoralty of Jacques Chaban-Delmas (almost five decades), the population of the urban core declined steeply, while the suburbs doubled in size. In the hope of changing this tendency, Chaban-Delmas launched an ideas competition entitled "Bordeaux Port de la Lune" in 1989, in which leading architects such as Rem Koolhaas, Zaha Hadid, and Jean Nouvel were invited to contribute forward-looking schemes for the historic left bank of the Garonne. In 1992, the mayor asked Dominique Perrault to prepare a study of nearly a thousand acres of industrial wastelands on both sides of the river.

In 1995, Alain Juppé, then the prime minister of France, was elected mayor and almost immediately gave the city a further wake-up call. By 2000, a new tram system linked peripheral neighborhoods with the city center. In 2007, Bordeaux was added to the UNESCO World Heritage List. That same year, Juppé and Vincent Feltresse, chairman of the Bordeaux Urban Community, declared their intention to grow Bordeaux to one million inhabitants by 2030. A decisive factor in the city's growth was its connection to France's high-speed, intercity TGV (Train à Grande Vitesse) in 2017.

The Garonne became the axis of development. In 2002, Juppé (now a member of the French Constitutional Council) asked landscape architect Michel Desvigne to define an approach to developing the city's green spaces. At the time, open areas were distributed unequally and were of varying quality. Rather than adopting a regulatory plan, the designer studied a dozen sites within the city in order to understand the typology of each: plaza, park, playground, and empty lot.

Based on his analysis, Desvigne tendered a plan to divide green spaces into categories and build a mock-up, or "pilot project," as Desvigne calls them, for each. The mock-ups were built in collaboration with the city's maintenance crew to test spatial conditions and care regimes at different scales and in different neighborhoods. The resulting Charte des Paysages, or landscape charter, is a guide for architects, developers, and administrators that documents what was learned from the pilot projects. Desvigne compares the method to that of the famous Second Empire engineer Adolphe Alphand, who worked with Georges-Eugène Haussmann to renovate Paris. Alphand's system of nurseries, greenhouses, and a gardening school ensured an ongoing process that could be continued by others.

City agencies will implement Desvigne's suggestions regarding modules, dimensions, typologies, grading, soils, plantings, and procedures and will also be responsible for upkeep. The city is gradually acquiring parcels of land and using them to expand green infrastructure. Desvigne says, "We have to be vigilant that our design intentions are maintained."

One of the pilot projects is Desvigne's own Parc aux Angéliques, which occupies approximately 185 acres on the right bank that Juppé was keeping in reserve for future development. An adjacent site became the location for Catherine Mosbach's Jardin Botanique (page 210). Buildings on the site had already been razed when the landscape architect began working on the scheme. The essence of Desvigne's design—strips of land perpendicular to the Garonne—recalls the seigneurial system of land division, typical of medieval Europe, which allowed lot owners access to the river. The French took this system to Canada and the United States, where parts of it remain along the Mississippi. Desvigne was also influenced by the existing irrigation canals that ran inland from the Garonne.

The designer defined his long narrow strips with rows of trees. The reduced planting palette includes European ash (*Fraxinus excelsior*) underplanted with quaking grass (*Briza media*), millet grass (*Milium effusum*), and switchgrass (*Panicum virgatum*). Within each row of trees, a diversity of spacing and rhythms gives a rich and dynamic impression.

Some of the old irrigation canals have been rehabilitated and others created anew to provide water for the depollution of old industrial sites, a process that takes three to four years.

The landscape architect thinks of the forest screens as "curtains framing a [theatrical] set made up not of filled and empty spaces, but of foreground, middle ground, and background with variable densities, and with passages connecting them." He points out that the trees planted in the Parc aux Angéliques were young saplings and that his team revises spacing, a strategy similar to that of a tree nursery. Trees spaced close together take on a more upright and vertical habit; those spaced farther apart develop more natural, open crowns. The soft, prairie-like grasses are left unmown, protecting the bark and root systems of the trees. The designer calls his approach, which considers landscape structures to be living environments, "intermediate nature."

Two notable remnants survived the clearing of the site. Long railway ties between the rows of trees distinguish between "rooms" intended for construction and those reserved for parkland. A wide cobblestone road running through the center of the park is parallel to the Quai des Queyries and the two Quais de Brazza. A new concrete path that responds to the system of future development runs perpendicular to the cobblestone course.

A fragile section of the riverfront, thirty-two to fifty feet wide, is off-limits to circulation, creating a protective buffer for the flora and fauna. Desvigne's design impedes the visual connection between the visitor and the Garonne at many points, allowing interaction only at key moments. To access vistas across the waterway to the row of spectacular eighteenth-century facades on the opposite bank, Desvigne selectively thinned the vegetation to create occasional view corridors. These punched openings contrast with the broad, unobstructed, and largely horizontal views from the left bank of the river, where the landscape architect Michel Corajoud (1937–2014), Desvigne's teacher, transformed nearly three miles of riverfront into a more structured pedestrian promenade (2009). As on the right bank, the riverside walk was enabled by the removal of warehouses and other transportation remains from the quai. It has been so popular that Juppé referred to it as "my own [Bilbao] Guggenheim."

Corajoud's formal language of parterres, linear walkways, and axial relationships contrasts with Desvigne's. The park on the left bank is in dialogue with the historic architecture in the city center, while the open green space on the right bank has a messy and more industrial aesthetic, which pairs with both the future residential blocks and the existing commercial remnants.

Inserted as it is between the river and a busy vehicular street, the Parc aux Angéliques is narrow along its length, and even more so toward the northern Brazza areas. Despite the relatively restricted space, Alex and I were immersed in rich textures when we visited on a cloudless June morning. The mix of trees, lawns, and prairie grasses gave the impression of being at the edge of a forest. As we walked toward the river, we looked at and through rows of trees at either side; varying rhythms and densities evoked a woodland. When we turned onto a path parallel to the river and perpendicular to the rows, we noticed a geometry and regularity that resembled a nursery. The park becomes more organic the closer it is to the river, much like Renaissance Park in Chattanooga. The numerous joggers, pedestrians, and cyclists that filled the walkways during our visit confirmed that this new post-industrial quarter is attracting a young population.

Juppé initiated other design projects during his time as mayor. The left and right banks of the Garonne are connected by a new bridge, soon to be joined by a second span. To the north is the vertical-lift Jacques Chaban-Delmas Bridge (2013), conceived by Lavigne & Chéron. To the south is the Simone Veil Bridge, designed by OMA and under construction in 2021: it will accommodate cars, trams, bicycles, and pedestrians and will also complete a riverside loop.

A limited number of buildings and plans is underway on the largely unbuilt right bank. The Dutch firm MVRDV has designed a master plan for the Bastide Niel neighborhood (2010), behind the southern part of the Parc aux Angéliques. The mixed-use development will include public buildings and affordable housing. If the plan is carried through, the new district will be granted a developing park grown from Desvigne's plantings immediately upon completion, which is perhaps the core idea. In the meantime, the city continues to develop additional green areas. A true evaluation of the Desvigne landscape must await its maturity—probably around 2030—as well as implementation of the city's ambitious plans to build in the spaces between his elegant bands of trees.

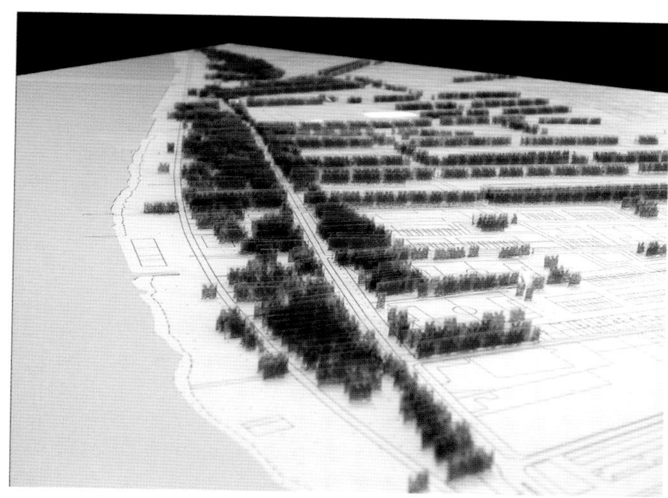

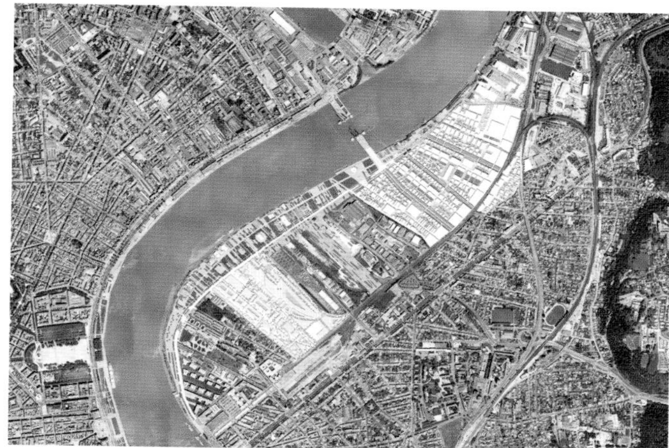

Parc aux Angéliques as adaptive planning, study model

Context plan

Ash trees in soft grasses

Rows of trees perpendicular to river

Cobblestone pedestrian path and concrete bicycle lane

View corridor to left bank

Trees in varying rhythms and densities

False Creek, view to north with Hinge Park (center left) and downtown Vancouver

Hinge Park

Vancouver, British Columbia
2010

PWL Partnership Landscape Architects

2.35 acres
cost: undisclosed

Landscape architect Margot Long of PWL Partnership began her work on Hinge Park in Vancouver with a single question: "Can you build nature in an urban environment?" Fortuitously, that same year the city launched a planning initiative entitled EcoDensity. The aim of the measure, like that of several earlier plans, was to find ways that density, design, and land use could promote environmental sustainability and affordability.

High-rise development took off in the 1960s in this large and scenic coastal seaport in western Canada. Expo 1986, located along False Creek (actually an inlet) and in a former railyard and industrial area, gave a boost to condominium construction there; when Expo closed, Hong Kong billionaire Li Ka-Shing acquired the site and commenced building yet more luxury residential towers. Vancouver currently has the highest population density in Canada.

Hinge Park is a small trapezoid and even smaller island just off the shoreline of False Creek in the Mount Pleasant neighborhood. The terrain is composed primarily of industrial fill, which was used to extend the coastline between the 1800s and early 1900s. Two street grids, laid out to follow the coastline of the inlet, meet at this location, hence the name "hinge."

When Vancouver was selected to host the 2010 Olympics, the planning committee chose land along the south shore of False Creek to build the Olympic Village, dramatically changing the demographics of the neighborhood. According to Canadian law, representatives from some of British Columbia's 198 First Nation tribes were invited to contribute to the planning process. The large residential blocks built to house athletes and located along the eastern edge of the park have since been converted to condominiums, many with roofscapes featuring urban agriculture.

Immediately apparent in Hinge Park is the importance of ecological performance, especially water management. The landscape architects wanted to draw people as close as possible to False Creek while also bringing water into the neighborhood, visually and physically. The location of the open space, at the terminus of Columbia Street, responds to local desires that streets end in views of the water, not buildings.

Among the various ecologies exhibited in Hinge Park, Long is most proud of a constructed wetland. It provides a key piece of infrastructure and also gives the landscape its primary character. Rainwater from the street along the eastern edge of the site enters into a bioswale; elsewhere in the park rainwater is directed into the wetland. In a cyclical process devised by the designers, plants clean the water as it moves north through the terraced wetland before it is pumped back to begin the cycle again. During severe storms when the wetland fills to capacity, water flows over a weir and into False Creek.

Adjacent to the wetland is a gentle rise studded with boulders for children to climb, at the top of which is a small pump designed for youngsters. Water from the pump can be redirected as it splashes into a series of metal runnels down the hillside. The water from this pump then feeds the wetland, which, in Vancouver's dry summers, is needed to support the plantings. In this way, a simple play feature is linked to ecology.

The wetland is remarkably successful as a habitat for fish and for feathered and furry animals, perhaps too successful. Shortly after the park was completed, a family of beavers moved in, decimating the young trees. Their presence, however, is much loved in the community, and the semi-aquatic mammals even have their own Twitter account. The beavers seem perfectly content in their new home, as do the otters and coyotes spotted on site. Meanwhile, the replacement trees have had their trunks wrapped in protective metal mesh.

The wildlife-focused Habitat Island is connected to the mainland by an earth and riprap footpath. Narrow dirt walkways encircle the tiny island, and logs and rocks provide areas for park users to perch and spot wildlife or take in views of downtown Vancouver. The improved water quality in False Creek, which evidences the widespread concern for the environment in Vancouver, has encouraged oysters and herring to inhabit the rocks. PWL also designed the adjoining inlet spaces to the east. Decking of heavy Douglas fir planks covers this area, which offers chairs that swivel to follow the sun and also connects to a sixteen-mile-long waterside trail.

To prepare the site for the park, Vancouver officials removed massive amounts of polluted earth and replaced it with soil in structured soil cells, a modular, suspended pavement system that accommodates large trees and controls storm water. Plantings are similar to those found on the Atlantic Seaboard of the United States. However, a mineral presence at

Steel columns from Canron Building and constructed wetland beyond

Play mound with water feature, sketch

Hinge Park is more pronounced than in the eastern coastline area, bringing to mind parks in Oslo and Switzerland.

As important as the park's introduction of nature to the urban context is its reuse of found materials. The landscape architects adapted an uncommonly large quantity of salvaged material: hundreds of unearthed Hardy Island granite boulders, whole or carved to resemble toy blocks, are incorporated into play areas; old city sidewalks, cut and reshaped, form the wetland's edge; concrete found on site was crushed to fill the gabions used as structure for the promenade; and pieces of the historic Canron Building have been incorporated into the structure of a bridge crossing the wetland. Bill Pechet, the architect who designed the pipe bridge, dug up underground pipes that were no longer needed for water control and made them into follies. Train tracks found on the site were retained as well as a jagged band of granite installed to follow the contour of the original coastline.

Like several of the public spaces we visited in Vancouver, Alex and I found Hinge Park to be unusually thoughtful and user friendly. It abounds in small gestures, like the children's water pump: the device alone might not ensure the wetland's survival, but it is a nice detail. The rich vegetation bordering the wetland itself is a pleasant surprise within the park's otherwise sparse plantings.

Regrettably, the park's condition has not lived up to its high quality. While a homeowners' group takes excellent care of the green spaces around the nearby condominium buildings, the Vancouver Board of Parks and Recreation has ignored the maintenance manuals provided by PWL and has implemented unauthorized, unsuitable changes: planting non-indigenous rather than native species, shaping shrubs as if they were topiaries, mismanaging the wetland. It is to be hoped that such oversights will be rectified in the future.

Pipe folly, Bill Pechet

The Beach, view to south across
Elliott Bay to Mount Rainier

The Beach at Expedia Group

Seattle, Washington
2019

SurfaceDesign, Inc.

2.6 acres
cost: undisclosed

Part of Puget Sound, Elliott Bay is the body of water that enabled Seattle's port to become one of the busiest in the United States. A series of waterside green spaces lines portions of the bay, from the Interbay neighborhood to the north to the Olympic Sculpture Park to the south. Running through these linear parks in Interbay is the five-mile Elliott Bay Trail. A promontory that extends into the bay is an ideal place from which to appreciate Seattle, its waterfront location, and Mount Rainier towering more than sixty miles away. This point of land is home to an exquisite 2.6-acre park, the Beach, created as part of a new forty-acre corporate campus for online travel giant Expedia.

Numerous major corporations are headquartered in and around Seattle. In the 1980s and 1990s, tech companies such as Microsoft and Amazon established themselves there. The city's growth and population surge at the end of the twentieth century has been compared to the post–Gold Rush boom at the beginning of that century.

Multibillion-dollar Expedia was founded in nearby Redmond in 1996 and for many years was located in Bellevue, across Lake Washington from Seattle. In 2015, the company announced its relocation to the property in Interbay. Along with three new buildings, and at the insistence of chairman Barry Diller, the new headquarters includes a public park. Stretching in front of and beside Expedia's new campus, the park is located on a sliver of the shore bound by water, industry, and active rail lines and consisting almost entirely of land that was previously occupied by piers and mixed industrial structures. Only the waterside space is open to the public.

SurfaceDesign principals James Lord and Roderick Wyllie described the parcel's dreadful condition, covered by rubble and debris, when they began. The bike trail, six feet wide and shared by pedestrians and cyclists, took a dangerous ninety-degree turn to follow the coastline. The designers separated the bike and pedestrian paths, realigning them to make a smooth, arcing path; oriented the site to take advantage of views to Mount Rainier; removed part of 16th Avenue as well as an asphalt-covered parking lot and remnants of an industrial landscape; and effected extensive soil remediation including the use of compost teas.

The landscape architects wanted to bring the bay into the site, creating an amplification of the water's edge. From the moment Alex and I approached the park along the bike trail, we were conscious of the shoreline's proximity. Every detail of the intervention is remarkably refined, including the mandatory emergency egress corridor. Instead of the typical wide expanse of paving, the designers created something akin to the Hollywood, or ribbon, driveway, where bands of cobble and grass border asphalt strips. The focus on materiality helps to visually reduce the scale of the drive while maintaining the width required by code.

At the widest point of the park, a landform studded with small stands of quaking aspen (*Populus tremuloides* 'Prairie Gold') planted in crushed stone rises gradually to create an overlook. According to SurfaceDesign, this dune-like feature was meant to feel as though it was a rock that dropped onto the site, resulting in a ripple effect. This effect is immediately evident as the rocky southeast slopes of the dune transition to stepped terraces composed of swooping arcs of concrete and soft lawn. The narrow terraces, intended to read as abstractions of regional geological conditions, flare out to reveal tiny lupine meadows. This waterside gathering space is not oriented toward the bay, as might be expected, but rather past the city's remaining industrial infrastructure and to downtown Seattle. In the other direction are two piers, each more than 2,500 feet long, where cruise liners dock, thus creating a link with Expedia's activities.

As we descended the steps of the terraces, we entered a beachscape like no other. Here, large driftwood logs—actually former booms—are positioned amid boulders and clumps of fox sedge (*Carex vulpinoidea*), tufted hairgrass (*Deschampsia cespitosa*), and American dune grass (*Leymus mollis*). The composition recalls the tidal marshes that occupied the area prior to development. Planted "islands" are studded with large boulders and surrounded by pebbles arranged in patterns that suggest the raked stone of a Japanese garden. We were struck

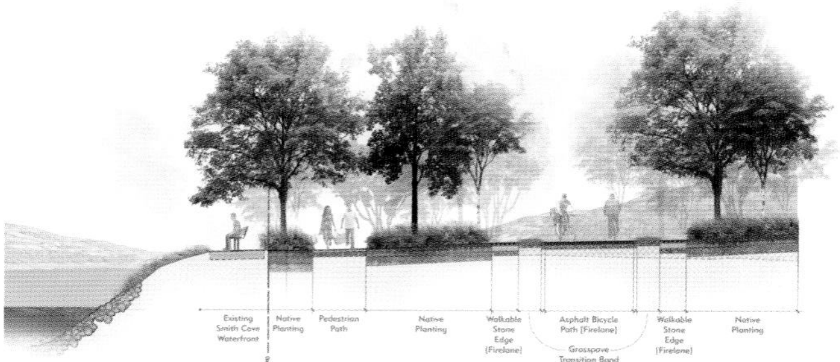

by how the soft gray tones of the pebbles echoed the concrete terraces. In fact, the designers took great pains to match the color of the concrete to the stone, bringing tinted samples on site to see how they would respond to the sun and water. Given the similarity in color, the landscape architects relied on texture to provide a contrast between the two areas: the strong mineral, irregular, and coarse texture of the beach against the smooth and sharply defined lines of the terraces.

The park owes its existence to Expedia (responsible for park maintenance), which wanted to give an elegant open space to the public; indeed, our sense when visiting the site was that the campus will feel like part of the public realm. Rain gardens (bioretention areas) act as the interface between the public landscape and Expedia's private campus, creating a visually porous perimeter. A ha-ha allows for 40-by-800-foot treatment beds for wetland meadow plants. Lord and Wyllie describe the plantings in this section as "wet toe plantings," that is, the species selected—Douglas iris (*Iris douglasiana*), lupine (*Lupinus* 'Gallery Blue'), pincushion flower (*Scabiosa columbaria* 'Giga Blue'), and others—like to have their roots a little wet but not saturated. The vegetation forms a "living quilt" that picks up reflected light from Puget Sound. The campus, once complete, will contain many different environments for Expedia employees and park visitors to enjoy, including a Pacific Northwest woodland, bosques and glades, perennial gardens, and an orchard.

As we left, we reflected on the varied spatial experiences offered in the Beach at Expedia: narrow strips of land opening to reveal the primary area of the dune and beach and then compressing as the trail enters Centennial Park; the pleasing contrasts between soft grasses, curvilinear paths, and sharp concrete and stone. Despite the awareness that the hand-traced pebble designs at the beach will surely be scuffed away by visitors, SurfaceDesign planned for these thoughtful details to be absorbed into the history of the park, eventually becoming just a memory.

Paths and fire lane, section

Expedia campus, plan

View to southeast past gravel beach and dunes to industrial structures

Stepped terraces of concrete and lawn

Overleaf: Driftwood logs and boulders in clumps of sedges and lupine

waterside industry: park systems

Before the advent of rail and air networks, waterways—rivers, ocean ports, and lakes—were essential to support the creation of cities. Transportation and communication were prime functions of rivers, along with irrigation, domestic use, and defense. Watercourses were also used to supply energy and for waste removal, with little thought given to the effect of such uses on the environment. Many of the world's major metropolitan areas—New York, London, and Shanghai—demonstrate plainly the role rivers have played in the history of urbanization.

Traditionally considered for their commercial potential, waterfronts have only more recently begun to be studied from ecological and environmental points of view. Riverfront park systems—generally devised by city or regional authorities at a n urban scale and incorporating commercial and residential facilities as well as open areas—offer the opportunity for spectacular transformations that address multiple waterside sites. Such a network may be thought of as a green chain bordering a riverside or other body of water with the individual parks as links in that chain.

Seventy percent of American cities with a population of more than fifty thousand are located on the edge of a river, lake, bay, or ocean; most of these urban areas are undergoing, or will undergo, redevelopment. New parks and recreation areas that fit into a larger renewal strategy take advantage of appealing, previously inaccessible shorelines. Waterside parks are also at the forefront of attempts to manage flooding from rising sea levels and storm surges.

The park systems in Shanghai and New York are large-scale projects that will drastically change their riverfronts: the East River in New York with numerous, individually developed open spaces; the Huangpu in Shanghai with a wholesale, government-sponsored reconstruction of the former industrial riverfront along with new territory created by a newly reinforced flood wall. These landscapes either continue older parks (as Hunter's Point South extends Gantry Park) or connect with new parks (or will connect, as with Brooklyn Bridge Park). Identified as sites for green spaces by government or developers' planning documents, such as a master plan, these parks transform post-industrial sites into dynamic landscapes.

The project now underway in Shanghai is one of the most ambitious of these schemes. A regeneration of the center of the city, which emblematizes the unprecedented urbanization throughout the country, was set in motion in 2010. Among the countless construction projects currently underway in China, including forty "new cities," is the replacement with parks of the docks, stacks, warehouses, and other manufacturing structures that were installed on both sides of the Huangpu River during China's industrial modernization in the 1950s. One important facet of the plan, stemming from a reevaluation of the river as a public amenity, is making views of the waterway available to the public.

The process of riverfront regeneration varies significantly between China, the United States, and Europe. The Chinese Communist victory of 1949 was followed by thirty years of isolation. But since 1978, Shanghai, with 27 million residents, has led the way in opening the nation to the rest of the world. In 1992, then-president Deng Xiaoping declared Shanghai to be the "head of the dragon" that would lead the country to prosperity, and indeed, by the mid-1990s, Pudong, an entirely new financial district, was rising across the Huangpu River from the historic city center, known as Puxi. By 2019, the new area, with five million inhabitants, was established as China's financial hub, proudly taunting memories of the remaining foreign concessions lining the waterfront of the Bund, once the center of financial activity.

The name Shanghai means "upon the sea," and for centuries the city has dealt with life-threatening deluges. Throughout the country, the customary response involves flood walls as well as devices like gates, locks, levees, and dams; even so, inundations remain an issue. The barrier in Shanghai has been and continues to be subject to regular improvements and adjustments: it was built in the 1950s as a simple levee along a portion of the river; upgraded to withstand a hundred-year flood in the 1970s; and fortified again, against a thousand-year flood, in the 1980s and 1990s.

In the first decades of the new millennium, flooding was again the first item in the brief for Shanghai's riverfront revitalization. Reinforcement of the protective edge on both sides of the river was completed in tandem with the parks. Running along the water's edge, the renovated wall is nearly twenty-four feet high at the north, where the Huangpu empties into the Yangtze Estuary, and twenty-one feet high at the south, which is farther from the estuary and the ocean. The flood wall allows views of the Huangpu but provides no contact with it; stark concrete esplanades as wide as one hundred feet isolate the public from the river in all but a few places. Waterfront parks built elsewhere in the world—for instance, Nansen Park in Oslo (page 68)—often allow visitors to dip their feet into the water, or even swim.

The United States and western Europe have led China in developing natural, or soft, flood control. As floods are now more frequent and more severe, it has become clearly preferable to accept nature rather than to attempt control, and more effective to accommodate floods in non-destructive ways, a method that also contributes to ecological diversity. This is the concept that drives the two New York parks: both allow tidal fluctuations to gush into marshlands and then to recede when the tide ebbs.

Contrasts between the various park systems, especially the transformative undertakings in Shanghai and New York, are instructive. Both the Huangpu and East Rivers are wide, fast-flowing waterways with a busy back-and-forth of ferries, freighters, and private vessels. Former industrial landscapes, the riverfronts were once forbidding. Clearing or repurposing these structures has opened views of the rivers and contributed newfound space to the public. Landscape architects have taken advantage of both scenic locations and sites that bear witness to past uses. All the parks provide sports facilities, performance venues, and various types of circulation—pedestrian, jogging, and biking. One notable difference is the separation between park goers and river imposed by Shanghai's flood wall.

There are also contrasts between China and the United States in industrial riverfront renewal. In 1989, then-mayor of Shanghai Zhu Rongji declared that the Huangpu had to be decontaminated, yet little was done in pursuit of this goal. In recent years, however, the Chinese government has become increasingly aware of the dangers of pollution. By contrast, cleanup of the Hudson River was promoted by environmental activists as early as the 1960s, and the first major remediation effort took place in the 1970s. Sightings of sturgeon and humpback whales in the Hudson River around the George Washington Bridge indicate the river's health.

Kongjian Yu is a leading voice in encouraging China to adopt the natural approach to flood control. Two recent parks by his firm, Turenscape, are examples of the new concept. Houtan Park (2010), at the northwest corner of a site for the 2010 Expo, stretches for one mile beside the Huangpu River. Incorporated into the park are a constructed wetland, settling ponds, aeration devices, and a series of cascades and terraces. The landscape architects replaced the rigid concrete flood wall with a new structure hidden below a riverside path without reducing protection from floods. Qiaoyuan Wetland Park in Tianjin (page 290) handles water in a similar manner. During a storm, twenty-one cavities fill and then gradually disperse water. Like Brooklyn Bridge Park and Hunter's Point South Park, Yu's green spaces welcome an influx of water, whether from high tides or heavy rains, and then allow it to subside.

Urban planning groups in China have encouraged architects and the public to speak up about small-scale improvements such as murals, pop-up events, and temporary exhibitions. Bottom-up processes for these interventions do not require formal approval from the authorities. Nevertheless, such efforts have been largely unsuccessful, and local communities have virtually no voice in projects of any size. By the same token, forecasts by planners and landscape architects of a regenerated "civic experience" in Shanghai had not materialized as of fall 2019. Established green spaces, like People's Park (1952) in Shanghai and Xuanwu Lake Park (1911) in Nanjing, are crammed with visitors in the early morning and late evening. Otherwise, the Shanghai riverside parks, like almost all new parks in China, were empty. While the completion of high-rise residential buildings may provide a constituency for these green spaces, the only users we found in the course of an evening stroll through the Shipyard Riverside Park were fishermen.

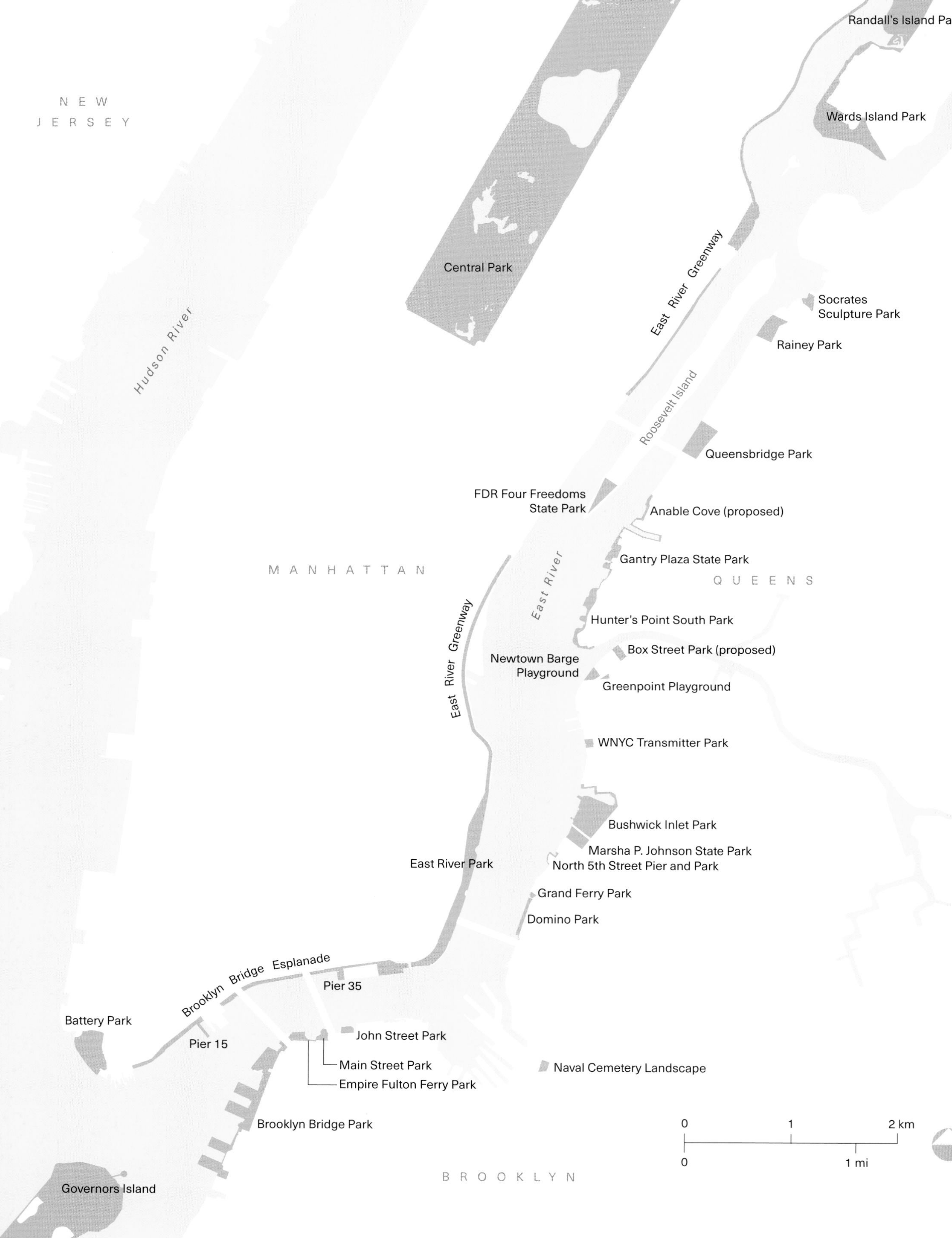

Randall's Island Park
NEW JERSEY
Wards Island Park
Central Park
East River Greenway
Socrates Sculpture Park
Rainey Park
Hudson River
Roosevelt Island
Queensbridge Park
FDR Four Freedoms State Park
Anable Cove (proposed)
Gantry Plaza State Park
MANHATTAN
East River
QUEENS
East River Greenway
Hunter's Point South Park
Box Street Park (proposed)
Newtown Barge Playground
Greenpoint Playground
WNYC Transmitter Park
Bushwick Inlet Park
Marsha P. Johnson State Park
East River Park
North 5th Street Pier and Park
Grand Ferry Park
Domino Park
Brooklyn Bridge Esplanade
Pier 35
Battery Park
Pier 15
John Street Park
Main Street Park
Naval Cemetery Landscape
Empire Fulton Ferry Park
Brooklyn Bridge Park
0
1
2 km
0
1 mi
BROOKLYN
Governors Island

New York City

Many people are surprised to hear that 2018—a year characterized by serious problems with infrastructure in New York City (subway system, bridges, and air terminals), not to mention political turmoil throughout the country—saw the completion, just a few months apart, of two of the most stunning new parks in the United States. These parks join several other landscape ventures along the waterways of New York City's five boroughs.

The ideas for both Hunter's Point South and Brooklyn Bridge Park were launched many years before, in the 1980s. In Long Island City, Queens, Gantry Plaza State Park (1998), a twelve-acre park on four piers in the East River, retained the towering industrial leftovers after which the park is named. Designed by Thomas Balsley, it was the first of two green spaces that would extend approximately a mile from Anable Basin south to Hunter's Point. The two phases of Hunter's Point South Park (2013, 2018), each five and a half acres, complete the design. Brooklyn Bridge Park in Brooklyn (2003–18), too, borders the eastern shore of the East River. The park stretches from the Brooklyn Bridge south to Atlantic Avenue and Brooklyn Heights.

On the other side of the waterway, in Manhattan, the two-mile-long scenic East River Esplanade, part of a revitalization plan envisioned in 2005, is slowly taking shape. Landscape architect Ken Smith Workshop and SHoP Architects initiated the project with a landscape promenade for bicycles and pedestrians built partially under the elevated FDR Drive and partially on a marine platform. Public features include a dog run (2010) and complex reconstructions of Piers 15 and 35. Pier 15 (2012), with a restaurant, generous seating areas, and upper level deck with lawns, is the most elaborate of these renewals. Despite the incongruity of the location, scantily clad sunbathers loll in full view of both the highway and the bridge above, obviously happy with this found space. Visible through a cutout in the pier, a sliver of the shoreline at Pier 35 has been made into Mussel Beach (2013), a mollusk habitat, created with the help of a tidal estuary that is restoring the river's mollusk population. Like oysters, mussels remove pollutants from the water, making it receptive to other marine life. On Pier 35 itself (2019), in front of an elegant steel mesh screen that hides a Department of Sanitation garage, is seating, including swings, that allows views of the Manhattan Bridge and the Brooklyn waterfront.

Farther south, where the East River and the Hudson River flow into New York Harbor, is Governors Island, a former military base. A five-minute ferry ride from downtown Manhattan, the island offers yet another magnificent park, the Hills, rich in views of the city. Dutch landscape architect Adriaan Geuze of West 8 won the competition for part of the 172-acre island, which was completed in 2016. One aspect of the West 8 scheme was to raise the southern part of the island by fifteen feet to acknowledge the rising sea level, at the time a novel concept in the United States. The former coast guard base includes more than fifty historic buildings, some of which have been adapted for cultural purposes.

Shortly after passage of the Coastal Zone Management Act (1972), New York's Department of City Planning drafted the first proposal (1975) for a continuous shared-use path along the Manhattan waterfront. The Byzantine complexity of the rules and regulations governing waterfront revitalization is attested to by the succession of mayors who have grappled with them.

Not until 1992, under the administration of David Dinkins, did the New York City Comprehensive Waterfront Plan materialize—the first long-range strategy for the entire shoreline. In 2011, Mayor Bloomberg built on that project with the announcement of Vision 2020, a framework for the city's 520 miles of shoreline. Hunter's Point South and Brooklyn Bridge Park are two of the major park projects in that grand scheme.

View to northeast with Hunter's Point South Park
and new residential development (background left)

Hunter's Point South Waterfront Park

Queens, New York
2013, 2018

SWA/Balsley and Weiss/Manfredi

11 acres
cost: $160 million

Hunter's Point was, until recently, an out-of-the-way neighborhood in Long Island City, Queens, populated by industry; affordable, low-rise residential buildings favored by artists and others of modest means; and such cultural institutions as MOMA PS1, Socrates Sculpture Park, and the Isamu Noguchi Museum. In 1993, however, the thirty-acre area was designated as the site for a mixed-use development: five thousand units of housing (of which 60 percent are meant to be affordable), three public schools, ample retail space, and open green spaces. That same year, the Greenway Plan for New York City laid out a vision for a system of landscaped paths connecting the city's residential and commercial neighborhoods to open space and waterfront areas. Four years later, the New York City Department of Transportation and the Department of City Planning produced the New York City Bicycle Master Plan, which incorporated the Greenway Plan's goal of expanding 350 miles of trails throughout the city into a 900-mile network of on- and off-street paths and bike lanes.

In 1983, Gruzen Samton Steinglass and Beyer Blender Belle prepared a master plan for the new development, or Queens West. The scheme occasioned the creation of Thomas Balsley Associates and Weintraub & di Domenico Architects' Gantry Plaza State Park, which occupies twelve acres of land at the widest part of the East River, affording exceptional views of the city. Balsley envisioned Gantry Plaza as the first portion of an uninterrupted green space, to be realized in phases, that would stretch from Anable Basin in Long Island City to Newtown Creek, the boundary between Queens and Brooklyn.

When Herbert Muschamp, then the *New York Times* architecture critic, came to write about Gantry Park, Balsley remembers that the journalist was so mesmerized by the panorama of Manhattan—from the Triborough Bridge (renamed the Robert F. Kennedy Bridge in 2008) at the north to the Williamsburg Bridge and the World Trade Center at the south—that he had a hard time concentrating on the park. Once he had readjusted his focus, however, Muschamp bestowed the highest praise on the green space, singling out as a welcome innovation the architect's retention of the giant gantries originally used to lift freight trains onto river barges. Since then, many other landscape architects have retained and incorporated industrial remnants in their designs in New York City.

For work on Hunter's Point South Park, the design team first focused on improving the site's water management by building a bioswale and gabion wall along adjacent Center Boulevard, which includes a cycling path. Control of flooding and finding vegetation resilient enough to survive salt conditions were additional tests. Alex and I visited the park with architect Marion Weiss and landscape architect Tom Balsley on a hot May afternoon. We arrived by car via the Queens Midtown Tunnel, which runs underneath the river and the park, and began at the first, northern section of the open space.

Two hundred years ago, all of Hunter's Point South was tidal marshland, and the team had to decide how to incorporate brackish water into the wetlands they would design, which are inundated twice daily by the river's tides. This first phase provides facilities for active recreation, including a small, sandy volleyball court and a large elliptical playing field composed partially of lawn and partially of artificial turf. The bowl-like, tilted lawn together with the seawalls surrounding it, catch flood waters and return them to the river. The field was under construction at the time of Hurricane Sandy; put to the test earlier than imagined, it worked perfectly, even saving nearby areas from flooding.

At the southern end of the playing field, a band of flowering Yoshino cherry trees (*Prunus × yedoensis*) arcs around an airy pavilion perched on a series of twinned, painted steel

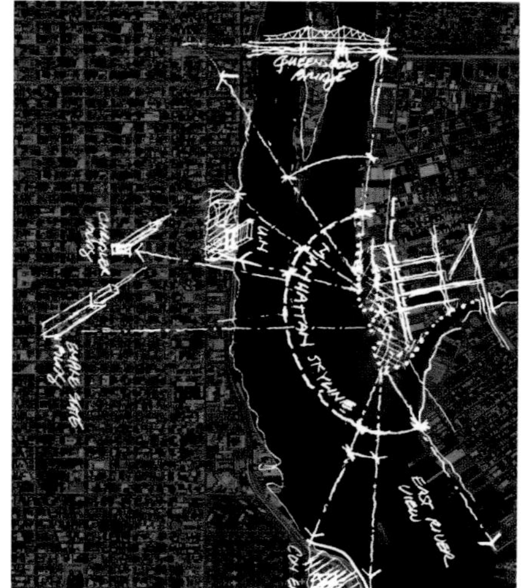

Overlook and view across Hudson River

View corridors, sketch

Center Boulevard, Queens

Oval playing field

columns. The structure contains an inviting outdoor café, as well as toilets, management offices, rooftop solar panels (which generate power for lighting), and a water collection apparatus. Nearby, a large terrace resembling a beer garden has large picnic tables and strings of lights (and overly amplified piped-in music in summer) and hosts picnickers and game players. Kebony wood was used for decking and site furniture throughout the park, and just steps away from the pavilion is the Hunter's Point South landing for the NYC Ferry.

The second phase of the park, completed in 2018, is designed for more passive activities. In contrast to the mostly flat northern end of the open space, the southern area features mounds that rise as high as thirty feet, composed of material excavated in the 1930s for construction of the Queens Midtown Tunnel. The landforms and the irregular shoreline create a natural feeling, which is helped by the subtle protective railings and barrier plantings toward the south.

At a curve in the shoreline, we crossed a gracefully slim bridge that descends mysteriously to a path encircling a small piece of land, which seems to become an island at high tide. On the central lawn was Nobuho Nagasawa's *Luminescence*, a group of gentle domes in white Portland cement, which illustrates the moon's effect on tidal flows. We followed the path as it spiraled up above the lawn, its cast concrete edge gradually increasing in height to become a bench. The new marshes which extend from this area to the southern end of the park are part of the system that absorbs storm surges by trapping and slowly releasing water back into the East River.

Our group returned to the mainland and continued walking south. A prow-like concrete and metal overlook, twenty-two feet high and fifty feet long, loomed heavily overhead. Weiss and Balsley drew our attention to the granite benches that skirt the water's edge. Always placed at a bend in the path, the benches have smooth, polished tops, jagged split-faced sides, and unobtrusive lighting. On the midweek afternoon of our visit, only a few of the many benches and even fewer of the "family rafts" (small platforms that jut out from a hillside lawn for seating and picnicking) were occupied.

The city's budget did not provide for irrigation; remarkably, the team was able to turn this into an asset. Reducing the selection of vegetation to native species capable of adjusting to the local environment fostered a look linked to the site's ecological history, one of the park's greatest aesthetic assets. Sedges (*Carex appalachica*), rush (*Juncus effusus*), feather reed (*Calamagrostis* × *acutiflora* 'Karl Foerster'), and switchgrass (*Panicum virgatum*) are among the tall marsh grasses that sway in the breeze.

The sound of water lapping against the shore's riprap edging enhances a sense of adventure. The feeling was evidently picked up by a group of teenagers we saw: they had climbed over the railings and were enjoying the sunset from atop the riprap. The paths brought us tantalizingly close to the water on one side and to the salt marsh on the other; we navigated the sliver of land along paths so narrow that Balsley compared them to a walk on the fortified walls of a medieval city. Among the park's most attractive features are its varied scales, from the large open spaces of the playing field to these little paths beside the river. We concluded our tour at an outdoor gym and a kayak launch at the southernmost tip of the park. This zone faces Newtown Creek, a wide bay that was once the city's shipping underbelly and remains active today.

On my first venture into the park—a preliminary research trip on a weekend afternoon—it was full of extraordinarily diverse young couples, some with children in tow, eagerly exploring the winding trails. The relative youthfulness of the park goers reflects the neighborhood's median age, which is roughly thirty-three, as well as the appeal of the park to this age group generally: the open green space attracts many such visitors from other areas.

The next decades will see the construction of massive residential buildings behind the park. In 2020, two residential towers were rising near a pair of apartment buildings that opened in 2015. All who are able to should enjoy this unexpected slice of nature before it is overwhelmed by the new population. The park is designed to engage the site's dynamics and reveal them to the visitor. The elevated walkways and high spaces of Hunter's Point take into account the tidal filling and draining of the marshlands and, periodically, the magical revelation of a near-island when the riverbank disappears.

Luminescence, Nobuho Nagasawa

Family rafts

Near-island

Park and proposed development, rendering

Overleaf: Tidal marsh

View to northeast over Brooklyn Bridge Park
to Brooklyn and Manhattan Bridges

Brooklyn Bridge Park

Brooklyn, New York
2003–2018

Michael Van Valkenburgh Associates

85 acres
cost: $400 million

As the second phase of Hunter's Point South was nearing completion, another even larger park project was finishing its most recent phase of construction nearly four miles to the south, in Brooklyn, under very different circumstances. The eighty-five-acre Brooklyn Bridge Park, sited on 1.3 miles of waterfront bordering the neighborhoods of DUMBO and Brooklyn Heights, offers a story unlike that of Hunter's Point South.

The inception of Brooklyn Bridge Park can be dated back to 1983, when New York City, together with the Port Authority of New York and New Jersey, closed its cargo operations on Brooklyn's piers. At the time, historic piers and 1950s industrial structures that served bulk cargo shipping and storage lined the waterfront. But one hundred years of marine life had rendered the 12,000 wood supporting pillars fragile and lace-like. To monetize the area, the Port Authority of New York and New Jersey envisioned selling all or part of the site to private developers.

While the local community in Queens had welcomed the city's plan for the new precinct of subsidized housing that accompanied Hunter's Point Park, the tonier neighborhood of Brooklyn Heights, represented by the Brooklyn Heights Association, fought the project tooth and nail. The disagreement produced years of infighting among community groups along with protracted negotiations with the Port Authority; city councilors and mayors; state governors; and state agencies—all of this in addition to the thousands of people unafraid of expressing their opinions at dozens of workshops and public forums.

Finally, in 2002, the groups reached a compromise in which the city and the state committed $360 million to the design and construction of a park on the Port Authority's property, along with market-rate housing. The agreement stipulated that the park would be self-sufficient in terms of maintenance and operations. The cost for both, $15–$20 million per year, is provided by tax revenues from private, market-rate housing, an arrangement that proved to be yet another bone of contention due to community fears that such funding would "privatize" the park. A new twelve-story condominium building, the conversion of a former warehouse facing the southernmost pier (Pier 6), furnishes some of the necessary ongoing financial support.

The well-to-do, predominantly white population of Brooklyn Heights had still another objection to register: a park with sports amenities would attract Black youngsters and teens from areas with few open spaces. The problem this time was that it was precisely such a diversified population that the city and the landscape architect, Michael Van Valkenburgh, envisioned for the park. Along with racial and economic diversity, Van Valkenburgh prioritized providing DUMBO and the adjoining neighborhoods to the south with their only riverside park.

The design challenges in Brooklyn were also different from those at Hunter's Point South. The Queens site was cleared of previous infrastructure, whereas in Brooklyn, the wooden pillars, the piers they support, and the piers' frames, newly painted blue, were carefully preserved. The condition of the piers severely limited the weight they could carry (350 pounds per square foot), which in turn restricted the amount of soil that could be brought in for the park; in addition, growing vegetation on structures above the river increased costs. Van Valkenburgh solved these problems by shaping the topography with layers of lightweight geofoam topped by two feet of soil and selecting plants with shallow roots.

Brooklyn also had a problem with noise: the ear-splitting traffic sounds of the Brooklyn-Queens Expressway, which runs along part of the park. To attenuate the rumble of the expressway, the designers built a series of thirty-five-foot-high berms of engineered fill (layered materials). Atop the berms are waving grasses planted in topsoil; a grid mesh holds the soil in place. Although the berms reduce noise by up to 75 percent, the din of the highway is still bothersome, and the berms, which can be seen from the beautiful Brooklyn Heights Promenade, are something of an eyesore.

Michael Van Valkenburgh's firm began designs for the park in 1999; construction began in 2008; and our visit took place in the summer of 2018. Alex and I met him at the intersection of Furman Street and Old Fulton Street to begin our tour at Pier 1 (2010), which extends south from Old Fulton Street. The thunderous roadway of the Brooklyn Bridge was almost directly overhead, and the classy new 1 Hotel Brooklyn Bridge stood nearby.

Brooklyn waterfront, 1983

Plan

Pier 5 uplands, berm

London plane trees edging Bridge View Lawn

Bridge View Lawn

Sumac trees along "secret" path at Pier 1

While the piers are similar in size (five acres each, except for the larger Pier 1), the paths that run through the park range from thin winding slivers to wide expanses. At the southernmost entrance (Atlantic Avenue and Furman Street), visitors walk along a narrow green corridor that cuts through one of the park's biggest attractions: a series of interactive playgrounds. By contrast, a broad promenade (excessively wide, in fact, because it conforms to the access requirements for emergency vehicles) runs the length of the park. Along the promenade is the Bridge View Lawn, which has an edge partially defined by a long row of London plane trees (*Platanus × acerifolia* 'Bloodgood'). Their thick canopies sheltered a gaggle of caregivers and their young charges, who occupied every inch of the bench running opposite. These and many of the other trees in this area (planted above a hundred-year flood level) are all multitrunked to create a richer effect.

The inviting paths on the Bridge View Lawn arc up to a ridge created from fill, in this case remnants of Long Island Rail Road tunnel excavations. The green space, bordered by trees that screen out the views, is one of several inwardly focused areas; these alternate with settings that have stunning vistas of New York Harbor; ferry, tugboat, and barge activity; and the Statue of Liberty. To the south of Bridge View, the Harbor View Lawn, its oval form partially surrounded by trees, offers both experiences. The Granite Prospect, nestled at the north of Harbor View, is a generous amphitheater constructed with more than three hundred blocks of granite left over from the Roosevelt Island Bridge rehabilitation. Another eco-friendly salvaged material is long leaf yellow pine: recovered from a demolished building on Pier 1, the wood was used for benches, tables, cladding, and decking throughout the park.

We followed a kind of secret woodland path that beckoned from a hill at the lawn's east side. Dense plantings of varieties of viburnums, rhododendrons, sumacs, catalpa, oaks, and magnolias enclose the narrow trail as it threads its way through an area of saltwater-tolerant plants and rain gardens. Here, and throughout the park, cisterns store storm water, which supplies 70 percent of the park's irrigation needs.

Emerging from this hideaway, we found ourselves once more in a wide-open area, this one with stone seating and steps down to the water. Van Valkenburgh pointed out a salt marsh, noting that it is the most popular and beloved of all the ecological areas in the park. It is also one of the designer's favorite places there. It attracts wildlife and contains many ecological benefits. He explained that a personal connection with the wetland comes from the fact that, because of its proximity to the brackish river, it is the only place in the park that can support a salt marsh.

To create the marsh, an old retaining wall was replaced by a riprap gravity wall, grasses such as cordgrass (*Spartina alterniflora*) were planted, grading was designed to allow for drainage, and the historic piles were preserved for protection from ice floes and debris. The construction was put to the test by record-breaking storm surges caused by Hurricane Sandy in 2012 but passed with distinction: the soft edge of the salt marsh and the park beyond were left largely unscathed. This concept is similar to, though executed differently from, the way in which Hunter's Point Park South and its marshes address the East River's tidal fluctuations. Another similarity is that the two green spaces attempt to create a relationship between the visitor and the river both spatially (by allowing visitors to come right to the water's edge) and experientially (through dynamic moments within the park as well as such programmatic features as kayak launches). Van Valkenburgh says that a future dip in the river is not out of the question.

We continued south to Piers 2, 3, 4, 5, and 6. Each of the constructions provides a distinct experience; as a whole, they offer a remarkable diversity both in plantings and in plant maturity, the latter because the park was built over a ten-year period as funding allowed. Between Piers 1 and 2 is an upland garden with a path through it. Pier 2 (2014) marks the beginning of a different aesthetic, where the romantic walkways of the earlier portions of the park give way to the straight, broad path for pedestrians and bikes (and emergency vehicles). Near Pier 2, the spine occupies a strip of land with little room for planting; nevertheless it is relatively lush. By contrast, the piers farther south have more open space along the greenway, which is used for gardens and lawns. Composed primarily of surfaces for play, Pier 2 offers basketball, handball, and bocce courts as well as a roller rink and the kayak launch. Similarly focused on active recreation, Pier 5 (2012) is devoted to soccer fields, while beside Pier 4 (2013) is a sandy beach with small, artificial tidal pools.

Only on Piers 3 (2018) and 6 (2010, 2015) are there echoes of the dense vegetation of Pier 1. On Pier 3, chiefly used for sunbathing, small events, and passive recreation, the undulating edge of a grassy bowl has created several semiprivate, room-like spaces. The bowl is bordered by meadow grasses, trees, and shrubs, and along the north side of the pier is a hedged labyrinth of play spaces surrounded by evergreens, multistemmed birches, and poplars. Pier 1's meandering pathways also reappear, some bordering the river, others snaking through the uplands. On one of my many return visits, this time on a sunny Sunday afternoon in December, an active road paralleling the greenway (and reducing the planted area dramatically) and the paths were equally popular: a diverse array of people, many with children and some with dogs, walked, jogged, and biked, cramming every route along the riverside.

We ended our visit at Pier 6, which has a quieter atmosphere, far from the tourists and crowds waiting for the ferry at Pier 1. Volleyball courts occupy one corner of this pier, a lawn with an edge of native plants wraps around a reconstructed marsh, and a picnic area occupies the riverside. Inland is a 1.6-acre suite of four playgrounds designed by Nilda Cosco and Robin Moore, professors of landscape architecture at North Carolina State University and specialists in nature-based play. On the hot summer day of our tour with Van Valkenburgh, the numerous features of the Water Lab were mobbed by children of all ages squealing in delight. Sandbox Village, Swing Valley, and Slide Mountain, each a distinct outdoor room enclosed by dense vegetation, offer something instructive and fun for youngsters from toddlers to teens. It is difficult to imagine a more diverse mix than this throng of children.

Clearly, it is this blend that is closest to Van Valkenburgh's heart. In 2016, the park received close to five million visitors between Memorial Day and Labor Day; an average of 330,000 people spend time in Brooklyn Bridge Park on a summer weekend. The gardens, marshes, playgrounds, sports fields, picnic area, and other attractions offer something for everyone. As Van Valkenburgh says, "Making a park is like cooking a Thanksgiving dinner: you have to invite all the relatives, and there has to be a dish everyone likes to eat."

Main Street Park, beach

Salt marsh and surviving wood piles

Water Lab playground at Pier 6, Nilda Cosco and Robin Moore

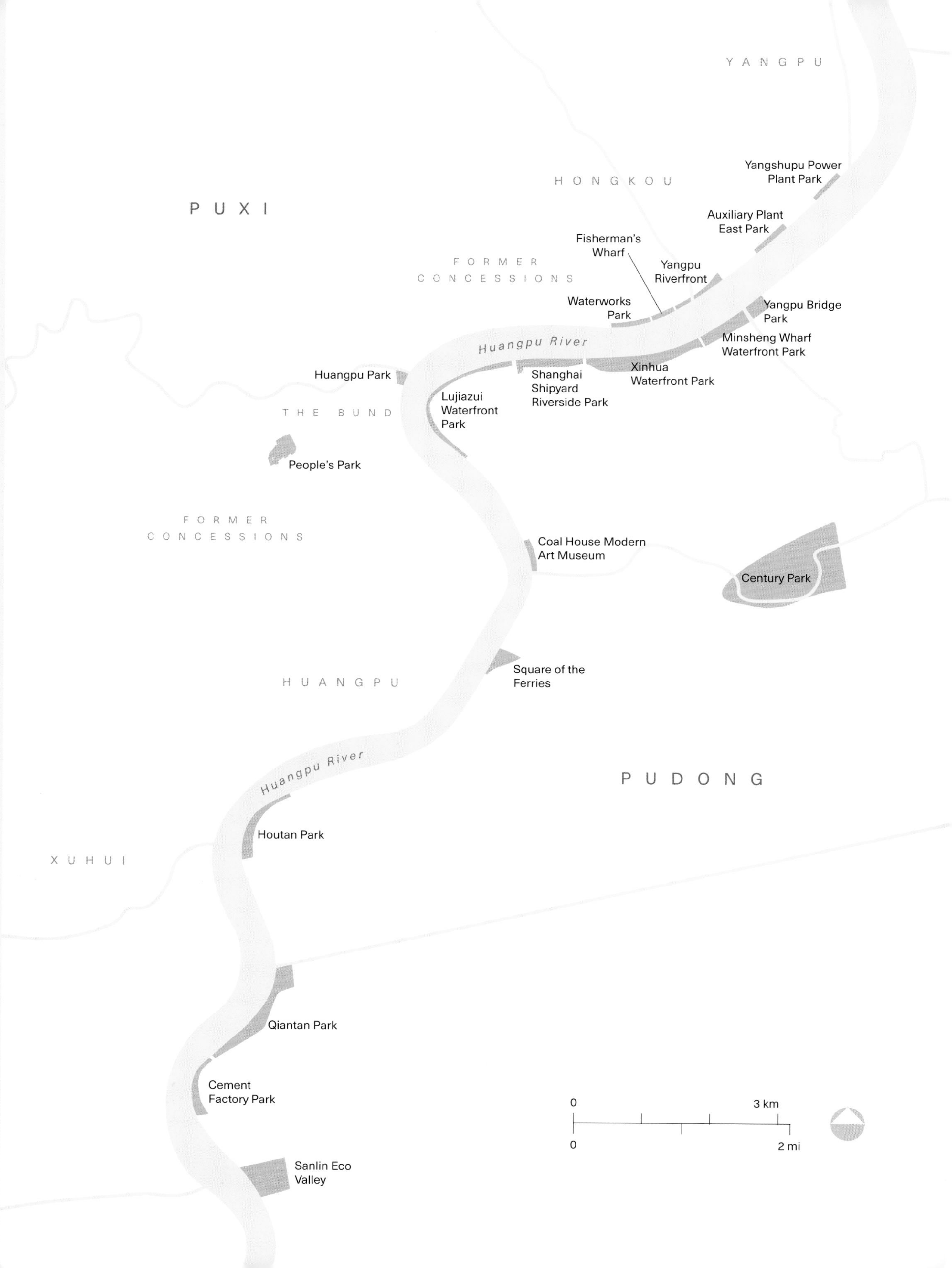

YANGPU

Yangshupu Power Plant Park

HONGKOU

PUXI

Auxiliary Plant East Park

Fisherman's Wharf

FORMER CONCESSIONS

Yangpu Riverfront

Waterworks Park

Yangpu Bridge Park

Huangpu River

Minsheng Wharf Waterfront Park

Huangpu Park

Shanghai Shipyard Riverside Park

Xinhua Waterfront Park

Lujiazui Waterfront Park

THE BUND

People's Park

FORMER CONCESSIONS

Coal House Modern Art Museum

Century Park

Square of the Ferries

HUANGPU

Huangpu River

PUDONG

Houtan Park

XUHUI

Qiantan Park

Cement Factory Park

0 3 km

0 2 mi

Sanlin Eco Valley

Shanghai

Shanghai is the "undisputed candidate" for a city to represent the twenty-first century, says David Koren in "Shanghai: The Biography of a City." Fiction and film have made China's largest city synonymous with mystery and intrigue, but Shanghai is, above all, a city of continual transformation.

The city's modern era began in 1842, when the Treaty of Nanjing made Shanghai a "treaty port" open to foreign trade and residence. The treaty allowed the establishment of concession areas in Shanghai, which still exhibit the neoclassical, colonial, and Art Deco architecture typical of the French, British, and Americans who occupied them. The French Concession, at the west of Shanghai's Old City, is characterized by allées of London plane trees; the former British and American Concessions are just north of the Old City, along the Huangpu River.

By the end of the nineteenth century, a mile of imposing buildings from that era along the western side of the river was among the extensive contributions by the flourishing imperial powers. Known as the Bund, the area was home to commercial companies from around the world, elite private clubs, and luxury hotels, all manifestations of the city's "golden age" in the 1920s and 1930s.

During this early modern period, most of Shanghai's public parks were built by the concessions in a European style and were restricted predominantly to foreigners. Astonishingly, one of Shanghai's oldest parks, Huangpu (1868), was barred for some time to Chinese visitors, a practice that continued in the concession parks.

In 1937, this cosmopolitan success was interrupted, first by the Japanese military occupation (1937–45) and then, after the Communist takeover in 1949, by the Great Leap Forward (1958–62), a government program designed to transform the country from an agrarian economy to a Communist society, and the Cultural Revolution (1966–76) initiated by Mao Zedong. Mao increased the early twentieth century's already gigantic industrial presence on both banks of the Huangpu River in Shanghai, an area where factories were abandoned in the 1980s.

At this time, the metropolis underwent yet another transformation. Awe-inspiring physical and economic growth, plus widespread modernization, spurred city officials to explore the idea of expanding the city across the Huangpu River to Pudong. Mayor Zhu Rongji, who made a practice of seeking foreign advice, looked to Paris's massive high-rise La Défense commercial district as a model for Pudong. The Huangpu River became the heart of the city's cultural, social, and civic life, with numerous museums and other art venues occupying repurposed buildings along its riverfront.

Yet the river itself, polluted and prone to floods, was still in need of attention. In the 1980s and 1990s, the government rehabilitated an old flood wall, now averaging more than six feet in height, with a two-tiered structure, similar to those in other countries. A lower terrace protects and absorbs flooding, and an upper terrace serves as a safe egress and, in Shanghai, provided the base of a series of new green spaces on both sides of the river.

In 2000, the US firms of Skidmore, Owings & Merrill and Sasaki, together with Philip Cox of Australia, were asked to develop ideas for the thirteen miles of the city's east waterfront. This initial proposal was never realized, and, in 2016, Agence Ter produced a new master plan for the east (Pudong) riverside that would be the basis for commissions awarded by the government to designers from several countries. The city had already implemented a seventy-mile greenbelt surrounding the outskirts. It connects to an automated purification system that removes petroleum hydrocarbons and organic pollutants from the water. Also connecting to the greenbelt are a number of urban parks, including several "wedge parks" that are meant to funnel cool air into the city center during warm months and block winter's strong winds.

The landscape architects who realized the waterside open spaces were usually presented with sites cleared by the authorities of their extensive industrial contamination. While the designers lost out to the city's site remediation, they were often more successful in persuading the government to retain the numerous industrial artifacts that line the waterway, recalling at least part of its storied history.

Pudong waterfront, aerial rendering of master plan, Agence Ter

Riverside Parks, Pudong (East)

Shanghai, China
ongoing in 2021

Cement Factory Park, Agence Ter

Coal House Modern Art Museum Park, YIYU Design and Atelier Deshaus

Shanghai Shipyard Riverside Park, Design Land Collaborative

Xinhua Waterfront Park, West 8

Minsheng Wharf Waterfront Park, Atelier Liu Yuyang Architects and Atelier Deshaus

According to the French landscape firm Agence Ter, the master plan for the east (Pudong) riverside in Shanghai is expected by the government to brand the metropolis as a Green City. More than thirteen miles of waterfront were divided into eighteen parcels for public/private development; half of this territory is owned by four companies, which are allowed to use only 2 percent of their lots for low-rise buildings. Some of the owners were permitted to engage the landscape architect of their choice, opting for American, Dutch, and Chinese firms; others followed the government's lead in choosing Agence Ter. The city government called for clearly marked tripart circulation for the greenways on both sides of the river. In Pudong, the planners determined the widths of a pedestrian "discovery" path, a red jogging path, and a gray asphalt bicycle path (occasionally elevated). Vegetation along the river was to be kept low to allow views of the waterway and its reflection of light; denser vegetation along the city side was to provide shade and fresh air. Restaurants regularly punctuate this side.

Alex and I started our exploration of the newly completed parks in Pudong at the south end of the string. The landscape architects met us at each site. As we drove to the first green space, gradients from urban to rural provided a shocking contrast. The dense urban form of Shanghai's city center gave way to the odd agricultural field on the outskirts of the city. This pastoral setting is under threat, however, as housing developments and shopping centers consume the landscape, a result of Shanghai's explosive growth. Within these new developments, only the occasional nondescript, partially demolished, two- or three-story concrete buildings provide a flashback to the relatively recent times when Pudong was known for rural farming rather than for its current dizzying skyline.

Qiantan District, which included the southernmost part of the completed riverside renewal, once consisted of small villages and a large cement factory. In 2018, Agence Ter converted the site into **Cement Factory Park** (2018, 30 acres, cost: undisclosed). The landscape design includes many new structures, notably elegant glazed "totems" every kilometer (required by the government, the totems, which continue along the river, contain comfort stations and an open space for reading and relaxation) and the Starry Night Pavilion. According to Emmanuelle Blondeau, Agence Ter's project manager, the large-scale impression of this park may have been inspired by the outsize design characteristic of the Danish firm BIG.

Of the many challenges the design team faced, the multilane vehicular tunnel running directly underneath the park proved to be one the biggest. Because of limitations related to building on top of this structure, the designers decided to create a broad lawn and plaza. Flanking the plaza—not over the tunnel—are two large forms (the designers call them "hills") built primarily of reinforced concrete. Inside are various programs, including a restaurant and park user facilities; outside are faceted exteriors painted in joyful colors as well as play space and a large amphitheater. The bicycle path that runs adjacent to the river—part of Agence Ter's master plan—is predominantly flat except where it ramps up the hills to provide a lookout over the park and river.

The expansive size of Cement Factory Park is in part a response to its intended use as a concert venue. The amphitheater and lawn provide ample space for festivals and massive gatherings. Yet elegant details emerge within these vast spaces, such as the long bench snaking through groves of oak and ash trees or the whimsical, reed-like lights within the meadow.

Alternating between walking and brief stints of driving, we passed the stretch of waterfront containing Turenscape's Houtan Park and Agence Ter's Square of the Ferries to arrive at the **Coal House Modern Art Museum Park** (2018, 19.7 acres, cost: undisclosed) by Atelier Deshaus and YIYU Design. The park, like the renovated Lujiazui Waterfront Park by Agence

Cement Factory Park, playground, Agence Ter

Reed-like lights

Coal House Modern Art Museum Park, Atelier Deshaus and YIYU Design

Ter, is at the heart of Pudong's financial district and faces Shanghai's historic Bund. The architects and landscape architects have adapted the remnants of an old coal works for the museum, cafés, and restaurants along the river. Entry to the complex is achieved by ascending a fanciful elevated zigzag path, built in steel and recalling the walkway in Huadu Lake Park (page 254). The designers were able to retain some of the existing trees along with the coal works and have surrounded the buildings with small gardens containing perennial grasses and swaths of white coneflower.

Farther north along the Huangpu's curve to the east was an especially interesting renewal. When he started work on the **Shanghai Shipyard Riverside Park** (2019, 30 acres, cost: $40.2 million), Dwight Law of the firm Design Land Collaborative was disappointed by the amount of advance preparation that had already been implemented by the local authorities. The existing flood wall prevented creation of the natural riverside that had been envisaged, and remediation had left a soil depth that was insufficient for the vegetation that had been planned. Yet Law deftly overcame these impediments.

The park offers multilevel lawns and amphitheaters terraced in a way that both accommodates seasonal floods and supports outdoor cultural festivities. Pedestrian bridges and ramps connect the cascading gardens with the linear paths specified in the master plan. A broad riverside path bordered by benches and boulders of green Hangzhou slate is a natural, hard presence within the soft landscape. We were captivated by the inviting human scale of this park. On the day of our visit, seductively rich plantings of scarlet Japanese blood grass (*Imperata cylindrica* 'Rubra') covered undulating hills; Chinese tallow trees (*Sapium sebiferum*) and muhly grass (*Muhlenbergia capillaris*) overlaid other mounds.

The Shipyard Riverside Park provides a magnificent setting for two elegant cultural buildings. One is a substantial red-brick former ship manufactory (1972) that was skillfully renovated by the Japanese architect Kengo Kuma into an international music hall and retail space; its restaurant and café overlook the river. The other is the Lujiazui Exhibition Center, part of which was designed by the Dutch firm OMA. The enclosed exhibition space functions as an urban theater, hovering over an outdoor area used for smaller events. The multiple

cultural facilities are more than most of the riverside parks can boast, although almost all have at least one (especially in Puxi, where they are installed in renovated industrial buildings).

In addition to the exhibition center, which sits on the ramp of a former ship cradle, where newly constructed vessels were slipped into the river, Design Land Collaborative created a space intended for festivals, Christmas markets, and other large-scale gatherings. The area is sheltered by grids of Chinese soapberry trees (*Sapindus mukorossi)* and camphor trees (*Cinnamomum camphora*) and serves as a food and beverage market. The east side of the plaza is bounded by a terrace paved in blue tile; a beautifully designed, wave-like pattern references the river. In the center of the plaza is a large reflecting pool with dancing fountains and mist. The water feature, which can be emptied to accommodate certain activities, displays a sectional representation of a ship, harking back to the site's history.

The entire Shipyard Riverside Park consists of two terraces, upper and lower, to mitigate occasional flooding; the terraces are connected by a zone of gardens on sloped terrain. At the lower level is a water retention area, or rain garden: a constructed, interactive wetland 164 feet wide that collects and cleans storm water runoff. The large stones strewn throughout the pond and a border of irises and bald cypresses (*Taxodium distichum*) provide a note of the natural in this orderly landscape.

Contrasting with the human scale of the Shipyard Riverside Park is West 8's **Xinhua Waterfront Park** (2018, 42 acres, cost: undisclosed). Here, West 8's requirement to keep the nearly hundred-foot-wide former dock has resulted in a park that blends an industrial aesthetic with a civic scale. Like the Shipyard Riverside Park, Xinhua Park is terraced to respond to flooding. The lower terrace occupies the zone of the former dock, and the upper terrace presents a woodland and rock garden. Along the lower terrace, ornamental annuals and trees in planters are the only vegetation on many of the broad swaths of granite-cobblestoned patterned paving. Robust metal structures along the waterfront provide shade to those wanting to stand along the railing and contemplate the river. Yet while the expanses are stark, and in warm weather unmercifully hot, they provide generous spaces for large occasions: festivals, food truck gatherings, and markets. Xinhua Waterfront Park is one of the few of the various riverfront parks capable of accommodating such activities.

An undulating retaining wall running the length of the park provides bench seating along the lower terrace. To shelter this bench, West 8 subtly tempered the arid quality of the open space by using bamboo formwork for the cast concrete that arcs overhead to create shade. This allusion to natural plant matter highlights the artifice of the protected bench and at the same time provides a sense of place and materiality.

The broad ribbon of paving on the lower level is contrasted by the dense plantings on the upper level, comprising 2,254 trees between rocky outcroppings and narrow paths. Generously scattered among the planting beds, the stones suggest a mountainous landscape. The rough-hewn, warm-colored stones selected by West 8 are repeated in the children's playground. The play area is shaped like a turtle—an animal that in China

Shanghai Shipyard Riverside Park, Design Land Collaborative

Muhly grass and amphitheater with international music hall and retail space beyond, Kengo Kuma

Rain garden

Ship Cradle Event Plaza and reflecting pool

symbolizes longevity. The shell, a domed structure with stairs and paths, allows children to run through a miniature forest of pine and flowering shrubs.

Xinhua Waterfront Park, although sophisticated in its materiality, was not without its challenges. Adriaan Geuze, the principal of West 8, calls it a "moving target." He bemoaned the extremely tight time limits, saying, "Something that would take five years elsewhere is expected to take a week in China."

We met Yuyang Liu and Yifeng Guo of Atelier Liu Yuyang Architects at their **Minsheng Wharf Waterfront Park** (2018, 6.7 acres, cost: undisclosed), the next landscape to the northeast. This park occupies a very thin sliver of space between the river and former warehouse structures that have been reprogrammed for various uses, including huge grain silos that have been transformed into an exhibition hall by the local firm Atelier Deshaus. Consisting primarily of a riverfront promenade and raised walkways, the park serves as a ferry stop, welcoming commuters and inviting them to pause underneath the curvilinear metal mesh roofs of its pavilions.

Most intriguing is the gracefully spiraling metal grate walkway that contains three levels: high (bikes), middle (joggers), and low (pedestrian) paths in accordance with the three-part circulation of the master plan. Liu and Guo told us that the small plaza where the walkway meets the ground level is a favorite dance spot for older people, who bring their own music-making devices. This plaza is one of the few places in Minsheng Park to offer vegetation. One reason for this is that the designers did not receive permission to alter the existing pier to plant trees, so vegetation is grown in modular metal planters. The silvery containers, chosen to convey the idea of technology, align in equidistant rows to provide seating, but they do little to relieve the dry quality of this expansive concrete platform.

We eventually crossed the river, leaving Pudong and heading to Puxi. Daily commuter ferries leave every fifteen minutes or so from the many Pudong terminals, and it takes another five minutes to reach the opposite shore. In contrast to the luxurious yachts moored in marinas along the Huangpu and the sight-seeing boats regularly plying its waters, the ferry we took with Liu and Guo was a modest conveyance, filled with male motorcyclists. We landed at the Shanghai Power Station Auxiliary Machine Factory, also designed by Yuyang Liu following a master plan for Yangpu District by Original Design Studio on the Puxi waterfront. Liu's parks on either side of the river preserve towering industrial equipment no longer in use, notably the bright orange tower cranes that line the two shores. The preservation of the sites' industrial legacy was something that had been largely lost on the Pudong side of the river; though we soon found that it defined the Puxi side.

Xinhua Waterfront Park, lower terrace, West 8

Shaded alcove seating

Rocky hillside

Minsheng Wharf Waterfront Park,
spiraling, multilevel (cyclists, joggers,
and pedestrians) walkway,
Atelier Liu Yuyang Architects

Riverfront walkway with cranes

View to southwest over Huangpu River and Puxi waterfront with Yangshupu Power Plant Park (foreground)

Riverside Parks, Puxi (West)

Shanghai, China
ongoing in 2021

Waterworks Park/Fisherman's Wharf, Original Design Studio

Yangpu Riverfront, da landscape

Yangshupu Power Plant Park, Original Design Studio

Referred to as the "cradle of China's modern industry," the 9.6-mile west shoreline of the Huangpu River hosted a series of firsts in China: water treatment, textiles, shipbuilding, and thermal power. The creation of what would become the Yangshupu Industrial Zone began in 1869, when the Shanghai Concession Project Bureau constructed the Yangshupu Road as a means to connect the Bund with the port of the same name. Following the 1842 Sino-British Treaty of Nanking, foreign industrialists gained the right to manufacture in Shanghai, and a flourishing industrial economy developed rapidly along the west bank of the Huangpu River. In 1913, British investors built the Yangshupu Power Plant, at one point the largest producer of electricity in East Asia and the tallest structure in Shanghai. It closed officially in 2010.

By the 1990s, however, the industrial landscape on this bank of the river was a ghost of its former self. Eighty-three percent of the area's industry had relocated, leaving behind a row of contaminated sites that obstructed public access to the river, and the number of workers had dropped from 600,000 to 60,000.

The rehabilitation project extends on the Puxi side of the river from Yangpu Bridge to the northern extremity of Yangpu District, an area as noteworthy for its history of intense industrialization from the late 1800s to the 1930s as for its magnificent views of the river and the Pudong skyline.

When Original Design Studio was awarded the master plan for the Puxi side of the Huangpu through a competition in 2015, the aim was to "return the river to the people." Sophisticated contemporary urban planning strategies, which layer park systems, transportation networks, and residential, commercial, and cultural uses, were pressed into service to replace the single-function industrial corridor. The government remodeled the former factories for cultural activities, and the landscape architects retained numerous industrial artifacts to allude to the neighborhood's identity.

Alex and I started our tour of the riverside parks in Puxi at the southernmost open area, just as we had in Pudong. At the paired **Waterworks Park/Fisherman's Wharf** (2016–18, 9.4 acres, cost: undisclosed), we were surprised to see Victorian neo-Gothic architecture beside the walkway—two building facades and a crenelated wall. The attractive red brick structures (1883) were built by the British during their occupation of Shanghai and still belong to the city's waterworks department. The colonial remains are rare survivors, given the many traditional Chinese buildings that have been demolished throughout the country.

It was this historic architecture, however, that presented the biggest challenge for the designer, Original Design Studio, in the Waterworks Park area. The master plan called for a continuous system of parks linked by paths, but the waterworks and its crenelated perimeter wall extended all the way to the water's edge. To solve this problem, the landscape architects repurposed an abandoned pier in front of the wall, creating a boardwalk over the water. The single boardwalk in the waterside park system, it is 1,755 feet long and varies in width from thirteen to almost forty-three feet.

Waterworks is the only park we visited that physically extends into the Huangpu, and the numerous tugboats and barges gave us an immediate sense of being on the river. This is also one of the few parks where industrial activity still occurs. Ships dock next to the boardwalk and unload materials such as liquid aluminum through large pipes underneath the decking and into the waterworks facility.

Large canopy trees inside the city waterworks complex arc over the walls, lending a richness to the public walkway. On the boardwalk itself, vegetation is limited to planters. The wide curved edges of the merbau wood balustrade, which matches the walkway, and the careful detailing of the shaded seating pavilions along the length of the boardwalk are of atypically high quality.

The Fisherman's Wharf portion offers a variety of experiences: river, with heavy boat traffic and lapping water on metal grate bridges, and wetland, which takes advantage of a pit left over from the site's previous occupant, a fish market. Connecting these two is an urban garden with beds of perennial grasses;

Waterworks Park with Victorian architecture, Original Design Studio

Waterside merbau wood boardwalk

Fisherman's Wharf, riverside seating, Original Design Studio

Wetland, walkway, and preexisting structures

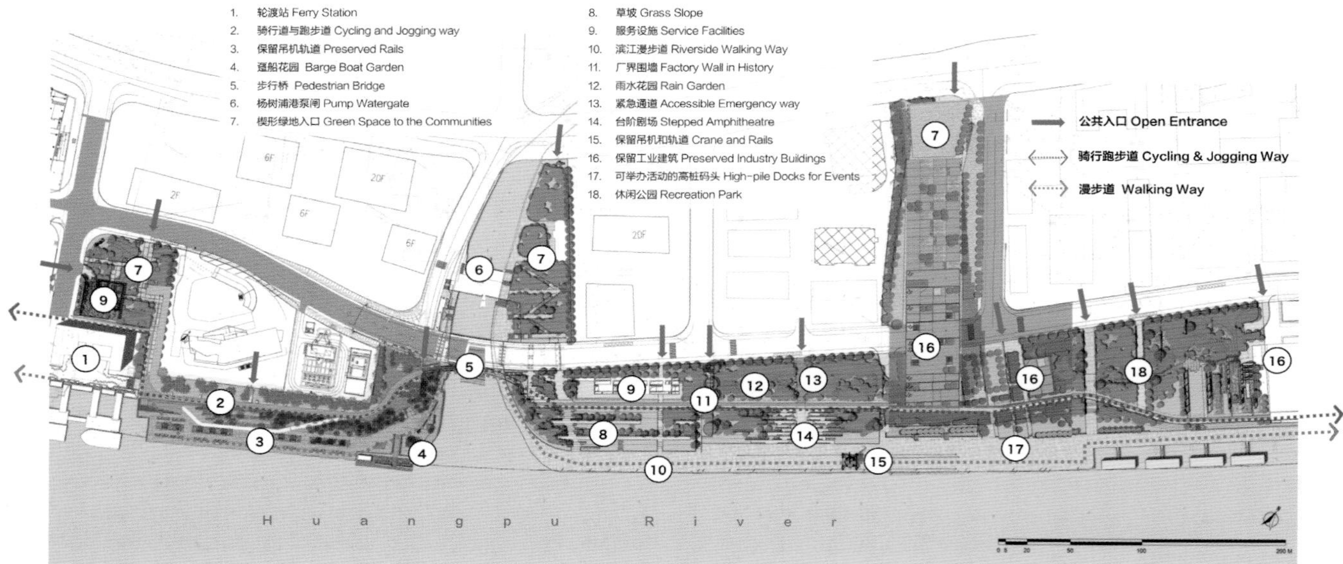

Yangpu Riverfront (Timber Market), steel walls with logs, da landscape

Plan

Terraced gardens and seating

Auxiliary Plant East, gabion walls on footprints of former industrial buildings, Atelier Liu Yuyang Architects, Atelier 2+, and Atelier Deshaus

seating areas provide a place for visitors to pause and watch the river traffic.

The paths through the park are equally diverse. Narrow footpaths and raised walkways over the wetland encourage visitors to meander. Wider paths paved in granite run through the center of the park, connecting it to various city spaces. Broad expanses of concrete adjacent to the river, formerly docks, allow for cyclists and rollerbladers to zip by. The formal tripartite circulation scheme of Pudong is relaxed in Puxi; designers have freedom to design paths that respond to site conditions.

In addition to the fish market, a British cotton mill once occupied the one-third-mile tract along the river, and the landscape architects embedded the history of the cotton mill in the wetland decking structure and in pavilions that look like looms, a nod to the weaving process. Statues of weavers and fishermen are less successful in this respect. Imagery showing the history of the site continues along the river; the designers have also added a narrow-gauge rail line in the concrete surface of the dock that rolls wide steel planters on wheels along it.

The generous stretch of planting between the Fisherman's Wharf pier and the wetland provides the park with its primary gathering space. Standing before a screen of gingko trees were vibrantly colored purple coneflowers, in bloom at the time of our visit, alternating with tall, swaying grasses and tidy lawns.

Original Design Studio calls Waterworks Park/Fisherman's Wharf a "demonstration section" for the riverside public space in Yangpu. The two parks are similar in character, richer and more distinctive than many of the parks on the Pudong riverfront, and the attention to detail is pronounced.

To the north of the duo is **Yangpu Riverfront** (2015–18, 16.6 acres, cost: undisclosed), designed by da landscape. Also known as the Timber Market, the park stands on a location that was a lumber company and, later, a ship salvage yard; large cranes and a ramped ship launch remain from the latter. The charming large green space, built partially on piers and partially on land that terraces upward, links to smaller parks that extend into the adjacent neighborhood. Newly built walls of weathered steel plates filled with precisely cut logs provide a rhythm to the site and also mark the property boundaries of the former industrial structures.

A small stream divides the site; nearby, along the waterfront promenade, is an interactive map of the neighborhood. Carved into the concrete paving is a shallow channel that represents the stream; park goers can fill the channel with a pump. The map indicates roads and bridges with bands of metal. An outdoor classroom composed of tiers of stepped seating and desks, each tier separated by planters full of flowering perennials, provides additional space for outdoor learning.

Within the park's amphitheater, benches in precast concrete display important dates in the history of the lumber company. The ends of the benches are stamped in a wood pattern, a use of natural materials as imagery similar to what we observed at Xinhua Waterfront Park. The concrete (produced by a German company) is smooth, well formed, and without stress fractures; such quality construction is a rarity in China.

Several parks under construction in 2019 occupy strips of riverfront adjoining Timber Market. Large, repurposed, early twentieth-century warehouses will be retained in some of the parks, including the Auxiliary Plant East Park by Atelier 2+, Atelier Liu Yuyang Architects, and Atelier Deshaus.

Finally, to the northeast of these sites is the most recently completed park on the Puxi side of the river, the **Yangshupu Power Plant Park** (2019, 4.3 acres, cost: undisclosed), created by Original Design Studio. Like many of the other parks along the Huangpu, this one occupies a site significant in China's rapid rise as an industrialized nation. To preserve this legacy of the site, Original Design Studio repurposed relics when possible, repaired the native landscapes, and connected the public with the river.

The park was scheduled to open the day after our visit, but cooperative guards granted us access. Our initial impression was of an otherworldly landscape consumed by the relics of an

industrial past: the foundations of a coal transportation trestle, pumps, wet and dry ash storage tanks, a coal hopper, conveyor belts, water storage tanks, and three massive tower cranes. China typically removes all traces of a site's former life, but in this case the designers were able to save them. The enormous size and quantity of remnants outdid anything we had seen until then. But it was the power station itself, with its soaring chimney, that dominated the scene. At 345 feet tall, the chimney, once a symbolic gateway to Shanghai's port, now stands as a terminus for the Yangpu Riverfront park system.

The primary open space is an industrial square defined by three stepped retention pools planted with reeds and grasses. The pools occupy the sites of two demolished buildings. Each contains a unique relic fragment: rectangular concrete piles piercing the surface of the water, foundation walls that frame three pavilions (one whose roof was formerly a coal hopper), and two large pumps set into a crushed stone terrace also containing waterlilies. Walls made from weathered steel sheet piling surround the ponds, and a restroom pavilion is partially buried underneath excavated fill.

Defining the river's edge are the three red tower cranes, as well as a 656-foot-long coal transportation trestle, converted by Original Design Studio into a lookout over the river. On the trestle, decorated by a long, linear planter filled with changing flower displays and accessible by a bridge, was the only place where we experienced the life of the busy shipping corridor.

One of the many singular aspects of this park is the articulation of the flood wall. In almost every riverfront park we visited in Shanghai, the designers raised the ground level to meet the top of the floodwall. In the Power Plant Park, Original Design Studio maintained the original grade as much as possible, exposing the wall. While this configuration obstructs views to the river, what is gained is a sense of occupying an industrial sunken garden.

Industrial structures have been repurposed as a museum, gallery spaces, information kiosks, cafés, and even a climbing facility. These pavilions might be difficult for those with limited mobility or acrophobia, because access is typically gained via long, narrow staircases that pierce or spiral around the skin of the structures to cantilever high over the park. The reward for reaching one of the many lookout spots is a panoramic view of not only this park but much of the Yangpu park system.

The tripartite circulation of the other riverfront parks is in evidence here, winding around rectangular planting beds and grassy areas as it leads from the park's entrance to the looming power station. The various paths in this area of industrial behemoths are like nothing so much as the Yellow Brick Road in the Land of Oz.

As we exited the park, we walked along a raised steel walkway through a grove of Japanese maple (*Acer palmatum* Thunb.). To our left were old concrete walls articulated with lace-like grilles, the remains of smaller industrial structures; to our right, decrepit machinery, the monumental remains of industry. It struck us that Original Design Studio's intended goal—restoration of a lost riparian ecology—may have dissipated, but it succeeded instead in creating an industrial *penjing* (mini-replication of a large landscape) within a vast sculpture park.

Yangshupu Power Plant Park, retention pools with relics, Original Design Studio

Tower cranes as follies

Industrial square with park pavilions

Industrial structure repurposed as information center/connection hub

Overleaf: Industrial *penjing*

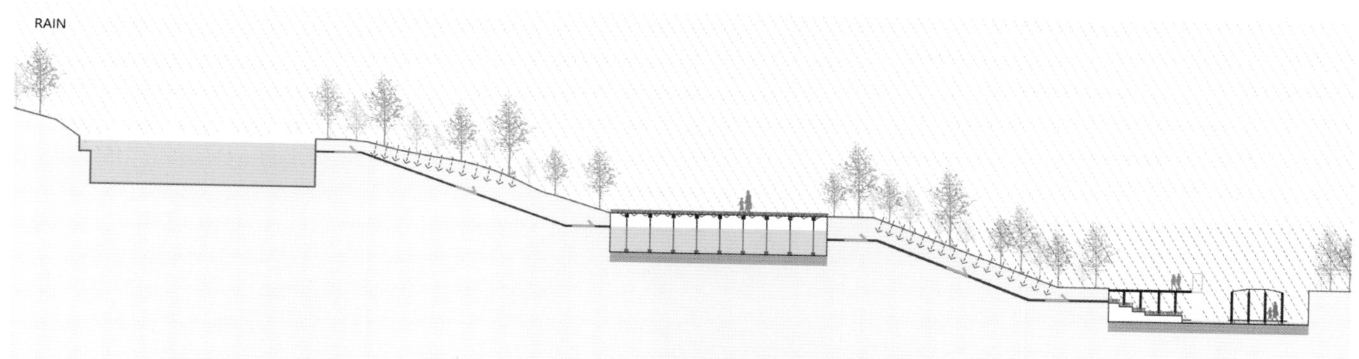

other materials including gravel, stone dust, and wood. These walkways complement the soft and permeable mulch trails that wind through the forest.

In addition to the natural conditions of the site, the landscape architects had to tackle remnants of the purification plant's infrastructure. The team covered ten of the plant's twelve large underground sedimentation tanks, which vary in size, with five to six feet of soil. One of the remaining two, already open to the sky, became a scenic lake. The other contains a rain garden/wetland.

The rain garden is a sunken garden whose long concrete walls divide the former storage chamber into two. Remains of concrete columns, with rebar protruding from the top, march through pools and planting beds. On one side, machinery original to the site acts as a garden ornament; judging by the young children intrigued by the industrial relics, this is a favorite destination in the park. On the other side, a permanent installation of sculpture stands on remnants of the columns, almost as if they were industrial pedestals. Nozzles built into the walls mist the entire space, creating a swirling haze. To the north, a building original to the site will be converted into a museum of water culture. To the south, a new café building completes the ensemble. The entire sunken public space, which recalls the rooms of the Mei Garden (page 248), can be viewed from the park's elevated metal walkways and from a bridge traversing the garden. In addition, there is an entrance via a stairway that has treads of metal bar grating; the treads match the project's industrial character and also allow a filtered view of the ground plane below.

The slope of the terrain, which rises 115 feet from east to west, was cleverly utilized in the original design of the water treatment facility and again by the park's designers. Originally, at the top of this incline, an open-air cistern captured rainwater. When this upper cistern, now a lake, became full, pipes

Rain garden with sculptures

Gathering circle built from repurposed materials

Playground

Forest walk

directed water into a series of lower reservoirs; the last in the sequence is the one now occupied by the rain garden/wetland. Other former cisterns store water for irrigation. Those that remain fully covered have had lawns installed over them.

At the time of our fall visit, the long entrance esplanade was ablaze with the fuchsia blooms of garden cosmos (*Cosmos bipinnatus*). This planting bed is atypical for the project: horticultural displays appear only around the foundations of some buildings, never within the forest ecology of the park. A trail, constructed from crossties recovered from a former railroad, leads to the elevated steel walkway that floats graciously through the forest at different heights. The meandering passageway took us within, or just below, the tree canopies. The curved course is lined by a railing of wooden pickets that reduce in height and slowly rotate to become an edge along the flyover.

Our stroll elevated above the ground provided a first-hand experience of the canopies, the quality of the leaf-filtered light, and views of the dense vegetation below. In a process of selective thinning, the landscape architects worked with a local agricultural college to determine which vegetation—a mix of native and non-native tree species and plants dating from the time of the purification facility and likely earlier—should be kept and which removed. This editing allowed the opening of key prospects, improvement of ecological performance, and reduction of invasive plants. As we continued along the raised walkway we saw the results of this task. High in the canopy layer, long views of the park alternated with dense stands of Japanese birch (*Betula platyphylla*) and a mixed deciduous forest that included Amur cork trees (*Phellodendron amurense*). One of the highlights is the lake-like tank, where we observed the water's abundant wildlife from a sturdy timber terrace.

An excursion through the forest is not the only attraction in this beautiful park. From the beginning, the designers' idea of creating an arts community ran parallel to their concept of retaining the natural condition of the site. Supporting this goal is the Art Square, a wide lawn on top of one of the sedimentation tanks that hosts contemporary art installations as well as a rich program of film, music, folk art, traditional Chinese opera, and Chinese crosstalk—an Abbott and Costello–like brand of stand-up comedy. A large exhibition pavilion, built by local university students, consists of a dense grid of thin white wooden members and recalls a Sol LeWitt sculpture. Nearby, several of the existing structures will be turned into additional exhibition spaces.

A polished aluminum tower, the Observation Tower, designed by the SHUISHI team, mirrors the surrounding forest. In tune with the landscape's lively habitat, the tower is shaped like an origami crane. Its highest level affords magnificent views of the forest and the historic architecture on the site.

The children's playground at the Culture of Water Ecology Park is as special as the other elements. It contains sophisticated activity equipment as well as numerous industrial relics. Located near a residential neighborhood, it is the only part of the site that was not covered by vegetation. A little farther on, and also close to an adjoining street, is a magnificent old Siberian crab apple tree (*Malus baccata*) encircled by a bench, evidently a favorite resting place for many locals.

The park is open twenty-four hours a day, seven days a week, and there is no entrance fee. It receives approximately 1,700 visitors daily and on special occasions has seen as many as 30,000 in a single day. On the weekday afternoon of our visit, the forest promenade and the playground were crowded. We regretted not being able to stay for an evening walk within the trees, when continuous LED lighting under the railings promises another kind of inspiring experience.

Raised walkway with lighting

Former open-air sedimentation tank

Art Square

Observation Tower

Vine on steel tension cable

Maschinenfabrik Oerlikon Park

Zurich, Switzerland
2002

Raderschall Partner

36,597 square feet
cost: $14.7 million

How ironic that in Switzerland, famous for its democratic procedures, there was little public participation in the creation of the Maschinenfabrik Oerlikon Park. But at the time of its construction, there was no residential or local community in Oerlikon, an eight-minute ride from the center of Zurich. The neighborhood had been occupied entirely by the factories of Maschinenfabrik Oerlikon, the maker of tanks and munitions.

In 1992, as Maschinenfabrik Oerlikon was closing, the architect Ruoss/Siress/Schrader won an open competition, organized by the city, to draw up a master plan for the new district; it included four new parks. The scheme called for design competitions for each new residential and service building; to win the right to construct, the developers of the buildings were required to cede land that would be used for parks. Three of the parks are programmed with more typical outdoor activities, so Raderschall Partner, winner of the competition for the central open area, could be more adventurous, even pushing the definition of a park.

When the main Oerlikon factory was stripped bare and reduced in size in 1999, Raderschall and collaborating architect Burckhardt+Partners devised a 328-by-111.5-by-59-foot steel structure as the skeleton for the park. The vertical composition is an inventive solution to the problem of increasingly rare open space in cities, and, in fact, new and old office buildings hem the park quite tightly on all sides. Before work could begin, a herculean effort to remove and clean polluted soil had to take place. The remediation included excavating and then replacing soil to a depth of over twenty-five feet across the site.

The project is an exuberant celebration of climbing vines—104 hardy species suitable for the region, but not necessarily native to it, including varieties of climbing perennials and woody creepers, such as Chinese and Japanese wisteria, various types of clematis, climbing roses, ivy, honeysuckle, hops, Virginia creeper, and silver lace. The climbers are planted in the ground and, on higher levels, in irrigated troughs. Each vine displays a discreet information tag for visitors. If one of the plants dies, it is replaced with the same species. But if a first and then a second substitute does not survive, the vine is removed, and neighboring climbers are allowed to expand into the vacant space. The park is maintained for the city by four individuals, two of whom are experienced mountain climbers.

The vines grow up steel tension cables that follow the geometry of the structure. Once installed, the vines grew rapidly up the cables, competing with each other for access to sunlight. Now, most of them have reached the roof of the structure and their vertical growth has slowed. Instead of growing horizontally to form a roof of vines, as the landscape architects had hoped, the vines form a wonderful frayed edge and a gradient of shadows. Many areas have grown so thick that they appear to be rich drapery. Burckhardt+Partners inserted metal stairways, walkways, and balconies within the walls; platforms of metal and spruce appear to slide out from the structure.

The north, mostly evergreen facade, which keeps its leaves in winter, is the most opaque; the southern side of the park is completely open. Along the two streets that line the long sides of the basic structure are numerous entrances to the park, which are signaled by alternating rows of waist-high European beech (*Fagus sylvatica*) and English yew (*Taxus baccata*).

When Alex and I visited MFO Park on a clear morning in July, mothers with strollers and young children, as well as a smaller group of teenagers, had begun to gather in the atrium around the park's focal point: a fountain sitting on a bed of recycled dark blue crushed glass. Lounging on furniture designed by Frédéric Dedelley, the mothers could be heard commenting on the giant rhubarb (*Gunnera tinctoria*) that fills the basin of the fountain. This species is famous for its huge leaves, which can reach a length of six feet and through which the sun radiates. Surrounding the fountain, four columns of Dutchman's pipe (*Aristolochia macrophylla*) further emphasize the verticality of the space.

Our climb through the four levels, or trays, of the armature was not only a visual experience but an acoustic and aromatic one. Birds flew in and out of the foliage, chirping amid an enchanting play of light and shadow, and wafting scents. The winged population has obviously taken as its own this extraordinary aviary.

A walkway built of metal grate runs along the framework's perimeter on every level, minus a few small areas that remain incomplete for lack of funding. Roland Raderschall compares this path and its directed views to the gardens of Stourhead in Wiltshire, England, which were designed in the eighteenth

Fountain and central gathering space

Suspended seating trays

Vines and climbing shrubs

Overleaf: Vertical vines and horizontal European beech and English yew

century by Henry Hoare II (1705–85). Each tray was unique, offering different views of the new neighborhood. The progression culminated at the roof terrace, where we could look down into the layers of structure and vines or look out onto views of Zurich.

As noontime approached, people poured into the park from the surrounding office buildings. The MFO Park is evidently a popular place for brown-bagging at lunch as well as for families picnicking in the evening, which we observed when we returned. Programming for the park includes a variety of community activities such as sports, concerts, performances, and film screenings.

At night, lighting made the large green enclosure as welcoming as it is in daytime. Inserted into the vine-covered columns, the lights created a lantern-like effect and a rich play of shadows. As we made our last observations, an elderly couple crossed the main, shadowy open space, and it was impossible not to see the scene as the spindly columns and mysterious figures of Giacometti's surrealist sculpture *The Palace at 4 a.m.*

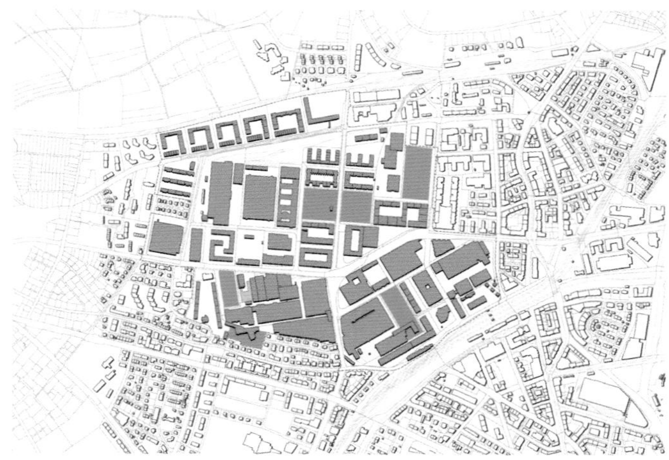

Redevelopment of Oerlikon district, master plan

Planting diagram, section

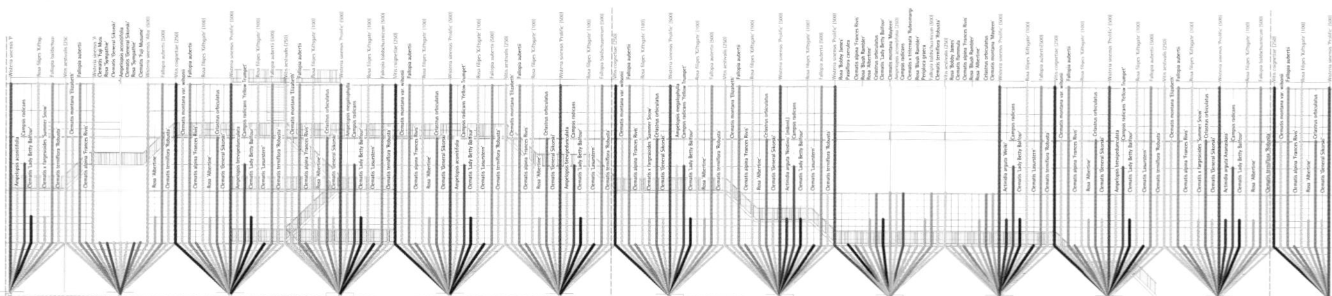

View to southeast over Novartis campus and Rhine River

The Square

Basel, Switzerland
2017

Good Form Studio

1 acre
cost: undisclosed

The Swiss city of Basel, with its population of 170,000, has long been a center for economic and cultural activity. Its geographic position within a trinational region (*Dreiländereck*) comprised of Switzerland, France, and Germany makes it one of Switzerland's most dynamic economies. Equally impressive is its long-sustained role as a leading cultural capital. In 1661, the city purchased the Amerbach Kabinett, a collection of Old Master paintings and drawings. This collection formed the nucleus of the Öffentliche Kunstsammlung Basel, the first municipally owned art collection available to the general public. Today, the city hosts Art Basel, one of the world's leading art fairs since its inception in the 1970s.

Building on Basel's cultural legacy is the fifty-one-acre Novartis headquarters, in the city's northwest St. Johann District. The site, once comprised of industrial uses, synthetic dye factories, and workers' housing, has been transformed into a collection of landscapes and architecture, all open to the public by reservation. Also ornamenting the campus is an extensive collection of contemporary artworks selected by the legendary curator Harald Szeemann. The result is a memorable display of architecture, landscape, and fine art.

Novartis is one of the world's largest pharmaceutical companies. In 2002, Daniel Vasella, then the CEO, presided over a renovation of the administration building and a redesign of the production site, transforming it into an enclave for "innovation, knowledge, and encounters." To facilitate these encounters, Italian architect and urban planner Vittorio Magnago Lampugnani was engaged to develop the campus as a pedestrian city set within a series of variously scaled open spaces. Lampugnani's master plan (2001) for architecture traces the original disposition of the industrial site, which was based on a highly rational composition of gridded streets and mid-rise buildings. Since then, seventeen new buildings have been constructed.

In 1999, PWP Landscape Architecture won the competition to create a master plan for the landscape and subsequently designed several of its green spaces. The scheme they devised introduced street plantings, courtyards, and urban squares. Like Lampugnani's urban design, the landscape plan includes strict guidelines. For example, all east-west streets are planted with fastigiate hornbeam, while north-south streets (other than the Fabrikstrasse, the main thoroughfare) are treeless. The Fabrikstrasse is defined by double rows of tulip trees and by arcades that contain cafés, shops, and outdoor seating areas. The absence of automobiles, which are largely prohibited on the campus, gave a delicious aura of calm and relaxation to the street; nevertheless, our impression was that of a vibrant urban space.

On a clear July day, Alex and I were accompanied on our tour of the corporation's sacrosanct precinct by Dorothée Imbert and Andrew Cruse of Good Form Studio, along with Novartis chief architect Marco Serra. An installation of massive boulders (3.6 by 92 by 26.2 feet) entitled *Wellenbrecher* (2007), by the German sculptor Ulrich Rückriem, defines the campus drop-off loop. The rough texture and dark, weighted tones contrast starkly with the sleek and elegant main gate pavilion, a light and airy cubic volume designed by Serra.

The primary gathering space on the campus, the Forum, was inspired by Basel's historic town squares and designed by PWP. A bosque of thirty-five pin oaks, which extends the eight-meter architectural grid of adjacent buildings, offers a shady respite. The ground plane is paved in White Moncini granite; works by Rückriem as well as a large reflecting pool containing koi, a symbol of good fortune, are placed within the space.

The adjacent administration building, Forum 1, contains a landscape that alternates the vastness and ceremony of the Forum with a delicate, densely planted birch forest (2004). Designed by PWP, the planting of more than two hundred Himalayan birches (*Betula utilis*) is set within the courtyard of the 1940s building, the only remaining building original to the site. A long, narrow pool, set within a surface of decomposed granite, brings the canopy onto the ground plane through its reflective surface. As we wove in and out of the birch forest, we paused to watch the sunlight penetrate through the leaves, sparkle on the pool, and set aglow the white bark of the trees.

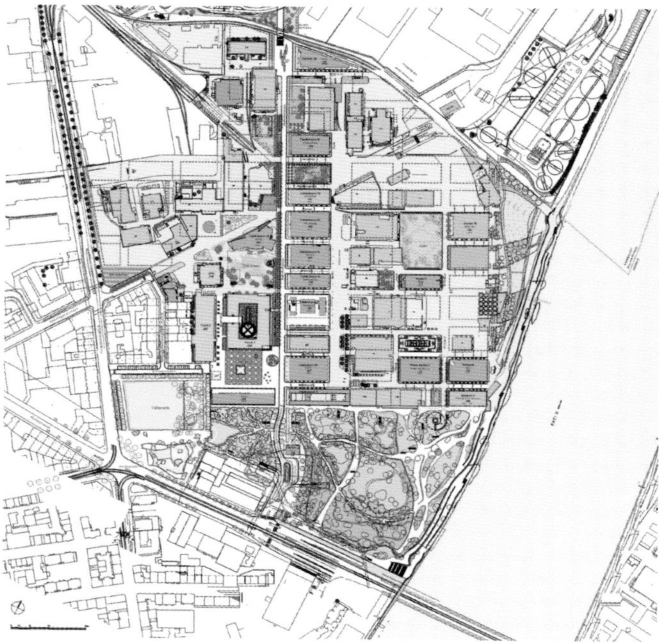

The Forum, PWP Landscape Architecture

Novartis master plan, Vittorio Magnago Lampugnani and PWP Landscape Architecture

The Green, Vogt Landscape Architects

Forum 1 Courtyard, Himalayan birch and reflecting pool, PWP Landscape Architecture

Physic Garden, Thorbjörn Andersson

The Square, aerial view, Good Form Studio

Another component of the campus design is the Green, which rests on the roof of an auditorium designed by Frank Gehry, where we had our first encounter with a robot lawnmower. Swiss landscape architect Günther Vogt, inspired by the Swiss karst (soluble rocks) landscape, devised the open area as a hybrid park and square. The thin soil profile (27.5 inches maximum) limits planting, though clusters of tall ash trees (*Fraxinus excelsior*) dot the perimeter. But it was Vogt's masterful manipulation of stone that most captivated us. Large blocks of limestone, transitioning from rough and irregular to smooth and precise, stretch like fingers into the Green. The blocks were cut to preserve their natural breaking edge, numbered, and then assembled like a puzzle on site. The passage from smooth paving to eroded limestone to green lawn, all built on structure, results in a design that marries geological processes and architectural geometry.

Purposely secluded, the Physic Garden (2012) by Thorbjörn Andersson with Sweco Architects is a nod to the medieval monastery garden; it provides a stark contrast to Vogt's ruggedness and PWP's ceremonial majesty. Intended as a reminder of the historic study of the pharmaceutical properties of plants, the garden is framed by a hedge of yew and hornbeam. Within this frame is a large sunken garden with tidy rows of thirty-two species selected for their importance in pharmaceutical research. Bronze edge strips set within the granite paving identify each species. It is a space of surprise and pleasure, one that allows visitors to learn about plants' medicinal properties while also making connections between Novartis and a legacy of pharmaceutical research.

The Square, designed by Good Form Studio, is one of the most recently completed elements in Novartis's landscape. Situated on the roof of an underground bicycle garage designed by Serra and flanked by buildings by Rahul Mehrotra and Fumihiko Maki, the Square offers smaller, more intimate spaces than some of the other green areas on the campus.

The project consists primarily of two green areas separated by a wide wood walkway. To the north, a quincunx grove of London plane, linden, and flowering cherry trees rises from the surface of crushed gravel. The trees have been trained as *dachform* (*dach* means roof), which creates a sandwich of space between the thin canopy and the gravel surface. (Dorothée Imbert studied at the École Nationale Supérieure du Paysage in Versailles, which has a legacy of pruning and manipulating plant material into highly geometric forms.) Within the grove is a rectangular pavilion constructed of low-iron glass. The absence of vertical mullions emphasizes the horizontality of the space. The parapet of the pavilion aligns with the top of the canopy; sliding glass panels blur exterior and interior spaces. A dense planting of crossvine within the pavilion's interior is spreading horizontally across steel cables, creating a continuous green ceiling.

The southern section of the Square, paved in *schotterrasen*, an inexpensive grass and pebble mix, is characterized by clumps of yew and circular garden rooms of tall clipped hornbeam. Here, geometric form, texture, and spatial layering combine effectively. Imbert credits the Geometric Gardens designed in the 1950s (and finally built in 1983) by Danish landscape architect C. Th. Sørensen (1893–1979) as her inspiration. The geometries of the "rooms" vary. Visible between the round garden rooms are glimpses of the pavilion, the grove, and the surrounding buildings. Each hornbeam ring provides a sense of privacy and protection and frames a disc of blue sky. Lightweight furniture can be easily moved into the garden rooms to encourage informal meetings. Imbert noted that in winter the exposed structure of the hornbeam branches creates a fretwork effect, providing a contrast between the void of the rooms and the solidity of the evergreen yew masses.

The wide platform of Accoya wood that bisects these two halves extends the Lampugnani-planned pedestrian street that links this part of the campus to the Rhine river. Here, Imbert states that the project expresses an analogy of the *cour et jardin* (court and garden), with the court represented by the more mineral and urban quality of the pavilion and quincunx grove and the garden by the hornbeam rooms. Imbert continues, "In French, you use *côté cour* [court side] and *côté jardin* [garden side] to refer to stage right and stage left. This relates to the scenographic aspect of people appearing and disappearing through trees or in between the hedge rooms and yew groupings."

We made a brief detour to see the Rhine River. Gustafson Porter + Bowman's Rhine Terrace (2018) and hanging garden cascade along the edge and connect to a riverfront bike trail. The park transitions between campus and river, its undulating form dissolving strict geometries into a sequence of lawns, meadows, and gardens.

As we left the Novartis compound, we found ourselves in its largest green area, the Park (2016). Designed by Vogt and resting atop an underground parking garage, this 15.5-acre open space portrays landscapes of the Upper Rhine Valley and provides a pause between the busy city and the rarified campus.

Vogt considers the concrete roof of the garage to be a new geological crust. The landscape on top of this crust expresses the natural phenomena of river terraces, glacial activity, and the *hohlweg*, a narrow depression in the earth formed after centuries of human use and environmental activity. Terraces comprised of woodland, meadow, and an artificial platform divide the space into distinct zones. Stone paths wind through a forest of oak, beech, and maple, while a vast meadow of native and non-native species is punctuated by stands of birch and poplar trees. It is the *hohlweg* that offers a special textural and spatial experience. Layers of lime, trass (volcanic tuff), clay, and loam rise like a giant trough, where uncontrolled growth and decay evoke a sense of release, a marked difference from the manicured campus greens. This open area, along with the other green spaces at Novartis, highlights a delightful display of landscapes that together promote a sense of expression and dynamism.

Dachform-trained trees in quincunx arrangement

Garden rooms

Overleaf: The Park, Vogt Landscape Architects

Stone path through verbena

Jiading Central Park

Shanghai, China
2013

Sasaki

172 acres
cost: $68 million

Jiading Central Park is an hour's train ride (both below- and above-ground) from downtown Shanghai. Like many other new parks in China, Jiading's was created to replace a polluted industrial site—a plastic factory and an electroplating workshop—and to serve as a social and ecological catalyst for the new district as well as to promote development. Indeed, beside the park rises a cluster of identical, poorly designed towers, which resemble countless other clusters across the country. Most of these residential buildings, including those in Jiading, remain underutilized. In this, Jiading is typical of China's numerous "ghost cities"—new communities where the government often doesn't build the necessary infrastructure until after a speculation period for real estate. In 2017, over 56 percent of China's population lived in cities; the nation set goals of 60 percent by 2020 and 70 percent, or one billion people, by 2030. Nearly six hundred new cities have been established across the country since the time of the Communist Revolution, and just about every existing city is doubling or tripling in size. The country's current fiscal system forces local governments to sell land in order to have the wherewithal to function; between 2000 and 2015, for instance, Shanghai's physical area increased by more than 25 percent.

According to official projections, residential ownership is expected to grow annually by 14 percent. But because there is no property tax, many Chinese buy apartments for investment with no intention of occupying them, and because people are reluctant to move into new buildings that lack necessary services, more than one in five apartments, roughly 65 million in all, are unoccupied. Owners do not rent the apartments because the profit margin is so low (1–1.5 percent), hoping instead to one day sell them at a profit. Unfortunately, not all such investors will be as lucky as a cab driver we met in Guangzhou. He told us that he sold an apartment four years after buying it and realized enough money to send his two teenage sons to college in the United States.

The site for Jiading Central Park was designated in the Master Plan 2035 for Shanghai, which was created by Shanghai's Urban Planning and Land Resource Administration Bureau, a government entity, and the Shanghai Grand Design Group, a private firm. The Sasaki team, winner of a bidding process for the commission, began work on the park by eliminating the cross-traffic envisioned in the master plan, relegating the routes that remained to under- and overpasses. This action produced an uninterrupted network of green patches and large sports fields. The designers were inspired by local artist Yanshao Lu, who creates contemporary interpretations of traditional Chinese art, calligraphy, and dance. Influenced by the majestic Three Gorges area, Lu depicted a dramatic scene of jagged cloud-topped mountains and turbulent waters. The park, whose name is itself fanciful—Purple Air from the East, based on a rich tradition of Daoist literature—translates these motifs into an artificial lake and undulating paths that may be interpreted as cloud forms.

Situated near the lake, a couple of the simple, stone farmhouses that formerly occupied the site stand in vivid contrast to the contemporary setting rising up around them. As it is in Central Park in New York, circulation is separated by type: pedestrian, cyclist, and vehicular. When Alex and I visited the park in May 2018, we found particularly impressive the wide variety and fine detailing of the various paving types. Among these were paths made from concrete pavers for the main circulation; narrower, secondary paths paved in rounded pebbles with a granite edge; and plazas covered in stone dust.

Chinese wingnut trees (*Pterocarya stenoptera*), which provide welcome shade, border many of the walkways. The canal that runs through the entire park enjoys rich riparian

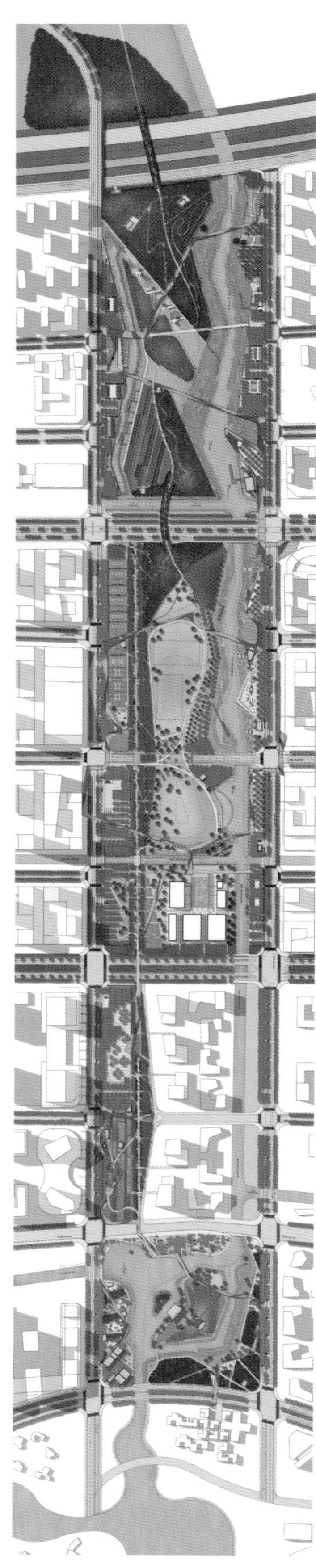

vegetation and feeds into a lotus pond. Unfortunately, maintenance of this beautiful park has been seriously neglected, in part because the local community is so small. Benches need to be repaired, paving is heaving, and some trees have died. Furthermore, structures that were built to house a library, a museum, and a café were never opened.

Our visit culminated in the captivating bamboo forest planted on an island within the park's artificial lake. A narrow path cuts through the forest and up a little hill; at the top are panoramic views of this fine but underutilized park.

In the course of our stroll we encountered some park goers who brought to life the cultural traditions and atmosphere that inspired Yanshao Lu. First, we observed a middle-aged couple gathering bamboo leaves to wrap sticky rice dumplings (*zongzi*) for the forthcoming Dragonboat Festival. The custom of eating these dumplings at the event commemorates the people's concern for Qu Yuan, a wrongly accused poet/minister who drowned himself in 278 BCE. So beloved was the poet that his admirers tossed *zongzi* into the water for the fish so that they wouldn't nibble on his body. We also came across a lone musician, an elderly man playing a traditional *huqin*. The expressive tones of this stringed instrument carried over the grassy hill just as they might have more than a thousand years ago.

Multiuse plaza with path

Bamboo forest

Old farmhouses in front of new towers

Plan

Shaded grove

Water-oxygenating weirs in waterway

Cultuurpark Westergasfabriek

Amsterdam, Netherlands
2006

Gustafson Porter + Bowman

28.5 acres
cost: $27 million

Gustafson Porter + Bowman won the commission for the Cultuurpark Westergasfabriek in a two-stage design competition organized by the district council of Westerpark, a neighborhood in West Amsterdam. The landscape architects met with the park's interest groups over the course of a year, using these gatherings to formulate a variety of uses. The end result is a study in contrasts: large and small, artificial and natural, old and new, planted and wild, open and intimate, commercial and leisure.

The clearly defined spatial diversity of the park makes it a valuable urban resource that meshes harmoniously with the locale. Large squares and plazas define the urban edge of the park and connect with the adjoining street grid. Meanwhile, the other edges of the park relate to an older open area at the east and to an agricultural area that includes a heritage-revival farm of community gardens to the northwest. Park boundaries edge the busy railroad line from Amsterdam Centraal Station and also the outermost of the horseshoe canals that encircle the city center.

The site of the Cultuurpark is adjacent to areas that have been studied for possible green space since the mid-nineteenth century. One of the earliest plans was Jacobus van Niftrik's of 1866, which sought to expand Amsterdam's urban form of U-shaped rings by creating an additional ring that would act as a greenbelt. Westerpark, a historic park directly adjacent to Cultuurpark, has its origins in this plan. A later study, the Amsterdam General Extension Plan of 1934 by Cornelis van Eesteren, aimed to provide increased recreational space, including parks, in the form of long, green corridors within the urban block; this program was largely implemented after World War II.

The site was previously home to Amsterdam's western gasworks, a complex that was built in the 1880s and became inoperative in the 1960s. Several of the buildings were designed in a simplified version of the Dutch neo-Renaissance style by Isaac Gosschalk (1838–1907) between the 1880s and early 1900s. The neighborhood district council began to use the seventeen buildings on the site and several of the former gasholders for the local arts community, and in 1981, the area was rezoned as parkland. The park is owned by the city and maintained by the council; all structures are managed by Westergasfabriek BV.

One of GP+B's core concepts was to move away from a traditional scheme and toward an ecological landscape by introducing diverse flora and fauna, from ornamental to naturalized to native. The design also follows the Dutch tradition of artificial polder landscapes: low-lying land reclaimed from a body of water and protected by dikes.

Before work could start, however, the soil needed remediation. The site was extremely polluted; at one point, coal for the city's lighting was stored there. The landscape architects helped develop a process by which rehabilitating the ground would create the desired topography. Polluted soil could not be removed from the site, so the team adopted a cut-and-fill method. The most harmful soil was stored and capped in the brick foundations of the gasholders; less harmful contamination was buried in berms and mounds beneath clean, imported soils. The softly graded terrain gives the park its distinctive form.

On a warm June day, Alex and I wandered into the Cultuurpark at the southern edge off Haarlemmerweg. The designers have labeled this area Market Square, and it is the starting point for a wide axial promenade that begins in front of a charming old Gosschalk-designed brick building left over from the gasworks. Dominating the eastern edge of the park is another one of Gosschalk's elegant structures. This building has been repurposed as the eco-friendly Conscious Hotel, part of a chain that features wind turbines and solar power, which aligns nicely with the park's focus on sustainability.

The northern edge of the park is defined by a man-made lake. The water feature begins as a narrow, shallow pool paved in granite, in which many children were playing. The pool widens into a small lake with fountains. As the water moves west through the park, this sharply defined feature transitions to a more naturalized state as it changes into a meandering stream.

The somewhat formal, urban landscape where we began our visit became more organic as we proceeded west. A woodland garden contains small greenery rooms; each is furnished

with a bench and suggests a romantic hideaway. These enclosed spaces are perfect antidotes to the expansive lawns, the huge event field (which can accommodate ten thousand people), and sports fields. Harking back to the site's history, the woodland garden led us to the so-called Village Square, where period structures, similar to those that face Market Square, line the park's southern periphery. The buildings in Village Square contain cafés and restaurants, and, in warm weather, diners spill out into the plaza.

While Village Square might raise questions about an extensive commercial area within a park, they are quickly dispelled by a second rich woodland garden. Here, varieties of flowering cherry trees planted in broad perennial borders line a gravel walk. The intimacy of the park's gardens is in stark contrast to the expansive squares and lawns found throughout.

Two small former gasholders have been transformed into lily ponds; they are skirted by weeping willow (*Salix babylonica*) and golden willow (*Salix alba* 'Tristis') trees, which have branches that trail languorously in the water. Both species thrive on remediated soil. The two pools face the park's largest gasholder, which is now used for cultural occasions and as part of the Westergas cultural venue. It is here that the lake also begins its transition from formal to more natural. Floating walkways, terraces, and stepping stones allow park users to move through and interact with the water.

The event field is a vast lawn, reinforced to allow for the transportation of the heavy equipment that is used to build temporary stages for concerts and large tents for festivals. In addition to hosting this type of large-scale function, the field is also a favorite place for picnics and recreational activities such as kite flying and ball games. At the same time, numerous grassy spots invite quiet relaxation; one of these settings offers exercise equipment. Many of the most tempting of such places are beside the scenic stream that flows through the green space.

The Cultuurpark's tremendous success has brought gentrification, via a mixed-use housing development, to what had been an industrial and working-class neighborhood to the south. Links are also planned to the new harbor city districts that are emerging northwest of the city center. But paramount among its achievements is fulfillment of the sponsors' original intention: to marry industrial artifacts with cultural context in a place that serves a maximum number of interests for the widest possible public.

Plan

Amsterdam General Expansion Plan, 1934, Cornelis van Eesteren

Water feature along northern edge of park

Village Square, repurposed historic structures

Lily pond in a former gasholder

Platforms along north canal

North canal

View to southwest over Parque Bicentenario with entry and Natura (foreground)

Evergreen tropical forest in greenhouse

Orchidarium in former waste tank

Re-creation of *chinampas* (artificial agricultural islands)

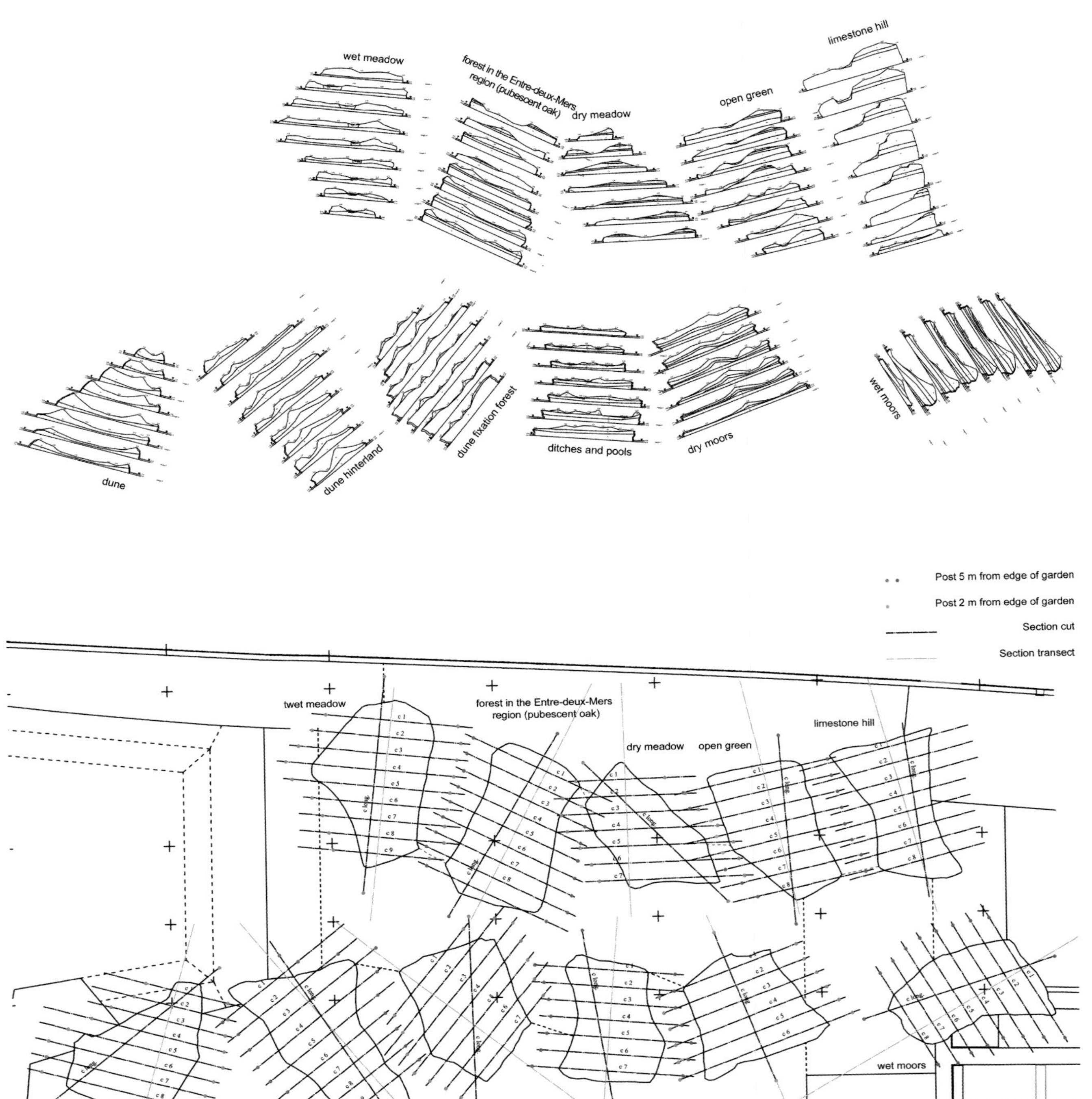

Earthworks in Galerie des Milieux, plan and sections

Jardin Botanique

Bordeaux, France
2007

Mosbach Paysagistes

11.6 acres
cost: $3.45 million

Dominique Perrault's urban plan for Bordeaux (1992–99) gave rise to many new initiatives in this southwestern French city, which was reinventing itself at the beginning of the millennium. Among them were two new bridges to span the Garonne River and Michel Corajoud's creation of a popular pedestrian promenade on the left bank. On the right bank, Michel Desvigne's Parc aux Angéliques (page 110), along with other green spaces, is also part of the city's rebirth.

One component of Perrault's plan was a park in the Bastide neighborhood, which within the decade would become the location of landscape architect Catherine Mosbach's Jardin Botanique; the buildings are by architect Françoise-Hélène Jourda. The Jardin Botanique is separated from the 185-acre Parc aux Angéliques only by the tree-lined Quai des Queyries. This is not the first time that Mosbach and Desvigne have worked on related sites: at the Louvre in Lens, Mosbach developed the museum park with SANAA, while Desvigne designed an inviting approach along the street that leads from the railroad station to the museum entrance.

The commission for the Jardin Botanique was awarded through a competition. A historical botanical garden, under the direction of Philippe Richard, already existed in the center of the city, and it was Richard who devised the brief for the new garden: a research facility for the study of natural resource management and biodiversity based on a new way to display plants. Claude Figureau, a botanist and specialist in urban biodiversity, became keeper of the experimental botanical garden. Working with botanist Patrick Blanc, Mosbach proposed demonstrating ethnobotany (people's relationship to plants through food, industry, pharmaceuticals, and so forth). To Mosbach, this view means treating plants and people as equals, without applied hierarchies. She says, "We are animals, like other animals." The designer is as unorthodox as the garden.

Mosbach grew up in the hilly Kochersberg area of Alsace (known for its cultivation of hops), an area that familiarized her with the land and with plants; trained as a metal worker; and finally attended the École Nationale Supérieure du Paysage in Versailles. Experience with public works readied Mosbach for the Jardin Botanique, where for the most part she had materials prepared on site. Upon meeting Alex and me, she warned: "My drawings and thinking are very abstract." Instead of conceptualizing shapes, she imagines masses and atmospheres—clouds, air, light, humidity—and then she proceeds by instinct, not by rational deduction. Her foremost preoccupations are temporality and environmental responsibility: she spends as much as eight to ten years on a project in a process that she feels is ongoing. Unlike most landscape architects, who take an inclusionist stance, Mosbach is outspoken in her opposition to community participation in a project; such involvement, she claims, assumes that the contributors have equal knowledge, when in fact each undertaking requires individuals with special expertise. "We belong to the planet," she says, "and we need to share."

Construction of the garden began in 2001, and, by 2003, Mayor Alain Juppé insisted that the completed portions open to the public that Christmas. Mosbach relates (with some satisfaction) that the mayor and the public were shocked by what she describes as "a garden of stones only—there were no flowers!" Almost twenty years later, the landscape she envisaged is completed.

By shunning an arrangement of plants according to Linnaean classification, typically used in botanic collections, the Bordeaux park also avoids the traditional nature of plantings in botanical gardens as installed in Kew in London or in New York City. Instead, vegetation representative of the surrounding Aquitaine Basin is organized in keeping with growing conditions.

During a trip to São Paulo, Mosbach visited the botanical garden and was intrigued by the Portão Histórico (1894), large iron gates that screened the trees. She decided to invite French artist Pascal Convert to Bordeaux; his huge laser-cut steel gates, inspired by child's play, mark one of several entrances to the garden. Mosbach surrounded the park with a three-foot-wide embankment, low enough to see over, creating a ha-ha. She stacked remnants of oak trees felled in a major 1999 storm to create a defined edge that is in keeping with the garden's interior; like those of many a descendant of the *hortus conclusus*, the wall is also a habitat for moss, lichen, ferns, and stonecrop. The wood, untreated and exposed to the elements, is slowly decaying, suggesting the idea of impermanence. Concrete

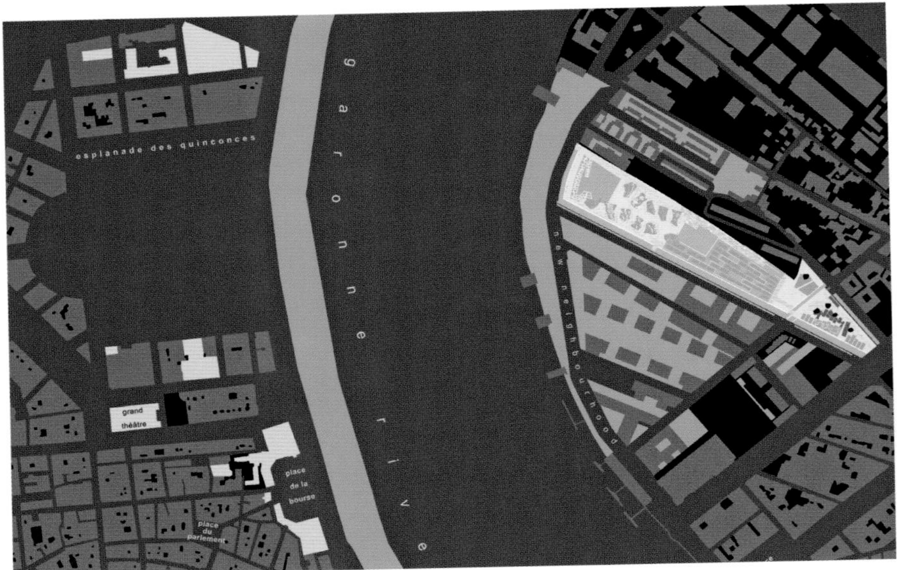

Plan

Steel gates, Pascal Convert

Champs de Cultures

bands alternating with grass strips lead to the gates and continue for a few feet within the garden to mark the transition to grass paths. The lawn creeps over the irregular edges of the bands, making them appear to erode: another gesture to impermanence and a nice contrast to the sharp edges of the steel planting beds. Grass paths change to narrow dirt, or occasionally concrete, walkways in the three main areas.

The first of these areas, the Champs de Cultures, consists of 49 metal planting beds approximately 15–24 feet wide and 44–66 feet long. The plinths have a defined edge on all sides, signifying that they contain something special. The narrow sides of each generous rectangular container abut water basins of varying widths, which use rainwater stored in eleven underground tanks. Each basin holds enough water to allow self-sufficient irrigation for the plot it fronts. Control of the soil conditions in each plot allows researchers to study how plants grow and adapt. The effect is like a museum gallery in which each sculpture is on a pedestal.

We traded the rectilinear geometry of this first section for a meandering arrangement of eleven relatively tall, cliff-like earthworks in the next section. This Galerie des Milieux supports landscapes depicting regional habitats. The vertical topography, which distinguishes the area from its flat surroundings, was created by compacting layers of material. In an unanticipated gesture, the mounds place at eye level the natural substrate and soil profile typical of the Aquitaine region. (Mosbach calls soil "the basis of humanity. Otherwise we would fly or swim.") The topography reveals the differences between the layers represented and also helps to make the narrow, approximately eleven-acre park feel much larger than it is. Views that stretch the entire length of the garden also contribute to the impression of enhanced scale.

The Jardin Aquatique, the third major area, offered a dramatic climax to our visit. Running along the park's western (riverside) edge is a pool, more than an acre in area and approximately two feet deep, that contains the collection of aquatic plants. Gridded, asymmetrical steel walkways cover part of the pond; as we walked around, we were charmed by the croaking of frogs and the serenity of the beautiful oasis beside the neighboring low-rise residential buildings. We were thrilled by a profusion of vibrantly colored water lilies with tall reeds behind covering the water's surface. Brightly colored climbing plants such as marsh morning glory (*Ipomoea sagittata*) and large tropical-looking pickerelweed (*Pontederia cordata*) rise up, and other species—white lizard's tail (*Saururus cernuus*) and American water plantain (*Alisma subcordatum*)—grow in underwater containers. As we turned back toward where we entered, we passed the large public lawn welcoming leisure activities. Elevated slightly and edged in concave steel, the green space was full of active young children.

The final component of the garden, completed in 2007, was the greenhouse with adjacent structures. These are separated from the entrance by a small pedestrian area, and, like many other features in the park, they are atypical in design and construction. For reasons of economy, the walls were constructed in timber and glass and crisscrossed by heavy glue-laminate beams. The ceiling, supported by sturdy Douglas fir columns atop steel socles, is composed of 7,500 square feet of photovoltaic panels that supply energy for the greenhouse.

The interior space contains what is called "seven Mediterranean greenhouses." These are designated by variations in the building envelope and different heights of skylight modules, of which 37.7 feet is the highest. Each area is devoted to a different type of vegetation, predominately plants from a dry desert climate or a humid tropical climate: broad-leafed South African plants, Australian vegetation, palm trees, and carnivorous plants. In a play of scales worthy of *Alice in Wonderland*, the garden has added magnifying glasses to some of the horticultural displays, allowing the smallest elements on the plant to expand dramatically. This immediate change of scale is repeated in the exterior garden: between the large regional mounds in the Galerie des Milieux and the small plants in the Champs de Cultures.

Support structures—reception, restaurant (no longer in service), studios, conference rooms, bookstore, and mechanical services—are housed in reinforced concrete protuberances coated in smooth granite resin, which resembles polished stone. The formal and material qualities, inspired by the mineral, organic, and vegetal worlds, are meant to be disconcerting.

Despite the emphasis on instruction and experimentation requested by the keeper, the Jardin Botanique is a place of pleasure as well. Unlike most such institutions, the green space offers free entry and functions like a neighborhood park. Circulation is also less structured than what is typically found in more conventional botanical gardens. The numerous entrances open the bounds of the space, encouraging visitors to cut across, rest on the lawn, wander through the planting exhibitions, visit the earthworks, or simply observe the captivating landscapes from sturdy concrete benches and movable metal chairs. This flexibility strengthens Mosbach's idea of equality between plants and humans. With 500,000 visitors a year, Bordeaux bears out her top priority: "The most important aspect of my work," she claims, "is for people to be happy."

Dune hinterland biotope in Galerie des Milieux

Lawn with steel edging

Jardin Aquatique pool with Galerie des Milieux beyond

Water lily and lotus in Jardin Aquatique

Paths over water

Overleaf: A place of pleasure

View to northwest over northern portion of park with vehicular tunnel

Taopu Central Park

Shanghai, China
2018, ongoing

James Corner Field Operations

231 acres
cost: $15 million

Located six miles away from Shanghai's Hongqiao International Airport, and nearly eight miles from the city center, Taopu Central Park rehabilitates a former industrial site that accommodated a soap factory, the Hero pen factory, warehouses, and a scrap yard. The park, parts of which were still under construction in 2020, was inspired by the concept of "new nature," specifically mountains and rice terraces, and by traditional calligraphy, dance, and movement. Additionally, like Sanlin Eco Valley (page 308), it joins the greenbelt corridor encircling the city.

Taopu itself is being redeveloped with more than four hundred residential, commercial, and other buildings on a thousand-acre-plus site. Shanghai Taopu Smart City Development and Construction Co. organized an invited competition for a substantial green space, an important amenity for the new community. Construction is being carried out in two phases: 103 acres at the north, completed in 2019; and 131 acres at the south, still being landscaped in September 2019.

The northern portion of the park is intended for passive recreation, while the southern part will be wilder in planting and will have active programming. Soil cut from the southern section and decontaminated on site was used for the northern area. Helping to ensure the success of the vegetation, planting soils were used throughout. Our impression was that this addition of high-quality earth is noteworthy, given that many of the parks Alex and I visited in China (sometimes visiting on days when planting was being carried out) used only soils that had existed on site. The result is trees in waterlogged clay pits and shrubs and perennials in similarly poor soils.

Competition winner James Corner Field Operations was disappointed that the site had been cleared of all industrial remnants, but the firm nevertheless invented numerous highlights, which were presented to Alex and me by Rui Li and Wejia Shuo from associate firm Shanghai Landscape Architecture Design and Research Institute. One of these was topographic variation. The landscape architects sculpted a "mountain" with construction foam (expanded polystyrene) under six and a half feet of planting soil; the smaller hills were made of soil alone. We observed many views of the surroundings, a rare phenomenon in flat Shanghai, when we walked through the new topography during our September visit.

Water is managed by means of a large underground cistern that can store 7.9 million gallons of water. Combined with this system is a small artificial lake with three charming islands with different themes. It was too costly to link the park's canal with the nearby Xinchapu River, so water in the site (with an exceptionally high water table) is isolated, although such a connection is planned for a future phase. The ubiquitous pine boardwalk along the shore connects to the three mini-islands via a traditionally shaped arched bridge in Merbau wood. The designers envisioned the islands as "dreamy" places, where visitors would feel as though they were walking in a poem. Indeed, despite their small sizes, once we had traversed the bridge, each islet felt very much like a place distinct from the rest of the park.

The client wanted to retain several municipal roads throughout the land to separate the north and south sections of the park. Field Operations suggested another solution, inspired by the four transections of New York's Central Park: to create a cohesive green area, all transverse vehicular traffic is relegated to twenty-three-foot-high, three-lane tunnels. Also buried are a café, restrooms, and commercial spaces.

The playground, likewise designed by Field Operations, is different from others we saw in our park visits. A handsome, intricately woven bamboo tunnel protected one side of the space, and bamboo was also used for some of the whimsical play equipment.

During construction, Field Operations increased the canopy cover from what the office originally planned. Another change was a switch from peach and cherry trees to hardier apple trees. There was, however, no explanation, except the client's regrettable capriciousness, for painting the bridges, given that the designers called for exposed Merbau. Also unanswered were our questions regarding ongoing maintenance: why has it been neglected—aphids infected the trees, grading is often uneven, and some paths have cracked—and by whom? Perhaps these matters will be resolved when the park is completed, allowing this stunning public space to enjoy the success it deserves.

N
0
100
250
500 M

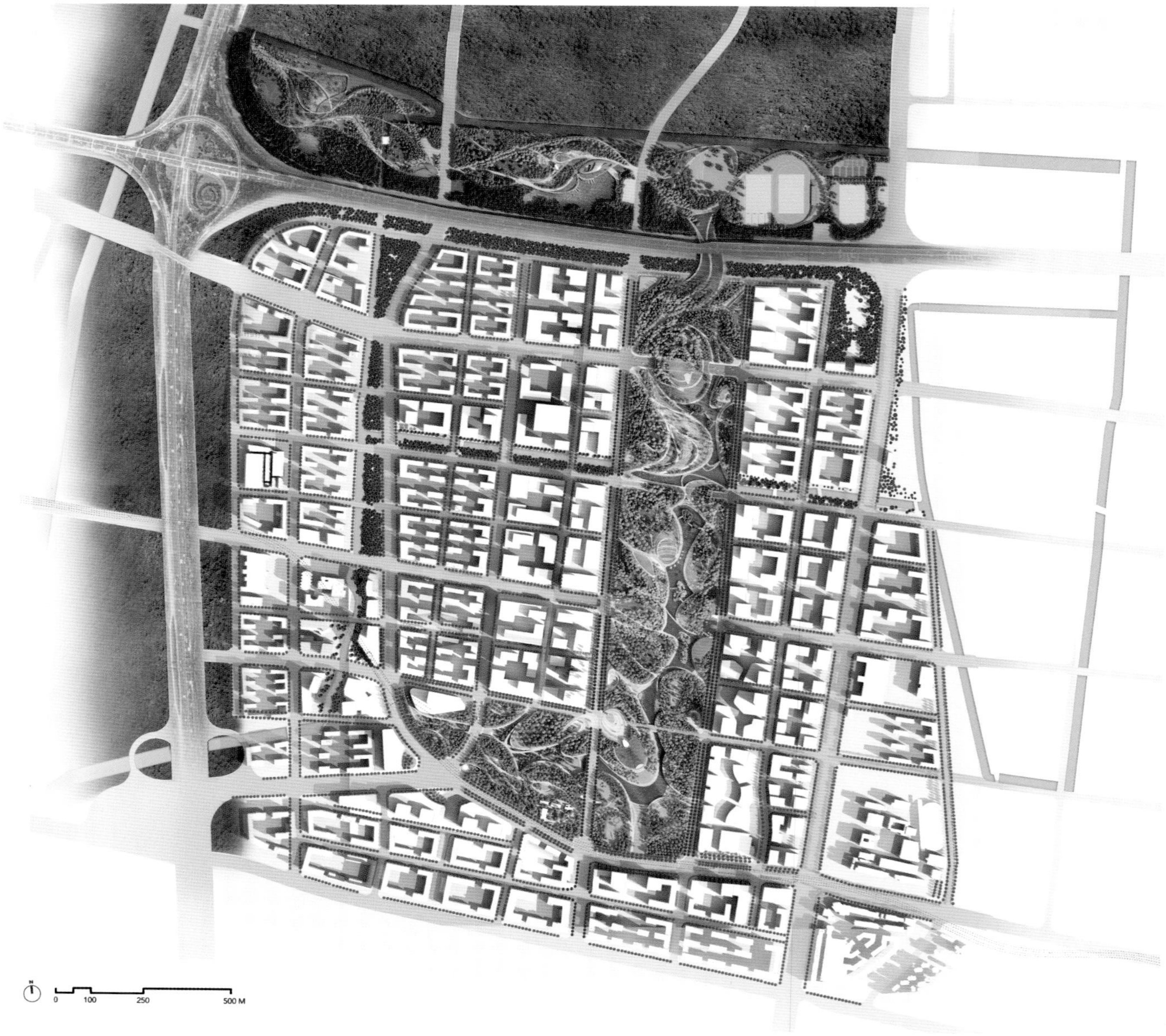

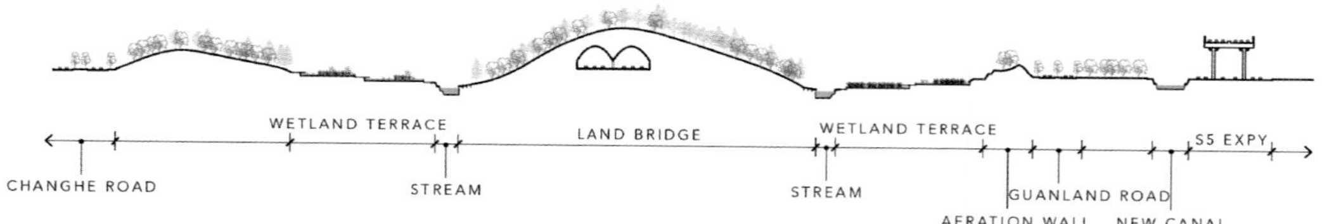

WETLAND TERRACE
LAND BRIDGE
WETLAND TERRACE
S5 EXPY
CHANGHE ROAD
STREAM
STREAM
GUANLAND ROAD
AERATION WALL
NEW CANAL

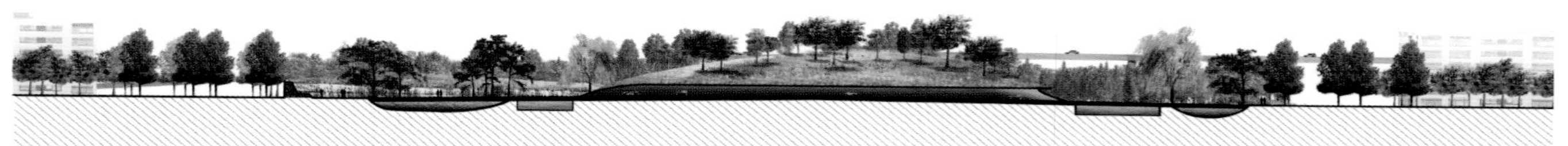

Taopu redevelopment, plan

Diagrammatic and illustrative site sections

Islands connected by arched Merbau wood bridges

Bamboo tunnel in playground

Summer Olympics, Beijing, 2008,
opening ceremony

Capital Steel Works Park

Beijing, China
2016, ongoing

THUPDI

1,927 acres
cost: undisclosed

The 2008 Summer Olympics in Beijing were inaugurated with an unforgettable hour-long spectacle, designed by celebrated film director Zhang Yimou, that showcased China's culture and history. Highlights included 14,000 carefully choreographed performers on the playing field of Herzog & de Meuron's Olympic stadium, itself a subject of global admiration, and a pyrotechnical display created by the famous fireworks artist Cai Guo-Qiang. This extravagance was characteristic of preparations for the event: in all, the federal government spent $42 billion on the 2008 Games, a large part of which was designated for improving the city's dangerously high levels of air pollution.

China's intention to position itself as today's prime world power suggests that, should the coronavirus pandemic abate, the 2022 Winter Olympics in Beijing will be equally ambitious. In the intervening years, however, the Chinese have taken note of the global interest in repurposing post-industrial sites. One such location is a densely industrialized area on Beijing's west side, once the headquarters of Capital Steel. The government seeks to use the factory's vast expanse as a demonstration zone of green transformation and urban renewal.

At over 1,927 acres and in 2000 employing over a hundred thousand people, Capital Steel was a veritable city within a city, containing housing, schools, shopping, recreational areas, and even historic sites. The facility has an almost mythological presence in the collective memory of Beijing residents. Yan Shuo, who visited the Chinese parks with us, remembers that the heat and steam emanating from the blast furnaces and the smell of sulfur dioxide floating through the air made the machines seem like living entities.

For nearly a century, the hundred chimneys of the steel works belched smoke, blanketing the area in a layer of soot and often blocking out the sun. As Beijing grew, however, the smog and dust produced by the facility transformed Capital Steel from a symbol of national pride into an archetypal bad neighbor. When the 2008 Olympics were awarded to Beijing in 2001, the plant was gradually relocated outside the city. Production at the original site finally ceased in 2010.

Planning for the future of the area began in 2013 and included identifying locations within the complex that could serve as venues for the 2022 Olympics. A master plan maintained the site's original division into three core zones, re-envisioning them as Olympic venues, cultural and heritage parks, and an innovation center (North Core). Being developed nearby are an international communications and exhibition center (South Core) and commercial and residential areas.

A limited design competition for the North Core was held among three local design teams—THUPDI, ECOLAND, and Walton Design & Consulting Engineers—in 2014. Instead of selecting a single winner, the Beijing Institute of Architectural Design integrated ideas from all three offices into a final master plan. This scheme envisions Capital Steel as a new culture hub with the North Core serving as a pilot project for the adaptation of post-industrial sites. Specific zones in the precinct have been slated for Shijingshan Culture Park, Winter Olympics Square, Capital Steel Heritage Park, Innovative Community Campus, and Service Amenities.

After the master plan was approved, the Institute of Architectural Design awarded sites within the North Core to various design firms including THUPDI, which formulated the park around the offices for the Beijing 2022 Olympic Games Organizing Committee as well as other areas. Using Latz + Partner's incorporation of industrial artifacts at Duisburg Nord in Germany as an example, THUPDI persuaded the city government to retain many of the industrial remnants. But according to Zhu Yufan, professor of landscape architecture at Tsinghua University and principal designer for the project, much of the machinery had been removed by the local administration when the landscape architects began work on the park.

Alex, Professor Zhu, and I began our visit to the park at its northern portion, where the offices of the organizing committee are located. Elegant paths, some paved in granite decorated with an interlocking snowflake design and others created from recycled porous pavers and square steel plates with decomposed granite joints, demonstrate the variety of materials used

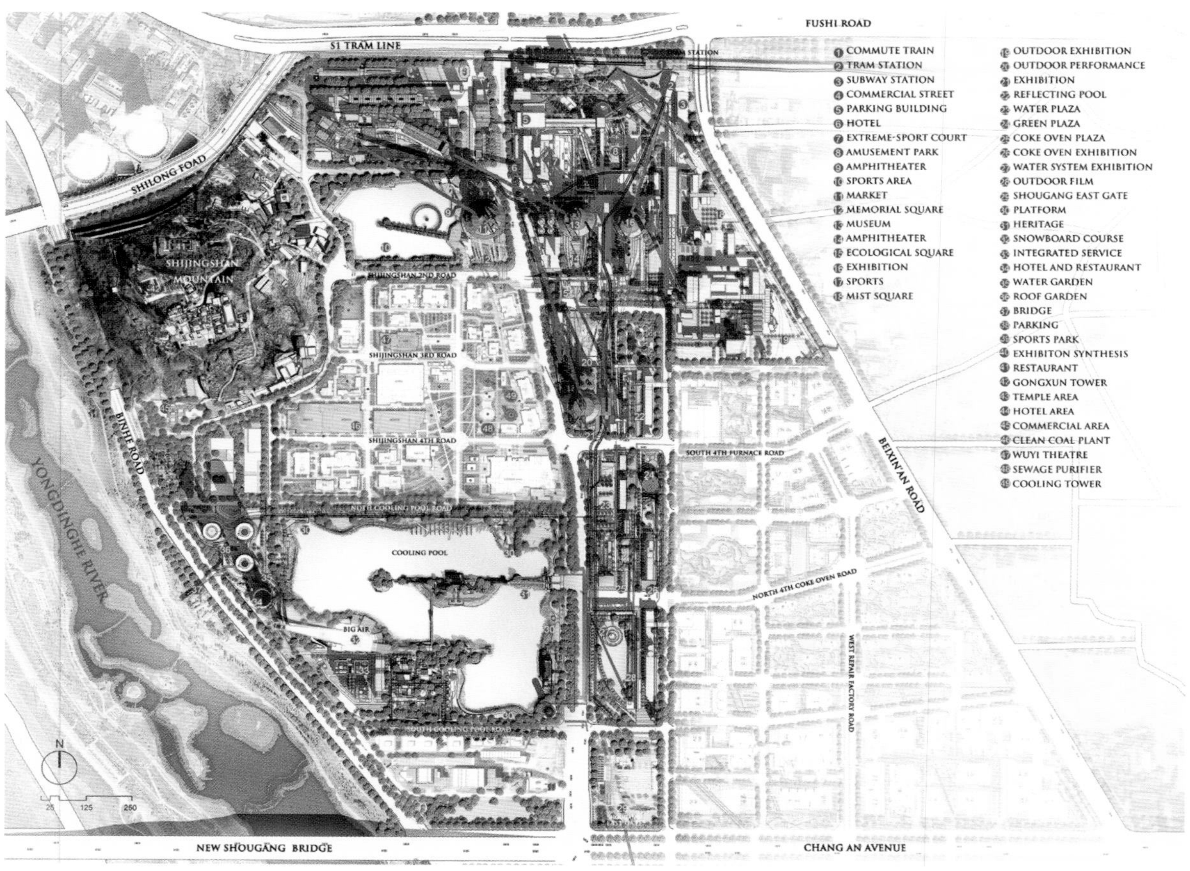

North Core, redevelopment plan

Ceremonial spaces

Qunming Lake

throughout. Circulation in the park, as well as the ceremonial lawns and other spaces in the overall site, is built on a scale large enough to accommodate the millions of people who will attend the games.

In 2018, I visited London's 274-acre Queen Elizabeth Olympic Park, designed by Hargreaves Jones with Field Operations. It, too, was constructed in a former industrial area (from the Victorian era) and was meant as an incentive to development in an economically depressed area. However, London's Olympic Park suffers from the overblown scale required of green spaces built for this kind of massive public event and is often deprived of intimate moments. Capital Steel park suffers from the same problem: only the Olympic committee offices offer small, human-scaled spaces within massive open areas. Near the offices, for example, narrow paths meander through flower beds with seating tucked into the borders. One of these is a traditional Chinese peony garden interspersed with multistemmed peach and ash trees. Blooming wild begonia vines climbing former silo walls add texture to the vertical surfaces. But it is the water management efforts and the repurposed industrial artifacts that are the main attractions of this small area. Rainwater is directed into a water garden with edges defined by walls made from the railroad ties found throughout the site. Existing rail lines provide context for a historic locomotive prominently displayed adjacent to the water garden.

As we moved south, the delicate, garden quality of the park near the committee offices changed into a landscape composed of broad swaths of ornamental grasses, including rose fountain grass (*Pennisetum setaceum*) and Chinese silver grass (*Miscanthus sinensis*). Farther along, the first of two large water bodies (both formerly used as cooling ponds) came into view. The smaller, Xiuchi Lake, contains visitor parking and the entrance to a heritage museum below its waters. The larger, Qunming Lake, is surrounded by cooling towers, coking plants, and power stations. It is here that Capital Steel's past is most evident. In an effort to beautify the campus in the 1980s, the government built a pastiche of historicist elements, including pavilions, bridges, and ornamental plantings. These traditional Chinese garden features contrast incongruously with the industrial remnants. Also visible are emblems of the site's urban renewal, including the dizzying Big Air, a snowboarding venue for the Olympics.

Before we left, our guides escorted us to the top of No. 3 Blast Furnace. This apparatus, the last Capital Steel mechanism to be closed, has been converted into a museum and a series of viewing platforms that allow visitors to take in the post-industrial scene. Professor Zhu noted that while the Olympics may have hastened the relocation of Capital Steel, the complex is being redeveloped for the Games within a vision of preserving an industrial legacy and reinventing a new community memory.

Repurposed materials in water garden

Metal-plate paving with decomposed granite

Walkway through Qunming Lake

Industrial relics with ornamental grasses

Aerial rendering

Parc du Peuple de l'Herbe

Carrières-sous-Poissy, France
2016

Agence Ter

280 acres
cost: $11.5 million

Constructed on a site previously occupied by an asparagus farm (beginning in 1895), a limestone quarry (1945–90), and most recently a landfill, the unusual Grass People's Park in Carrières-sous-Poissy, a suburb of Paris, resembles almost no other park we encountered. The 280 acres of land are on an alluvial plane adjacent to the Seine River and provide a rare taste of nature in the developing Yvelines district. Immediately to the west of metropolitan Paris, Yvelines is undergoing construction of major residential and commercial projects, creation of eco-friendly enterprises, and possibly development of a riverside port. The low-income, socially diverse, and relatively young community of Carrières-sous-Poissy is accessible by commuter rail from Paris. In the future, the town of Poissy and the RER Railway station, across the river, will be connected to the park by a pedestrian bridge, under construction in 2021.

The landscape design was awarded in 2010 through two competitions, one for the park and one for the architecture. Entrants were judged on originality and ambition, multidisciplinary qualifications, and approach to the project's value and management. The winner, Agence Ter, was entrusted with devising a program for the former quarry based on strategic and political objectives: priorities were environmental quality, public usefulness, community access to the Seine, integration with nearby green corridors (specifically those of the waterway), and satisfactory transition between city and nature.

The Parc du Peuple de l'Herbe is characterized by a wild, natural aesthetic similar to what we observed at Alter Flugplatz in Bonames (page 62). Both favor the restoration of sites of human disturbance by means of a keen understanding of natural processes and ecological networks. Like Bonames, Carrières-sous-Poissy lies in a region subject to strict environmental regulations. In 2010, the Department of Conservation designated it an *espace naturel sensible* (sensitive natural area), that is, an area where endangered animal species are present. The ENS designation allows the government to acquire these sites to preserve habitat and landscape and, where possible, to make them accessible to the public.

The animal species targeted for protection at the Parc du Peuple were largely insects. The year 2014 saw a 45 percent decline in monitored species, and in 2018 the *New York Times Magazine* called the cataclysmic drop in the insect population worldwide "the insect apocalypse." The park's designers and managers, considering the protected nature of the area and in partnership with the European program LIFE+, decided to build an entomological visitors' center (originally 1,076 square feet, as built 8,600 square feet). The facility, designed by AWP France Architecture, prepares the public to see the insects by displaying various species and explaining their vital role in pollination and decomposition.

In order to reveal the existing ecosystem, Alexandre Moret of Agence Ter removed invasive black locust trees; besides proliferating aggressively, the trees were obscuring views of the park and river from the adjacent residential development. The park edge closest to this development is the noisiest, most active, and most disruptive to the habitat. Between the edge and the river, the park's focus gradually shifts from human to insect and wildlife populations, and from dry to wet ecosystems. A forest band of willows, maples, and oaks separates the river from the dryer areas, while openings within this band allow views to the watercourse.

A tall lookout tower, constructed in metal and painted white, provides visitors with an impressive overall vista of the expanse with its tall grasses, relatively large trees, and a widening of the Seine filling the former gravel pit. Among the wet areas is a network of small ponds that prevents flooding: when one pond fills, it connects to the next via a bioswale. The designers retained the earthen pathways of the quarry, some of which lead to wooden platforms. Benches on the platforms, thrust partway over each pond, allow a leisurely appreciation of the flora and fauna. When Alex and I visited on a warm June day, the latter was particularly well represented by loudly croaking toads.

A major part of the rehabilitation was the excavation and reuse of over fifty-five thousand cubic yards of soil. This material was taken from the banks of the Seine and used to create a gentler embankment, protected by riprap from soil erosion, for the enlargement of the river. New views of the waterway from the park have produced scenes worthy of a Poussin landscape. Boardwalks of recycled black locust (not from the site) and oak define the water's edge.

In contrast to the low-income community adjacent to the Parc du Peuple de l'Herbe are the luxurious villas that dot the hills on islands in the Seine that face the park. As has been experienced in many a NIMBY phenomenon, the wealthy homeowners vigorously objected to the new views of housing. The district government prevailed, however, and now owns this serene oasis at the periphery of the city. Véronique Brondeau, who manages the park and the visitors' center, admits to the park's shortcomings: the lack of shade and the presence of mosquitoes in the summer is a problem for humans, if not for the park's preferred animal inhabitants. Even so, twenty thousand people came to the park's inauguration in 2017, and the open space continues to be well attended.

The cost of creating the Yvelines park was relatively modest, as is its yearly maintenance budget of $345,000. Agence Ter's design strategy presupposed that conditions in the park would change constantly and of their own accord. When species in the forest band are outcompeted and die, they are likely to be replaced by other species. This successional approach to a park that will evolve continuously contrasts with some of the other parks we visited. At Race Street Pier (page 84), for example, the death of a swamp white oak entails its replacement by a tree of the same species and comparable size. Race Street will mature, but it will never evolve into something other than what it started as, whereas this park in the suburbs of Paris will grow and change.

Plan

Dry meadow

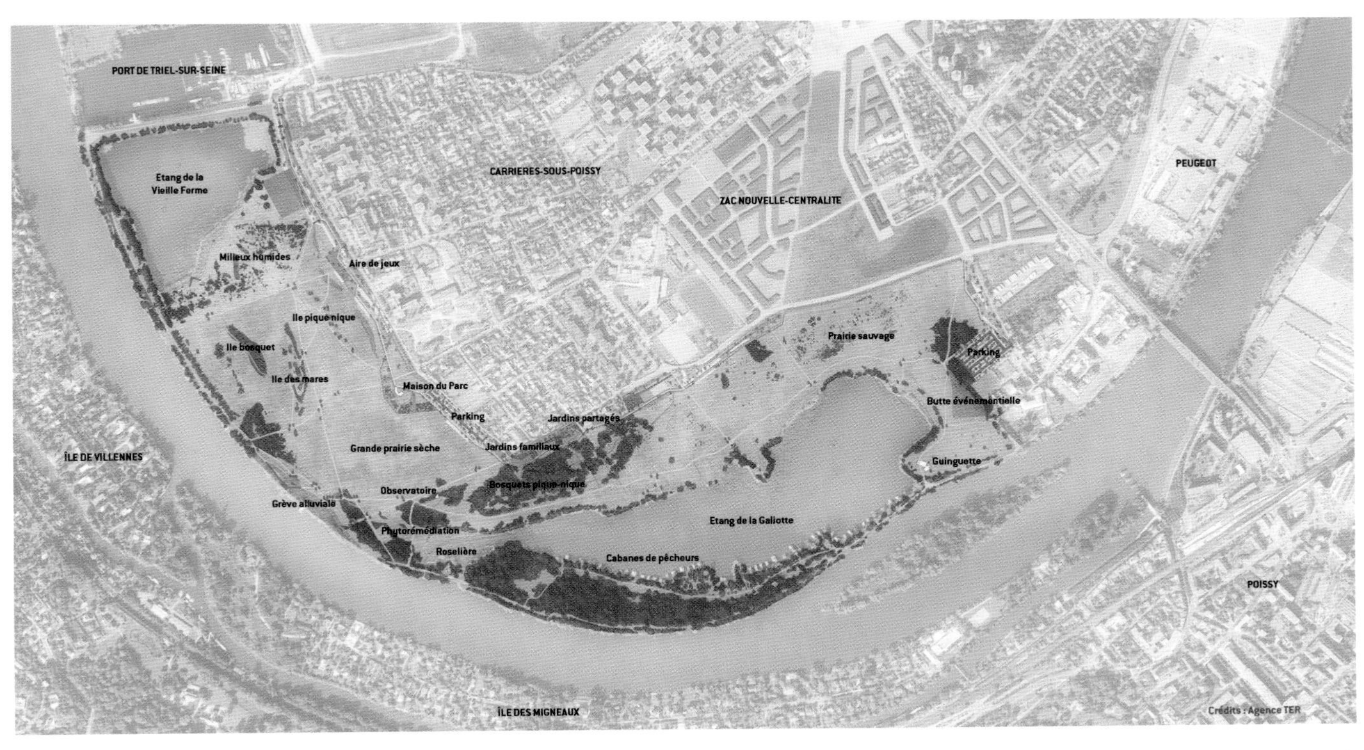
PORT DE TRIEL-SUR-SEINE
Etang de la Vieille Ferme
CARRIERES-SOUS-POISSY
ZAC NOUVELLE-CENTRALITE
PEUGEOT
Milieux humides
Aire de jeux
Ile pique-nique
Ile bosquet
Prairie sauvage
Parking
Ile des mares
Maison du Parc
Butte événementielle
Parking
Jardins partagés
ÎLE DE VILLENNES
Grande prairie sèche
Jardins familiaux
Guinguette
Observatoire
Bosquets pique-nique
Grève alluviale
Etang de la Galiotte
Phytorémédiation
Roselière
Cabanes de pêcheurs
POISSY
ÎLE DES MIGNEAUX
Crédits : Agence TER

Riparian edge along the Seine

Boardwalk of black locust

Fisherman's huts along Galiotte Pond

Small ponds

Overleaf: Galiotte Pond

View west over wetland

Zhenshan Park

Suzhou, China
2007–2017

Turenscape

106 acres
cost: $5.2 million

Each year, millions of tourists visit Suzhou to see small, carefully restored scholars' gardens. These gardens were made between the sixteenth and eighteenth centuries, for the most part, by the owners of houses along the town's numerous canals. The unparalleled Western expert on Chinese gardens, the late Maggie Keswick, compared such gardens to the plans of Gothic cathedrals. Both are cosmic diagrams that reveal a profound and ancient view of the world, and of humankind's place in it.

Scholars' gardens were designed to be an escape from everyday life (as the countryside, or *res rustica*, was for ancient Romans) and an inspiration for the imagination, but ironically, sightseers have made them into places for selfie-taking and Instagram-posting. So the private place for reflection has been made available by social media as a backdrop for snapshots offered to millions of viewers. The new Zhenshan Park, by contrast, which is ten miles from the city center, is more successful in capturing the original intention of these historic gardens.

The green space is located within a high-tech development zone—an area where foreign investment is encouraged. The national initiative started in 1980 in four cities, extended in 1984 to fourteen cities, and currently includes more than forty-nine cities. Suzhou is home to thriving agricultural enterprises, iron and steel industries, and trade entities; to date, it has attracted more than seventeen thousand foreign-funded enterprises, and the accumulated actual use of foreign capital exceeds $130 billion. Indeed, so prosperous is the city generally (population 6,339,000, with one of the highest growth rates in China) that since 2000 it has been competing with Shanghai in production.

Water and mountains (represented by rocks) are the two linchpins of the traditional Chinese garden—the yin and the yang of these designs. Historically, water symbolized positive energy; its presence (in ponds, small waterfalls, and streams under zigzagging bridges) and its sound (gurgling, splashing, and so on) were ever present. Limestone scholars' rocks, eroded by the water, were taken from nearby Lake Tai. Famous for their use in Chinese gardens, they were positioned as focal points and intended to infuse perceptions of temporality into the garden.

Garden paths were never straight but rather twisted, meandering, or curved to reveal a sequence of unfolding spaces. Height changes, achieved by the construction of artificial rocky hills, inclined walks, steps, and bridges, contributed to the variety of experiences in the scholars' gardens. Changes in path articulation and design also affected the visitors' experience. For example, footbridges without railings gave the user a feeling of walking on water. The result is a *penjing*, or space that re-creates a large landscape in miniature.

Although the Zhenshan landscape differs tremendously in design philosophy (straight instead of meandering paths, for one), scale (106 acres as opposed to an average of about three acres), and purpose (park rather than garden) from the nearby historic gardens, they share many conceptual similarities. Many of the new green spaces in China, including Zhenshan Park, include water in some form or other as well as topographic changes. One of the most notable ideas adapted from the scholars' garden is the use of borrowed landscape, epitomized at Zhenshan by view corridors that take advantage of Zhen Hill, a rise hovering beside the park.

A noteworthy difference between gardens of the past and those of the present is equally evident in Suzhou. In older gardens, small paths from which visitors would experience specific moments dictated a highly choreographed procession: tiny stone bridges that cross a stream, for instance, or rocky paths that culminate in a tea pavilion perched on a hill. Visitors would be allowed to see only controlled views of the landscape. In fact, traditional Chinese gardens are like scroll paintings, as Charles Jencks has observed. In more recent parks, paths still guide visitors along a predetermined route, but it is easy to stray from the walkway and set foot in the landscape itself, like the forested areas at Zhenshan.

The site proposed for the park included an abandoned granite quarry filled with rainwater; the property had also been used as a landfill, and the pit was packed with refuse. Suzhou's Department of Urban Planning commissioned landscape architect Turenscape, known for expertise in remediating brownfields, to design a low-maintenance park that

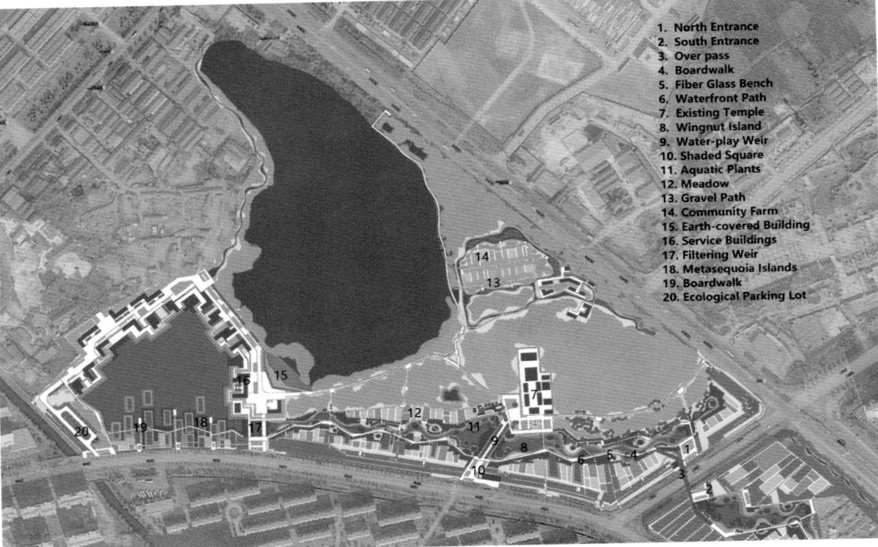

Humble Administrator's Garden (Zhuozheng Yuan), Suzhou, China, c. 1513

Plan

Zhen Hill

Water flowing from constructed wetland to pond

would rehabilitate the quarry and decontaminate surface water in the region.

Surrounding the open space is a residential development occupied by newly urbanized migrants, primarily relocated farmers who lost their land due to various government development projects. Kongjian Yu, principal of Turenscape, surveyed this community on the subject of the new park and discovered the need for a place to jog, a setting that would allow gatherings of both young and old, and land for small-scale cultivation of crops and vegetables.

The designers developed a park in four sections—lake district, farmland, wetland, and forest—within an area bordered on three sides by busy four-lane roads. Two key strategies for the design were Sponge City (Yu's concept for increasing site porosity and responsiveness) and the use of native and low maintenance plants. A half-mile-long water channel collects rainwater from the site and the surrounding neighborhood and filters it through a constructed wetland. The quarry was filled and rubble was used to build the park's varied topography.

Alex and I entered the park through a plaza planted with bright chartreuse ginkgo trees and surrounded by gabions, which serve as benches. The shades of light green and the textures of the pond cypress trees beyond the plaza contrast with the darker green shades of Chinese privet (*Ligustrum lucidum*), Japanese blueberry (*Elaeocarpus sylvestris*), schima (*Schima superba*), and other broad-leafed evergreens growing on Zhen Hill. Similar layered plantings throughout the park expand its spatial depth. At times, the hill blends with the trees in front of it; at other times, it almost disappears.

An existing Buddhist temple is a surprising, and surprisingly popular, presence. The government had intended to remove the religious complex, but the community succeeded in opposing this scheme. The place of worship, with the usual subsidiary pavilions, appears as a found object within the artistry of the new landscape.

We followed a half-mile-long boardwalk made of bamboo and steel grate and slightly elevated above ground level. Water is visible below the walkway, and wetland grasses penetrate the grated surface. The result is that the grasses act as a visual safeguard in the absence of railings (except on bridges), which lends immediacy to the experience of the park. Several fishponds were chock-full of yellow pond-lily (*Nuphar pumila*), pygmy waterlilies (*Nymphaea tetragona*), and patches of tall, thickly packed reeds. The water is bordered by pond cypress (*Taxodium ascendens*); embankments are protected by stacked pine logs that prevent erosion. The planting strategy is often textural: plants like canna lily (*Canna glauca*) and powdery thalia (*Thalia dealbata*) dapple the water's surface, while dawn redwood (*Metasequoia glyptostroboides*) flank many of the paths, reinforcing the effect of a shaded glen. Dawn redwood is paired with pond cypress within the wetland to help clean the eutrophicated water.

In other areas, gridded bands of pond cypress grow on small, artificial islands that recall the Mexican *chinampas* (pages 206, 209). This highly regular planting scheme is repeated in the denser, more forest-like sections. Additionally, patches of farmland within the park nurture productive, seasonally rotated crops such as canola, rice, and sunflowers. We saw visitors resting on red fiberglass benches—a Turenscape hallmark—that run alongside the boardwalks through many of these areas and occasionally slip into the forest.

Bridges with views of the park over dense vegetation and waterways join one of the two paths that return to the main entrance. A shaded, dappled ridgeline of poplars (*Populus × canadensis*) also provides vistas into the landscape, to a large lake and an even larger meadow filled with wildflowers; on the day of our visit, young people were flying kites in the meadow. These quiet, bucolic areas are a far cry from the noisy and overrun scholars' gardens in the center of the city. A planned second phase will add active recreation and additional amenities to Zhenshan Park; we hope that these new insertions will not destroy the peace we experienced.

Metal-grate and wood walkway over water

Artificial islands planted with grids of pond cypress

Rotating crops recalling the site's agrarian history

Plum blossoms in spring and garden room

Mei Garden

Jinhua, China
2013

Turenscape

32 acres
cost: undisclosed

As Kongjian Yu's birthplace, Jinhua has a special sentimental resonance for him, which was certainly a factor in his firm, Turenscape, receiving the commission for a new park there. The site designated, a drive of about ten minutes from the city center, is on a riparian plain created by the construction of a hundred-year flood wall along the Jinhua, or Wu River. The land was contaminated not by industry or material extraction but as the byproduct of human settlement and activities. Once in place, the wall limited water flow, producing a swampy lowland with heavily contaminated water. The pollution on the site was exacerbated by its use as an informal dumping ground. As at Qiaoyuan Wetland Park in Tianjin (page 290), the community helped to initiate this park by petitioning for its replacement.

The fully realized Mei Garden is not built on a preexisting structure; it is included here because of its expert remediation of a brownfield site, its exceptional beauty, and Yu's declared merging of contemporary Chinese parks with traditional gardens like those we visited in Suzhou. The new green space is based on ideas suggestive of historic precedent, including scale shifts, materiality, and a consideration of the garden as scenographic endeavor.

At the historic Lingering Garden in Suzhou (created in the sixteenth century and altered in the eighteenth and again in the nineteenth century), spaces are often slightly obscured to heighten a sense of discovery. Alex and I experienced this feeling as we wound our way through the garden, seeing bridges and pavilions with no clear means of access. We had a similar sensation at the Mei Garden as we glimpsed small garden rooms through openings punched in vine-covered walls.

Despite the allusions to China's rich garden tradition, the Mei Garden is a contemporary landscape dealing with contemporary issues. The plantings—large swaths of monocultures chosen for their phytoremediative benefits—respond to environmental concerns. And the landscape architect's agrarian references would never be found in a traditional garden.

Turenscape addressed problems at the site by using a cut-and-fill technique to make the park's thirty-two acres into a twenty-foot-deep terraced valley. The valley is divided into two parts—a nine-square garden and a wetland. Urban runoff and polluted water pumped from the river move through a biofilter that retains and remediates the water, which then flows over cascades to a constructed wetland. Recapturing the brownfield site started with massive aquatic beds of canna lilies, which efficiently remove pollutants from the water. Every day two and a half acres of wetland can clean up to 20,950 gallons of water.

The plantings reflect the site's terrain and, to a certain degree, inform visitors of their location in relation to water movement. Pines, which shun saturated soils, stand on the top terraces along with bamboo; these species form a backdrop for the Mei (Chinese plum) groves on the middle terraces. Naturally, the wetland is in the low-lying, floodable area.

Chinese poets and painters have celebrated the Mei blossom over more than a thousand years for its moral characteristics: modesty, righteousness, and courtesy. The plum flower is hardy, and its ability to blossom in snow and cold weather, as well as in windy micro-environments (the shady side of a space, for example), make it a symbol of persistence. Traditionally, the soft colors, delicate forms, and intoxicating fragrance of the Mei flower (which blooms only from early February to early March) were hidden, to be enjoyed only as the result of exploration or an unpredicted encounter. And indeed, the long approach to the garden rooms in which the plum trees (*Prunus mume*) are elegantly sequestered re-creates this secretive feeling.

The Nine-Square Plum Garden—six garden rooms with poetic names such as Jade Butterfly or Colorful Jade enclosed by fifteen-foot-high walls and a central lotus corridor—is located toward the north. The form is based on the Lo Shu Square—a perfect square used in traditional Chinese culture as a symbol of the unique normal magic square of order. The generous rooms, each 6,200 square feet, exhibit the Mei flowers. Many historic gardens are surfaced in delicate stone patterns;

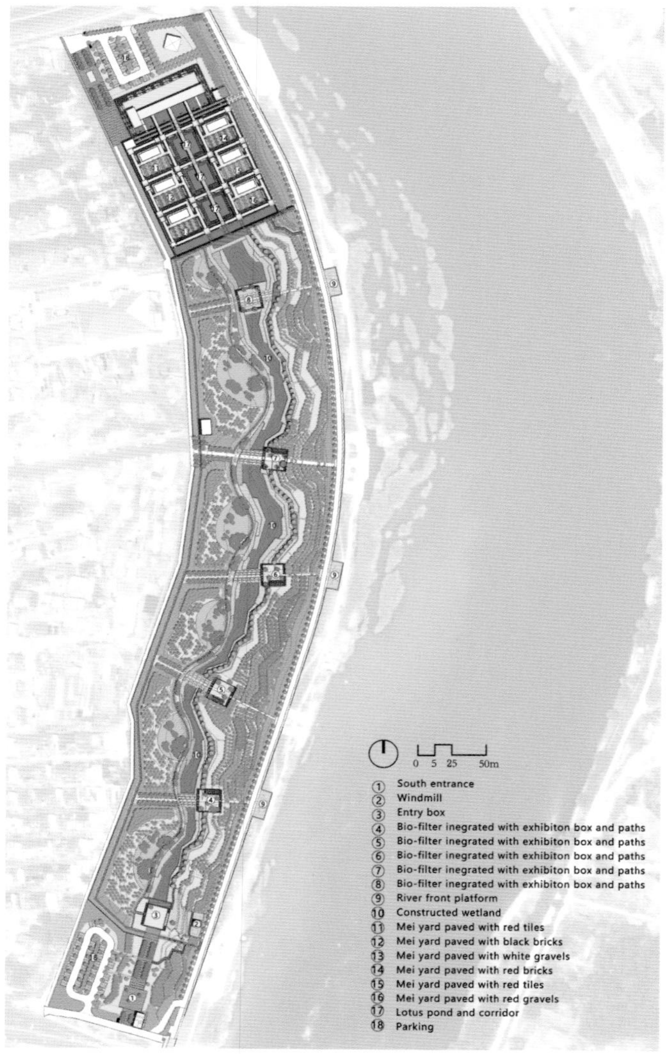

here, the rooms are paved with a local material—black or red bricks, red tiles, white or red gravel. Innovative crafting of traditional materials—notably the roof tiles and the pure white gravel—gives these spaces a human scale. Three corridors are filled with a profusion of lotuses, which bloom in the summer and symbolize cleanliness and purity. Four weirs slow the flow of water as it descends from the highest terraces; they also create a pleasant gurgling that together with melodic bird calls adds to the sensual richness of the park. Boston ivy (*Parthenocissus tricuspidata*), which turns bright red and gold in the fall, covers the gray slate walls, pierced by window-like apertures, that delineate the garden rooms. The square spaces are connected by a paved pathway covered with a glazed wood lattice canopy that protects from both sun and rain.

During our visit, on a warm day in May, we observed the focused intimacy of the Nine-Square Garden opening to broad vistas, a progression similar to what we experienced at the Qiaoyuan Wetland Park and the Culture of Water Ecology Park (page 168). One wide view offered a massive field of bright yellow tickseed (*Coreopsis*), its scale and grandeur especially effective in the absence of surrounding buildings. A stunning field of six-foot-tall orange and red canna lilies is divided by raised, stone-paved pathways wide enough for just one person. The giant plants obstructed distant views, and their leaves brushed our skin, making us keenly aware of the sensuous textures and colors of the plantings.

Approximately one million visitors come to the Mei Garden each year. "The plums and the lotuses are the biggest attractions here," we were told by one of the matrons accompanying crowds of children. Many youngsters were playing excitedly in the Nine-Square Garden, and many more had discovered another absorbing attraction: the tiny snails that live in the garden's water channels.

Site, preremediation

Plan

Constructed wetland with garden room

Mei Yard

Paving in traditional materials

Boston ivy covering slate walls

Bamboo plantings screening views

Beds of canna lilies on either side of stone-paved pathway

View to northwest over Huadu Lake Park

Huadu Lake Park

Guangzhou, China
2018

Palm Design

570 acres
cost: $20.5 million

The rich subtropical vegetation along the highway between the Guangzhou International Airport and Huadu, a northern suburb of that major metropolis, is quite different from the flora in the north: it includes a rich sampling of Persian silk trees (*Albizia julibrissin*), blackboard tree (*Alstonia scholaris*), and banyans. Guangzhou (population nearly 14 million in 2018) is one of China's four largest and most important cities; the others are Beijing, Shanghai, and Shenzhen.

Formerly known as Canton, Guangzhou has been open to foreign trade for centuries thanks to its advantageous location: the Pearl River (Zhujiang), which flows through the city, faces the South China Sea, with Hong Kong seventy-five miles to the southeast. Guangzhou is the manufacturing hub of the Pearl River Delta, the nation's most populous and prosperous region, with 70 million people, 37 percent of the country's exports, and 12 percent of its gross domestic product. The government's plan to link Guangzhou with eleven other delta cities, including Hong Kong, Macau, and Shenzhen, in an integrated economic and business conglomeration, has made competition between the cities fiercer than ever, and one of the ways in which they compete is the quantity and quality of their parkland. By 2015, Guangzhou had built seven wetland parks and was planning for an additional seven. One of these is Huadu Lake Park, commissioned by the Huadu district government and exemplifying the increase in power and autonomy granted to Chinese towns and cities starting in the 1980s. The park is intended to meet local needs.

The decision to construct a park in the wetlands and mudflats at the mouth of the Tieshan River and adjacent to Huadu Lake (a former limestone quarry) was a practical one, arrived at for reasons of safety; but it also aligns with the long-held Chinese belief that a great lake contributes to the serenity of a garden. Three existing rubber dams along the Xinjie River equalize the water levels between river and lake.

Furthermore, the Xinjie River was subject to flooding and was heavily polluted by storm runoff, contamination from a pig farm upstream (today converted into a traditional Chinese garden), and trash. Significant areas of land adjacent to the river had been abandoned, and the waterway itself divided the city. Sewage interception has improved the quality of the river water, and an existing levee between the river and the lake, with a road on top, was opened to connect both sides.

The former quarry had furnished raw materials to a cement factory atop a hill at the east of the site; a second levee provided access to the pit. When the excavation closed, the narrow levee eroded and the islands in the lake, used for fishing and vegetable cultivation, became dangerously unstable. The rehabilitation effort included securing the levee and building a pathway through the park.

The district government held a competition to award the commission. Winner Palm Design, in a nod to the government's promotion of local cultural aesthetics, looked to the regional tradition of Cantonese gardens in its entry. This tradition is exemplified by the "Four Famous Gardens of Guangzhou," created in the late nineteenth century. These featured materials, like glass, concrete, granite, and coral, from nearby locales and incorporated towering pavilions, higher than the comparable architecture that Alex and I saw in Suzhou. Huadu Lake Park strictly follows the traditions of Cantonese landscape design, which replaces topographic metaphor with a greater emphasis on water and rich plantings of the subtropical species native to the region. Lushness is the hallmark of this park.

The path through the park zigzags wildly; according to tradition, this course avoids evil spirits, who are believed to move in straight lines. The islands that support the path also accommodate numerous roofed pavilions that provide pleasant, shaded rest areas, a response to the hot and humid local climate. Some of the shelters offer a second level within the tree canopy; the deliberate opening of view corridors at this level gave us directed views of specific moments within the landscape. The ground level puts forward a different experience: the deep green hues of the trees and the colorful shrubs are like a scrim enclosing the pathway. The contrast between envelopment and openness echoes the contrast between the park's naturalistic environment and the surrounding city.

Yu Yin Shan Fang garden, Panyu, 1866

Plan

Former cement factory

Lake Park is divided into two parts: a simple 7.6-mile looped path on and around the islands and a green space that stretches into the city from the eastern bank of the river. At the midpoint of the park, a wide walkway climbs the hill to the closed cement factory, which may one day become part of a new artists' community. We slipped into the north end of the park through a narrow, unobtrusive opening in the vegetation to discover the partially hidden zigzag passageway. Quite narrow and protected on both sides by heavy guardrails, the wood-plank walkway connects a three-and-a-half-mile-long chain of islands.

Both the path and the park presented problems for the designers. Palm Design wanted to retain some of the industrial relics in the hillside industrial area, including a kiln through which they had made a path, but the government turned down the idea. The deep quarry pit destabilized nearby roads and walkways; although reinforced as part of the park construction, these paths remain closed to the public for safety reasons.

In addition to using the principles of Cantonese gardens, the landscape architects inserted literal references, giving the landscape a conservative air. The concrete guardrails painted to look like wood recall similar details in nineteenth-century parks in Western Europe; certain architectural elements also hark back to earlier designs. It seems that this look was favored by local residents, who asked for a "beautiful park in which they could exercise." Judging from the numerous visitors of all ages in all parts of the park on the warm Sunday of our visit, people got what they wanted.

We, too, were delighted by our experience in the Huadu Lake Park. Its simplicity was a welcome relief from the many overdesigned parks we had seen in China and elsewhere. This quality is especially conspicuous in a comparison to the excessive artifice in the Thousand Lantern Park in nearby Foshan: instead of a public green space, this area felt like a garden akin to a Disney amusement park.

Historic view over quarry lakes

Pathway on former levee

View toward city center through existing vegetation

Zigzag walkway along former levee

View to southeast over Tangshan Quarry Park

Tangshan Quarry Park

Nanjing, China
2019

Z+T Studio

100 acres
cost: $13.3 million

A pleasant forty-five-minute drive from the center of Nanjing brought Alex and me to the nearly hundred-acre Tangshan Quarry Park on a hot September day. We entered through the neat little modern visitors' pavilion and were immediately taken aback by the steepness of the mountain we had to ascend to reach the quarry. An asphalt path edged by a runnel at one side and a swale at the other ran straight up the incline, suggesting a "stairway to heaven" at a religious shrine.

The one break in the ascent is a turnoff halfway up the hill, which leads to the children's area. The playground, and especially its extremely long slides, have proven to be the park's main draw. Despite an entrance fee of 8 RMB ($1.16) per person—atypical, since most parks and playgrounds are free to enter—parents drive from Nanjing just to visit this playground, which gets between one and two thousand visitors a day on weekends.

Nanjing (population 8,270,500 in 2016) sits beside the Yangtze River 160 miles west of Shanghai. For three thousand years, it has served as the capital of various dynasties, kingdoms, and republican governments, notably of the Republic of China established by Sun Yat-sen in 1912. Today, it is merely a provincial capital, one where the administration depends on upper-level government. In fact, it was the central government that in 2005 designated the area for rest and recreation. Two years later, landscape architect Z+T Studio suggested repurposing the large quarry, which had ceased operations in the early 2000s.

The designers focused on restoring the landscape, in particular remediating the limestone quarry pits. In the absence of official construction specifications for this type of project, the design team adopted (for the first time in China) international standards for sustainable initiatives and worked in collaboration with other disciplines. Z+T struggled to protect wetlands and forest in the face of the client's indifference to issues of preservation. Part of the effort to preserve hydrological conditions consisted of transforming an existing pond into a water garden.

There were, however, many matters to which the client was not indifferent, and numerous unfortunate interventions handicapped the landscape architects, a situation unlike the exceptional circumstances at the Culture of Water Ecology Park in Changchun (page 168), where the designers profited from more freedom in their work on the part of the local government. The large expanse of lawn, for example, ignored ecological objectives.

As we trudged up the hill, we came to the monumental weathered-steel ramp that hugs the quarry's formidable rock facade. The wonderful serenity of this spot was unfortunately marred by intrusive Muzak piped throughout the area by the government via fake stone loudspeakers. The ramp brought us close enough to the quarry wall to appreciate its geological formation, explanations of which are provided on signage throughout the park. We were also able to see the delicate plants that have established themselves in the cracks. The twists of the ramp provide changing views, including one that reveals a massive tourist center—another government imposition.

The park is rife with sumacs, pines, and golden rain trees, which began to establish themselves from seeds that found their way to the site during its ten-year fallow period. Flower beds, planted at the insistence of the client, likewise bedeck the park. The return path from the quarry leads down the other side of the mountain. As we descended, we encountered construction workers busily trying to complete the project. The one-and-a-half-year schedule originally foreseen by the government was evidently a low estimate.

Even considering the client's unfortunate design demands, we found the concept of the park sound for this sensational site. Yet at the same time, it felt like a small-scale design blown up to fit a large landscape.

Oxygenating weirs

Playground

Plan

Mixed deciduous forest surrounding lake

Elevated metal walkway clinging to cliff face

Observation pavilion

View to east with Thomas C. Wales Park (bottom center), Lake Union, and Gas Works Park

Thomas C. Wales Park

Seattle, Washington
2011

Site Workshop

1.3 acres
cost: $350,000

This charming park sets itself apart from other quarry parks in numerous ways. It is much smaller, for one, just over an acre in size. And it is situated in a surprising place: Queen Anne, a residential neighborhood north of downtown Seattle. The excavation crater, lodged in one of the city's innumerable steep slopes, operated for a short time in the early 1900s as a gravel quarry. After it was shut down, it was taken over by a variety of uses; in recent years, the city used the property as a staging area for construction equipment and materials.

Thomas C. Wales Park is a stunning example of how effective even a small landscape intervention can be. Unlike most new green spaces, this one is entirely passive, without a playground or any other amenities. Portland artist Adam Kuby's five-part sculpture *Quarry Rings* is installed around the site. Even the namesake of the park—Thomas C. Wales (1952–2001), a federal prosecutor and gun control advocate who was the victim of an unsolved murder—is unusual.

The Seattle area has long been known for well-maintained, popular hiking trails, which wind through wild growth and around magnificent cypresses. Trekkers are rewarded with framed views of Puget Sound and the state's towering, usually snow-capped, Cascade Range, which includes Mount St. Helens and the fourteen-thousand-foot-plus Mount Rainier. In addition, Seattle has been at the forefront of park innovation since John Charles Olmsted, stepson of the celebrated Frederick Law Olmsted, was hired by the city in 1903. The senior partner at Olmsted Brothers (the sons and successors to Frederick Law Olmsted) planned thirty-seven parks and playgrounds in and around the city and linked together a system of boulevards and green spaces. The boulevards, themselves linear landscapes, connect city residents to areas of natural beauty. The city's early recognition of the importance of preservation and ecology has continued through the twentieth century, with Gas Works Park (1975) and Freeway Park (1976), and into the twenty-first, with Olympic Sculpture Park (2007), which involved the rehabilitation of three urban brownfields.

Given this extensive tradition, it was perhaps inevitable that city officials would designate for renovation the overgrown site where Thomas C. Wales Park now stands. Clayton Beaudoin, principal and project manager at the Seattle firm Site Workshop, says the land was "like a jungle" when he began work there. Himalayan blackberry plants, aggressive and invasive, that had taken over the hillside had to be removed along with the soil surrounding the plants. The slopes were regraded and stabilized and the existing wetland restored, providing a focal point for new plantings.

When Alex and I passed through a screen of tall cedars and walked up a few steps at 6th Avenue North to enter the park, we were immediately caught up in its magic. The small, mysteriously dark, and wild wetland in front of us was the first feature to grab our attention. Bridging the wetland, a fallen log allows visitors to cross through dense plantings of rose spirea (*Spiraea douglasii*), salal (*Gaultheria shallon*), and Nootka rose (*Rosa nutkana*). Floating above this scene was the large, airy *Quarry Rings*. Its five gabion rings have a fairy-tale quality in themselves: for me, they conjured crowns the giants Fafner and Fasolt might have worn in *Das Rheingold*. Each of the constituent rings—fifteen feet high and ten to fifteen feet in diameter—contains nesting cavities for the birds and bats that now flock to this habitat.

Stone from King Creek Pit in Washington State partially paves the paths and fills the extensive, curved gabion that follows the arc of the hillside in addition to Kuby's gabion rings. One of the biggest challenges for the landscape architects was to provide accessible features on the steep slopes that rise above the central wetland. Benches and railings of locally salvaged cedar facilitate the climb up crushed-rock paths; alternative paths at gentler inclines can be used to circumvent grade changes.

Our climb up and along the paths presented prospects to Lake Union and the Cascade Range to the east and to different areas of the park as well. Beaudoin claims that these vistas are one of his favorite aspects of the park; another is the ever-changing spatial experiences produced at different times of year.

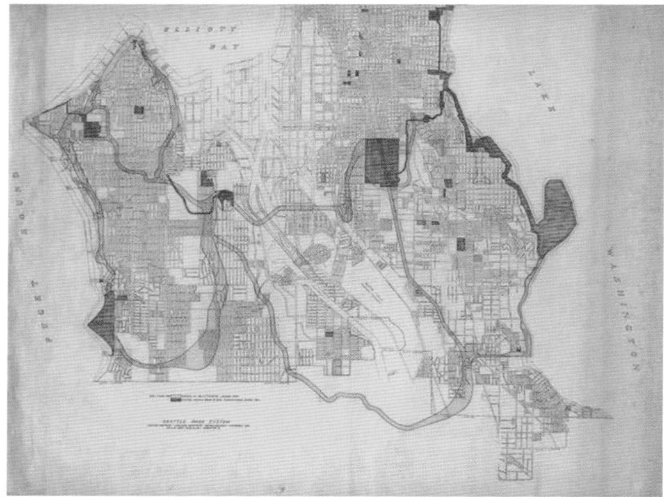

Seattle park system, 1928, Olmsted Brothers

Plan

Restored wetland

Gabion walls

Overleaf: *Quarry Rings* in winter

strongholds

The term *stronghold* conjures images of the historic forts and defensive walls characteristic of innumerable cities throughout Europe and Asia. Like quarries, fortifications are one of the oldest types of repurposed infrastructure. Many walled cities turned their defenses into roadways or parks once there was no longer a need for fortified security. Two notable examples are Paris's Boulevard Périphérique and Vienna's Ringstrasse.

Such is the case with the fortresses in Luxembourg City, which were altered over nine centuries by a series of military engineers, including the celebrated Vauban, who served under Louis XIV. Fort bij Vechten in Utrecht belongs to an extensive defense system with a strategy distinctive to the Netherlands: flooding low-lying areas to impede advances by foot or by boat. Both the forts in Luxembourg and the Netherlands, which retain parts of the original architecture, are now green spaces.

The Carolingian Abbey of Lorsch, Germany—a spiritual rather than military stronghold—has experienced numerous periods of strife, ending with its near total destruction in the seventeenth century during the Thirty Years' War. The remains of this famous complex evoke salient relationships with Lorsch and the surrounding countryside.

Besides exemplifying some of the ways in which military architecture developed, ruins are also cultural relics, witnesses to past eras. Twentieth-century installations are also subject to rehabilitation and reinterpretation. For example, a former shooting range in Tianjin, China, which has been transformed into a busy local recreation area, demonstrates the Sponge City system for mitigating floods devised by Kongjian Yu. Fuzhou, in the Fujian province of China, retains a military role because of its proximity to Taiwan. However, military camps, which deterred access to the steep slopes of Jinniushan Mountain overlooking Fuzhou, have been marginalized to allow construction of a daring elevated trail that crosses the peak in exciting roller coaster loops.

View over west entrance with Torhalle (bottom) and abbey ruins (upper left)

Lorsch Abbey

Lorsch, Germany
2014

Topotek 1

14.8 acres
cost: $5.9 million

Lorsch was one of the most important monastic communities among the thousands that flourished throughout Europe in the Middle Ages. Founded in 764 in a simple hall-like church with a few conventual buildings on an island in the Weschnitz River, the Benedictine abbey received the body of St. Nazarius, which inspired the monks to build and relocate to a new abbey just a few years later. Renamed the Monastery of Saint Nazarius, the new abbey, about a half-mile from the previous one on a plateau atop an Ice Age sand dune, was given additional prestige by Charlemagne's presence at its consecration and later King Louis the German's (817–876) choice of Lorsch for his burial place.

Over the centuries, the abbey underwent architectural changes and additions, was converted to a secular college in 1555, and was finally destroyed in the Thirty Years' War (1618–48). While the abbey's buildings have almost totally disappeared, the preeminent writings, illuminations, and manuscript bindings created there, including the *Codex Aureus of Lorsch,* are now held at the Vatican and elsewhere.

In 1991, Lorsch was designated a UNESCO World Heritage Site. In 2009, the State of Hesse initiated a year-long, two-part interdisciplinary competition for a park that would respond to the legacy of the abbey but not disturb the physical remains of that legacy; the competition was accompanied by a series of public meetings. The city also began to raise money for site research and preservation, since the land includes two royal cemeteries in addition to architectural remains.

Topotek 1, the only landscape architect to propose connecting the park to the site of the eighth-century abbey—allowing visitors to trace a pilgrimage route—won the competition. The course winds along the Weschnitz River and through the countryside, passing a modest historical museum, old tobacco barns, and a buttressed, twelfth-century retaining wall, all set against a view of the scenic Odenwald mountains. To encourage visitors to experience the circuit, even in inclement weather, the designers developed umbrellas (as well as rain capes for dogs).

The west entrance to the park—used by the majority of visitors—starts at the edge of Lorsch's main square. The transition between civic and historic precincts is delineated with a wide strip of granite pavers. Instead of the town's cobble paving there is dark ironspot Roman brick, which alternates with bright green strips of grass. The arrival sequence culminates at the steps of the Torhalle (gate hall), one of the best-preserved Carolingian structures in the world. The route continues through the lower arcade of the hall and ascends to the former abbey site on the ancient dune, the bands of lawn gradually becoming wider. The walkway leads to a continuous lawn that acts as a spatial frame for the park, setting off the large canopy trees and the remnants of a medieval church.

Alex and I arrived in Lorsch, a town of about fourteen thousand, on a cool day in September 2018 and went looking for the park. We discovered the eighth- or ninth-century gatehouse, its long sides inlaid with patterns composed of white and red sandstone plaques, a short distance from the central square. It may have served as the entryway to a forecourt of the monastic area, a gateway to honor Charlemagne's victorious return to Lorsch in 774, or a triumphal arch intended for the future emperor's coronation. Lulled by the peace of the fine morning, we were overwhelmed by the phantom presence of the abbey.

The area around the abbey is an archaeological site, valued for its insight into the great abbeys of Europe. Any ruins have been reburied, as required by law, to preserve them for future excavation and study. Topotek 1 has suggested the monastic complex by transcribing its plan onto the ground plane. The outlines of the church, the walled entrance court, and the enclave with its cloister are indicated via topographic devices: low but sharply extruded segments of the lawn held in place by discreet steel edgings. Hermann Schefers, who heads the management of Lorsch for the Administration of State Palaces and Gardens, likens the imprints on the lawn to the impressions of jewels displayed on a velvet cushion: "If you take away a ring, you can still see the indent in the velvet. You can imagine that a ring or brooch must have been lying there." How effective that conceptualization is! This is exactly

Plan

Pilgrimage route through countryside

Sunken lawns delineating former abbey

View to Odenwald Mountains

how we read the park, as the abstraction of a lost history. The design ingeniously renders the invisible visible.

Brick paths are elegantly set within the lawn at the perimeter of the green space; they intersect in a pattern inspired by the children's game Mikado (pick-up sticks). As we walked along these paths, we noticed that there was little park furniture, apart from a few benches. The Topotek 1 team discouraged installing any three-dimensional objects in the park, whether lighting, trash receptacles, or signage, in an effort to avoid visual clutter. For the same reason, the landscape architects removed specimen trees planted randomly on the site by the Forestry Department, former stewards of the abbey site.

Among the specific challenges of the site was erosion related to a nineteenth-century road cut thoughtlessly into the ancient sand dune. Excavation might have disturbed the archaeological record, so the designers introduced a steep embankment stabilized with geotextiles and engineered soils; it purposely lacks protective barriers.

The dramas around the complex are not relegated to the past. As soon as it was introduced, the landscape design met vigorous opposition from the town: residents considered it too radical and forced significant details to be abandoned. The most "dramatic situation," says Lorenz Dexler of Topotek 1, "arose when we moved the existing herb garden; it was almost like a civil war."

Starting in 2000, the citizens of Lorsch had developed a garden based on the famous Carolingian *Lorsch Pharmacopoeia* (now in the Bamberg State Library), the earliest compendium of herb-based classical remedies in the Greco-Roman tradition. But the location of the plantings interfered with the new design. After tremendous public protest against its removal, the landscape architects and the town came to an agreement that the garden would be moved to a different location within the park. The new garden is larger than the original, allowing the inclusion of additional species from the *Pharmacopoeia*.

Martin Rein-Cano, the founder and principal of Topotek 1, is "convinced that the perception of landscape is highly dependent on the stories that are told about it." Whatever the subject of these stories—the abbey's glorious founding in the eighth century, its sixteenth-century secularization, wartime demolition in the seventeenth century, or twenty-first-century controversies—the Lorsch Abbey narrative continues.

Terraced garden with species from *Lorsch Pharmacopoeia*

Twelfth-century wall

Criss-crossing brick paths

Fort bij Vechten and nearby forts, context diagram

Wattle fence (left) stabilizing bank of moat

Mixed deciduous forest within fort
and along moat's banks

Restored landforms

View to northwest over park entrance

Qiaoyuan Wetland Park

Tianjin, China
2008

Turenscape

54 acres
cost: $10 million

Located 71 miles southeast of Beijing, the Qiaoyuan Wetland Park in Tianjin, commonly referred to as Bridge Park, breaks with custom in several ways. Its realization came about not as a result of municipal government fiat or a developer's effort to increase real estate values, as many new Chinese parks do, but at the request of the local population. Occupants of low-cost residential buildings to the south and east of the site objected to the unsightly informal dumping ground that had replaced an abandoned military shooting range and demanded better.

Kongjian Yu wanted to create a park that would provide recreation and natural pleasures for urban residents. He also hoped that the project would educate residents about the environment, indigenous plants, and ecological systems. To accomplish this, the Turenscape team dug twenty-one pools throughout the park that sequester water runoff, allow it to be filtered by plants, and return it to the aquifer while decontaminating the soil; they also recolonized the regional landscape with low-maintenance, high-performance vegetation.

The park is distinctive in another way: it teemed with activity the morning Alex and I arrived, despite 90-degree temperatures that had reduced visits to many other parks in China. Older couples social danced to popular music on radios, cardplayers were intent on their games, a gentleman practiced calligraphy on the pavement with a large brush dipped in water, and a lone saxophonist performed.

Furnished with benches and planted with large canopy trees, an entrance plaza at the southeast corner of the park is intended for lively community gatherings. The plaza leads to a walkway over water; we felt a more subdued atmosphere as soon as we crossed the bridge. At this point the circulation split: one walkway provided overviews, while the second ran at ground level. High points throughout the green space—elevated, bright red metal walkways, towers, and bridges, which give the park its popular name, as well as lower planted terraces secured by weathered steel panels—introduced thrilling panoramas of the otherwise relatively flat park.

We saw themed plazas between the towers; vast, lush expanses of vegetation; a large lake planted with willows (*Salix matsudana*); and slight rises along the peripheries crowned with rose of Sharon (*Hibiscus syriacus*) and Kaido crab apple (*Malus × micromalus*) trees. Turenscape had specified poplars for these areas, but the government replaced them with the showier species. Also visible were trees shielding the far side of the park from a curving elevated highway. Rising above the highway was a skyline of towers.

At ground level, the park is a series of individual encounters. A network of discreet red asphalt paths bordered by narrow granite pavers accentuates the primary circulation system of light gray granite pavers flanked by wide borders of cobble setts. The trails weave through wild native marsh grasses, reeds, tree stands, and water retention areas. Generous wood platforms off the walkways offer respite: visitors can enjoy a picnic or simply observe the landscape. Informal expanses of flowers such as plains coreopsis, garden cosmos, and flowering shrubs captivate viewers and add dramatic color to the predominantly green palette. The interplay between broad overviews provided by raised infrastructure and more intimate, tactile experiences is a frequent theme in Turenscape projects, including Houtan Park and Mei Garden (page 248).

Bridge Park is a straightforward demonstration of Kongjian Yu's Sponge City system, which here is intended to protect low-lying areas from frequent floods and to remediate contaminated soil naturally. The twenty-one pond cavities—33 to 130 feet in diameter and 3 to 16 feet in depth—synchronize with the topography, which slopes down from the northeast to the southwest. Lower elevations feature deep ponds; shallower basins are distributed across the landscape. In the rainy season, some of the cavities fill with water—some become wetlands, some seasonal ponds—while others remain relatively dry. Water is filtered within each of the cavities and then released into the aquifer. This process improves the soil condition of the dry cavities and deposits nutrients in the deeper ponds, which collect storm water runoff for irrigation.

The landscape architects chose a mixed yet minimal plant palette. These selections were joined by spontaneously growing native plants, and by 2012, the initial 20 species had developed into 126. The resulting "wild" look, sought by Yu in many of

View southwest to entry bridge

Cosmos in dry pod

his designs, has been compromised in places by the government's imposition of large beds of neatly planted roses and a sizable grove of multistemmed tree of heaven (*Ailanthus altissima*). Further, upon taking over management of the park in 2013, the Tianjin city government inexplicably removed plants and furniture (though Turenscape replaced them after protests from the community). The government added uninspiring sculpture, also at odds with the original design, as well. However, Turenscape reissued a set of construction documents for a second round of planting, and numerous species have been restored to the site.

None of these alterations have tempered the community's enthusiasm for the new open space. Besides the crowds at the entrance angling for photos with my tall companion, we saw an elderly woman with her three-year-old granddaughter. The older woman told us she loves coming to the park at least once a day for a health-giving stroll and for her charge to see the ducks. Another gentleman, who commutes two hours by bus to visit the park, opined that it "is good for old and middle-aged people." His only criticisms were insufficient shade trees and the absence of backrests for the benches. But his pronounced delight and amazement, that a park so beautiful could flourish despite its inauspicious origins, eclipsed these few omissions.

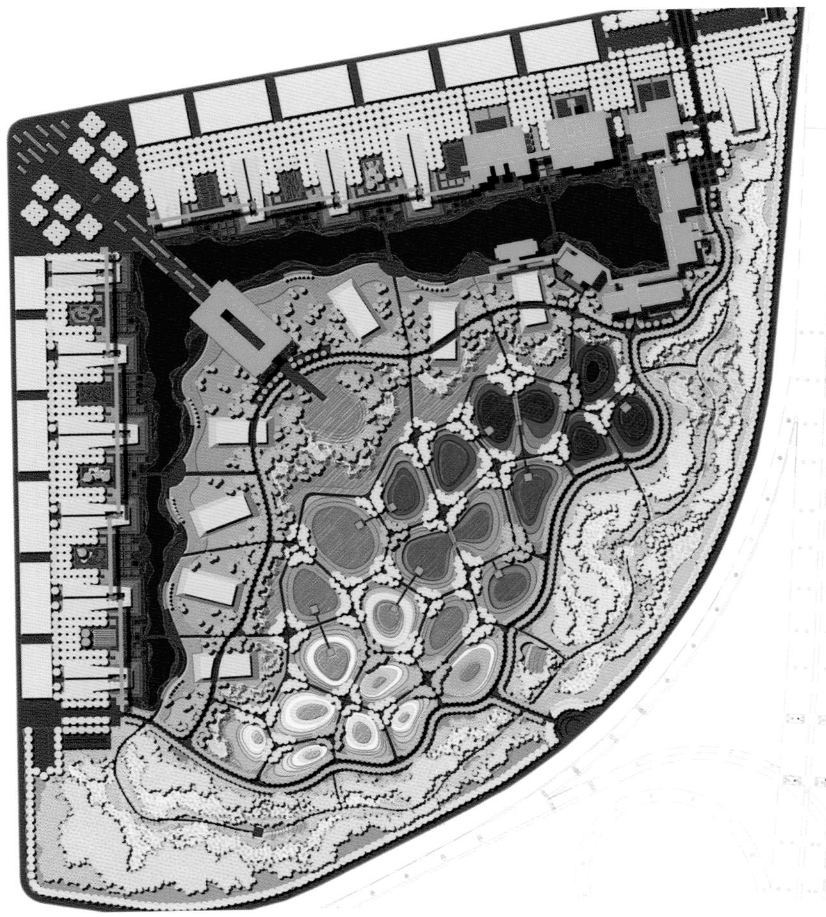

Plan

Constructed wetland pods with seating platforms

Rose plantings imposed by government

Trail through existing forest

Fuzhou Forest Trail

Fuzhou, China
2017

LOOK Architects; Fuzhou Planning, Design, and Research Institute

12 miles
cost: $50 million

Accompanied by Chua Liang Ping and Loh Kin Kit of LOOK, Alex and I embarked on the Fuzhou Forest Trail at the West Station, the only one of the ten entrances with stairs rather than ramps. The elevated trail spans the steep, 330-foot-high Jinniushan Mountain in daredevil, occasionally vertiginous loops. On the day of our visit, in late May, temperatures were in the upper nineties and humidity was high. Even the relatively gentle 6 percent incline of the walkway didn't make the climb easy.

The elevated trail winds through the forest near Fuzhou's historic Sanfang Qixiang area. Until recently, the extremely steep terrain, military camps (some still in operation), burial sites, and a quarry prevented anyone from crossing the mountain. The Forest Trail solves the problem with an urban connector, traversed by thirty thousand people every day, that also provides a sheltered corridor below to usher migrating animals between the Min Jiang River at the south and West Lake at the north.

Located 380 miles south of Shanghai and surrounded by scenic mountains, Fuzhou is a city of nearly eight million inhabitants. Part of Fujian province, it is roughly eighty miles from Taiwan across the Taiwan Strait. This proximity has discouraged heavy industry, giving Fuzhou cleaner air and water than other areas in China; in fact, it is one of the greenest cities in the country, famed for the luxuriant banyan trees that line its streets.

The municipal government selected LOOK Architects of Singapore for the project based on the firm's Alexandra Arch and Forest Walk (2008; not to be confused with this project, the Forest Trail), a pedestrian bridge and elevated walkway in the designers' home city. While the Forest Walk and the Forest Trail both furnish elevated, gridded metal walkways, there are significant differences between the two in approach, scope, and complexity. The former is much shorter (a little more than one mile as compared to nearly twelve miles), narrower (5 feet 3 inches as compared to 7 feet 10 inches), and less dramatic. In addition, the Singapore project is primarily a recreational green area, while the Fuzhou design includes a complex series of public spaces such as rest shelters, viewing decks, teahouses with washrooms, a columbarium for tombs collected from the site, and subsidiary parks—all equipped with internet connectivity and up-to-date information technology. Both trails use robust materials as a precaution against strong winds and possible earthquakes. Yet the Forest Walk is generally rectilinear, and the Forest Trail is a curving composition that responds to the form of the land and also refers to the style of traditional Chinese painting that poses the question: "How to make people wander in the mountain?"

Finally, the trail in Fuzhou is far more complicated structurally than the one in Singapore. In Fuzhou, the steel walkway is constructed with a prefabricated six-part modular system that can be adapted to different building methods and different territories; it will serve as a prototype for large-scale elevated paths in other parts of the nation. The components—three curved, two straight, and one flat—are assembled in varied configurations.

Because the steep terrain ruled out traditional building techniques, construction was executed by means of a rail track built under the metal decking. A crane on the track transported, hoisted, and attached each segment before sliding down to position the next. This procedure eliminated the need for access at ground level, which could have affected the existing vegetation. Even so, the contractor had to use horses and mules to transport certain materials, such as lightweight concrete blocks.

Local landscape architect Fuzhou Planning, Design, and Research Institute assisted with plant selection. The elevated trail, made of perforated metal interspersed with recycled bamboo panels, puts visitors in close contact with the lush vegetation of the region and fosters a richly layered vertical experience. Some portions of the trail hover slightly over the ground, where we appreciated the stems and lower trunks of the plantings; other sections are raised to the level of the tree canopy, where we admired the vibrant colors of banana palms and flowering vines. Trees arch over the path, creating dappled light, projecting patterns onto the metal walkway, and conjuring a sense of enclosure.

The air was absolutely still, and only birds, fragments of visitors' conversations, and the soft metallic sound of shifts in

Path around and walkway through bioretention basin

Route of Forest Trail, plan

Bioretention basin (formerly part of fish farm)

Moses Bridge, Halsteren, Netherlands, 2011, RO&AD Architecten

the platform broke the quiet of our aerie. All of the shaded seating areas, which are staggered regularly along the trail, were filled by younger women with baby carriages and older people seeking respite from the sun and the climb. Many of these individuals were enjoying mid-morning snacks carefully wrapped in aluminum foil.

A unique aspect of the Forest Trail is how it reveals the topography of the site. As the walkway gently rises and descends, the terrain does just the opposite. Abrupt rises and falls disclose the sequence of forest floor, canopy, and views. Trail segments in contact with the forest floor often run along the ridgeline; sections engulfed in the canopy are typically along the face of the mountain. Close to the top, we emerged from the treetops to expansive views of the city. The effect is magical.

The aluminum handrail that lines the entire trail slants outward; this gesture of openness to the surroundings immerses visitors in the park—as most Chinese gardens attempt to do. With the exception of small adjoining parks, the trail doesn't create a landscape but rather exposes the twelve miles of natural landscape that it covers.

A particularly stunning wide loop of the path descends gradually into Meifeng Hill Park, a former village fish farm that has been transformed into a bioretention basin. This aquatic environment, which is animated by ducks, geese, and vociferous frogs, captures and purifies runoff from the surrounding mountain. Its natural soft bottom gradually returns water to the land. During the wet season, the water overflows into a rocky area, slowing the runoff speed, and then into a lower, shallower basin near one of the entrances, ensuring that the civic sewer system is not overloaded.

It was a pleasure to enjoy the plump water lilies and sleeping lotus flowers of this space from a horizontal rather than an inclined surface. The weathered, steel-sided bridge that cuts across the basin at water level was particularly exhilarating. Because the passageway has low sides and is barely wide enough for two people, we felt as if we were gliding over the surface of the pond. The effect is not lost on visitors to the park, several of whom traveled from one end of the bridge to the other and back again for the benefit of the youngsters who accompanied them: the children were obviously entranced. The basin's shoreline was another popular destination, hosting families gathered to enjoy the aquatic plants and watch fish.

Other projects have attempted to achieve a similar effect. The Moses Bridge (2011) in Halsteren, the Netherlands, for example, by RO&AD Architecten is a slice through the moat of one of the fortresses in the New Dutch Waterline, Fort de Roovere. But the striking natural setting of Meifeng Hill and the placement of the bridge in the center of the spiral make it the most memorable.

Unrelated to the park's natural beauty are planters of sedum at either side of the trail. These were imposed by the government, as was an extremely tight construction schedule. Chua and Loh explained that the duration of building (one-and-a-half years) was shorter than the time for design (two years). The time frame, radically reduced even by Chinese standards, led to further construction considerations: LOOK had to work with two separate contractors, develop details on site, and source materials from multiple vendors. Happily, no sign of this haste is evident in the Forest Trail. Instead, its remarkable diversity, detail, and responsiveness to site conditions lend an immediacy and vibrancy to a singular feat.

Forest Trail and Fuzhou

Autumn color along the Forest Trail

future

What does time mean in relation to landscape? A green space is not like a building, for which a completion date remains fixed. On the contrary, parks are never completed. Landscapes take time to mature and to reveal themselves. Landscape architects, together with architects, continue to respond to changing environmental conditions and to users' needs and interests. Attractions such as playgrounds, sports fields, amusements, and food facilities are easily added to existing parks. Competition entries for the Parc de la Villette in Paris (1982) by architects Rem Koolhaas and Bernard Tschumi, the winner, made this kind of flexibility a keynote of their designs.

The four future parks included in this chapter are not yet completed. Graffiti Pier Park in Philadelphia, the smallest of the parks, and the Los Angeles River renewal, one of the largest, are still only concepts. Construction on Freshkills Park on Staten Island, another behemoth, began in 2012 but will continue until the 2030s. Only the Sanlin Eco Valley in Shanghai is currently expected to open to visitors in the 2020s.

Like James Corner's Race Street Pier (page 84), Studio Zewde's compact project in Philadelphia is part of the master plan for the rehabilitation of Philadelphia's waterfront, devised by the Delaware River Waterfront Corporation in 2011. The two abandoned industrial piers that are the starting point for Zewde's work served different functions and are given new life by distinctly different means. Tom Leader's Sanlin Eco Valley, an expansive landscape for a large residential neighborhood in Shanghai, exemplifies China's rapid urban expansion as well as the country's recent efforts toward environmental improvement.

Freshkills Park on Staten Island and the Los Angeles River project are enormous swaths of land that may be considered rehabilitation first, public parkland second; the two are comparable in many aspects. Both are completely artificial, created landscapes, dependent on complex engineering solutions. Both are controlled by rigorous government policies, among them water and soil management. Both have been shunned: Los Angeles due to greed and to an indifference to environmental considerations, Freshkills due to its prolonged hazardous nature. Both are subject to widespread community engagement. Finally, both owe their existence to local visionaries and designers who are able to see the latent qualities and inherent potential of the sites.

Landscape architects—in the West, at least—generally agree that it takes a long time to develop a park. Sara Zewde predicts that four years will be needed to complete the six acres of art space, trails, and landscape of Piers 20 and 18 (Graffiti Pier). Time is a prime influence for this designer, who has traced the history of the site to its occupation by Native Americans in 8000 BCE. She has also allotted ample opportunities to meet with the participants.

Extended undertakings in China are in sharp contrast to those in the United States and Europe. The almost six hundred acres of Sanlin Eco Valley will be nearly a decade in the making. The absence of public engagement in the design process in China fuels the amazing speed of construction there. Furthermore, construction and installation are controlled in such a way that parks appear mature even in their early years.

A frequent question for the two huge projects in this chapter is the amount of time that will be needed to conclude them. In 2020, OLIN, Frank Gehry Partners, Geosyntec, and Studio-MLA, all studying ways to improve the aesthetics, ecology, and flood control abilities of the Los Angeles River, talked of 2035 for completion. In fact, many issues, including both not having enough water and having too much water, have ignited heated controversy in Los Angeles throughout the twentieth century. It would not be an exaggeration to say that the landscape design and flood control measures that finally emerge from the contentious studies of the project will have taken over a hundred years to formulate. As for Freshkills, James Corner Field Operations began to work on the park design in 2001; in 2020, Corner anticipated that it would be complete in roughly 2035.

Among the many pleasures of a stroll in a park is the constant change—change brought about by season, by weather conditions, by the time of day. How many switches in plant species take place over the lifetime of a park? Michel Desvigne has said that his projects in Bordeaux, including the Parc aux Angéliques (page 110), will be implemented over twenty or more years. "A garden is never finished, and neither are our landscapes," he comments.

The careful preservation of historic artifacts in many of the parks in this book, including Graffiti Pier and Freshkills, reveals the designers' efforts to capture time within a changing environment. Freshkills, like Parc du Peuple de l'Herbe in Paris and Alter Flugplatz in Bonames, among others, welcomes the changes that self-propagation brings to a landscape. So yes, the completion of a designer's work is only the beginning of a park's life.

Proposed view of Canyon

Graffiti Pier Park

Philadelphia, Pennsylvania
2024

Studio Zewde

6 acres
cost: undisclosed

Pier 18, the site of the Graffiti Pier Park project, is unique among the dozens of other piers projecting into Philadelphia's Delaware River. A "coal tipper"—coal chute and trestle—operated clamorously, bringing the product of mines in central Pennsylvania to barges in the Delaware River via the Reading Railroad. The pier was shut down in 1991 primarily because of dwindling coal shipping dating from the 1950s. The second pier, number 20, accommodated a shipyard that was already inoperative in 1947; the structure is more deteriorated than Pier 18. Both piers belong to a 150-acre property owned by Conrail.

Plans to rehabilitate the site are the work of the Delaware River Waterfront Corporation, a non-profit founded in 2009 to address 1,200 acres of private and public waterside lands. In 2012, the city adopted a master plan created by Cooper Robertson, OLIN, and Kieran Timberlake, which focused on public space and waterfront trails; the plan also serves as a framework for private development to follow.

The corporation's first initiative, Race Street Pier by James Corner Field Operations, was commissioned in 2009. According to Karen Thompson, director of planning for the DRWC, the project demonstrated "who we were and what we were trying to accomplish." Modest rehabilitations of four more piers followed the Race Street project; as of 2021, there were plans (as yet unscheduled) to combine four additional piers with Pier 68 to create a wetland at the southern end of the waterfront plan. Studio Zewde won a competition for the design of Graffiti Pier Park, toward the northern end, in the summer of 2019.

Unlike most of the abandoned and inaccessible industrial sites reused for parks, Piers 18 and 20 are well frequented. Philadelphia, in the mid-1960s, was allegedly the birthplace of modern graffiti in the United States. In recent decades, aerosol art has been adopted as an important art form (as with the critical and commercial success of graffiti artist Jean-Michel Basquiat, among others). Even so, in the 1980s, the Philadelphia government proved inimical to graffiti on the streets, and the defunct Pier 18 emerged as a place where painters were able to work, as graffiti painters have done at Dequindre Cut in Detroit and Natur-Park Schöneberger Südgelände in Berlin. Providing expansive surfaces able to support art, the robust concrete trestle has been referred to as a hidden gem. Pier 20 is less visited than Pier 18: it is significantly overgrown, and large portions have been lost to the river. Because of its secluded nature, it is known colloquially as "Lovers' Pier" or "Pebble Beach."

The site's popularity, with both artists and non-artist residents, posed a difficult problem for the designers. Sara Zewde, founder of Studio Zewde, has organized barbecues and other social gatherings to encourage the public to participate in the design process, and in 2019, she invited an advisory council to comment on the best and worst things that could happen at Graffiti Pier. The clear answer: best would be to leave the site "untouched," worst would be a "new park."

It took a good deal of persuasion to convince the community, first, that rising tides caused by climate change would submerge the piers within thirty years and, second, that the area's beloved seclusion would soon be lost to development. Gradually, more constructive responses followed, among them: to make a safe and accessible space that feels "found"; to continue the expansion of art; to keep the site vegetated and passive; to keep it gritty. There was also a desire to maintain the park's connections to the neighborhood and the Delaware River Trail.

Zewde's team devised a buffering strategy to address rising tides and nearby urban construction. In the upland area, already home to an enchanting forest, the designers plan to add vegetation and trees such as box elder, red maple, river birch, sweetgum, American hornbeam, and sycamore. These species will screen the entrance to the park, which is at the junction of Cumberland and Beach Streets in the Olde Richmond neighborhood, from future developments at the southwest and northeast. Soft pathways will lead visitors the short distance from the entrance either to the two piers or to a hillside to the north where old, graffiti-covered freight cars will be installed as a reference to the past. The landscape

Existing forest

Proposed shade garden

architects will maintain much of the existing vegetation on Pier 20 and add seawalls for art.

Removal of existing bulkheads will allow the creation of an artificial, sloped intertidal landscape on either side of Pier 18. A shoreline edge with tidal marsh vegetation will adapt to rising tides, while a new wetland will absorb increased storm surges. The street directly opposite the park entrance, which passes under the I-95 highway and elevated railroad tracks, will be upgraded to improve the connection between the city and the park.

Zewde's commitment to defining local values within an urban area is clear in her concept for Graffiti Pier. The scheme addresses the importance of street art and seclusion to this community as well as environmental threats. Graffiti Pier Park promises to be not only a harmonious blend of nature and culture but also a dramatically different aesthetic experience from the other new parks on this riverside.

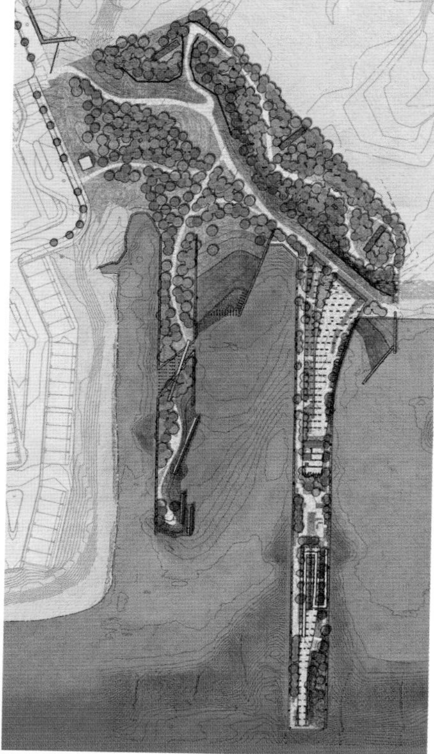

Pier 18 edge and tidal marsh

Proposed view of south trestle

Plan

View of Sanlin Mountain through arch

Sanlin Eco Valley

Shanghai, China
2022

Tom Leader Studio Landscape Architecture

596 acres
cost: undisclosed

The nearly six-hundred-acre project for Sanlin Eco Valley is by far the largest and potentially the most complex of the new riverside interventions in Shanghai (page 144). The site, formerly occupied by industrial, farming, fishing, and nursery uses, is being transformed into a model for large-scale urban development that emphasizes environmental responsiveness and ecological diversity.

The competition to design the master plan for this undertaking (2014) was initially won not by Tom Leader Studio, but by AECOM. However, two years later, the client approached TLS and commissioned the firm for the design. Well into construction in 2020, the project consists of a dense urban core of mixed residential and commercial uses surrounded by expansive green spaces that will offer diverse experiences. In addition, the development will connect to the 13.5 miles of bike and pedestrian trails that run along the Pudong side of the Huangpu River and also expand the larger regional network of green corridors, or "wedge parks," encircling Shanghai.

Sanlin Eco Valley will join 285 other ecological, or eco-, cities in China. The goal of the eco-city program is to create resilient, self-sustaining models for human settlement that respond to natural ecosystems. Although there have been many failed attempts, Luxelakes Eco City near Chengdu, one of the more successful eco-cities in China, helped us imagine what Sanlin might look like once complete. Luxelakes's bamboo forest is not dissimilar from Sanlin's recently completed cypress swamp in providing a place where people can lose themselves in nature.

The site for Sanlin has its own challenges and controversy. The Chinese government relocated nearly ten thousand people who inhabited the land to a new, nearby housing district for nearly half a million residents. The area, adjacent to the Huangpu River, is flat and prone to flooding. The parcel is subject to flood control regulations similar to those of the linear parks directly to the north. Tom Leader commented that the various agencies responsible for the management and quality of Shanghai's water were in reality concerned only with flood control. The designers proposed rebuilding the riverbank above the flood wall, creating a soft edge—in this case, a vegetated levee. Canals existing on the site will be connected to an expanded network of smaller waterways, lakes, and streams to collect and treat storm water; water will then flow into wetlands, swamps, and other designed ecologies able to handle flooding.

A major problem the design team faced was the direction of water flow into the site, which changes throughout the year. Sometimes, water from the river flows onto the tract of land; at other times, water from the canals flows into the river. Pollutants brought into the site from the river are primarily heavy metals from industrial activity; the canals carry runoff, typically water with high nitrogen levels, from the surrounding agricultural areas. The wetland system designed by the landscape architects, which Leader calls a "treatment train," will respond to this mix of pollutants with a series of terraces, each planted with material that will remove specific contaminants.

TLS's design concept is based on five artificial valleys, each with a theme: Water, Wind, Forest, Earth, and Sports. The designers sculpted the terrain, digging depressions to create emergent wetlands, cypress swamps, and even rice paddies. Within each of the valleys will be an ecology related to the theme.

Linked pedestrian and cycling paths will connect Sanlin's five valleys, and new land bridges and wildlife corridors will ensure that different species can safely traverse the open space. Park programming will relate to the valleys with an ecological research center (Water Valley), pollinator meadows (Wind Valley), amphitheater (Forest Valley), demonstration farm (Earth Valley), and active pursuits (Sports Valley).

The traditional Chinese practice of feng shui, which positions built works to take advantage of positive energy, says, "Dig a lake, build a hill," and indeed, the most impressive landform will be the hundred-foot-high Sanlin Mountain in Sports Valley. Views of this landmark will be framed by a second major component, a huge rectangular arch that shelters a large outdoor performance venue by the river. Leader has drawn other design elements from aspects of Chinese culture: "The park . . . is energized by weaving together diverse strands of Sanlin culture—symbolized by the local 'drunken lion dance.'"

Leader guided Alex and me through a five-acre demonstration park, essentially a full-scale mockup of one section.

The testing ground is a constructed cypress swamp within what will become Forest Valley. Views from a bamboo and metal walkway, elevated in case of seasonal flooding, showed how the designers manipulated soil and grading to define the different ecosystems. Undulating topography, generated via a cut-and-fill process, has resulted in indentations for the streams, small pools, and canals that will wind through the site. A fairly homogeneous forest of dawn redwood (*Metasequoia glyptostroboides*) and bald cypress (*Taxodium distichum*) provides the canopy layer.

The demonstration park is critical to the success of the project. The plot has allowed Leader's team to test planting, construction, and design strategies. It also supplies a tangible landscape experience to the client and various government authorities that makes clear the long-term goals and vision of the open green space.

Leader notes that the client's dissatisfaction with the lawns, flower beds, and ornamental trees characteristic of many parks in China spurred the choice of a city rich in ecological diversity instead. Sanlin Eco Valley achieves this goal and more, addressing environmental issues by creating a city that has been planned and engineered with landscape at the fore.

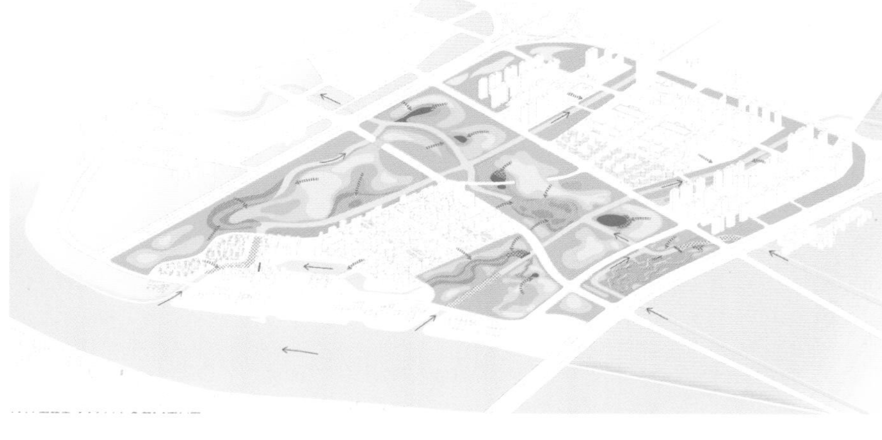

Plan

Green corridors around Shanghai

Water management diagram

Eco Bridge in Wind Valley

Trails in Forest Valley

Los Angeles River after a storm

Los Angeles River Revitalization Plan

Los Angeles, California
2007 (plan), 2028 (Taylor Yard)

Studio-MLA

42 acres (Taylor Yard)
cost: $252 million (Taylor Yard)

Los Angeles River Master Plan

Los Angeles, California
2018

OLIN, Gehry Partners

51 miles
cost: $1.4 billion

Constructing a park near a body of water is often unusually complex because of the inordinate number of laws, regulations, rules, and other considerations that govern these sites. The Los Angeles River is no exception; its intermittent hydrological state, mixed adjacencies, multiple constituencies—not to mention political infighting—have set the stage for what might become the city's largest public works project to date.

The fifty-one-mile-long Los Angeles River was originally an alluvial watercourse: its bed and banks consisted of loose sediment, and its channels were formed by the size and frequency of floods. When Southern California was sparsely settled in the early nineteenth century, large areas of the Los Angeles Basin were covered by a floodplain that contained a forest of cottonwoods and willows. But due to excessive pumping and channelization of the streams that fed into the river—largely to manage floods—the mixed ecologies of the basin vanished. In addition, the digging of wells in the Simi Hills and Santa Susana Mountains above the basin caused the springs near the heads of the waterway to disappear. By 1900, the original environment had been almost entirely eradicated.

At the same time, the city's burgeoning population required more water, and floods continued to wreak havoc during heavy rains. In 1913, an aqueduct was constructed by the city and overseen by William Mulholland, the controversial civil engineer who famously built the infrastructure for Los Angeles's water supply. It stretched from the smaller Owens River nearby to Los Angeles, but by 1931, this conduit proved inadequate, and another aqueduct, in this case extending from the immense Colorado River to the city, was built. Even though the city finally had enough water—thanks to distant sources—Los Angeles was growing beyond its resources.

The Los Angeles River runs through seventeen cities, each with its own mayor and municipal government, each of which must be dealt with individually. Furthermore, the question of how to control flooding remained contentious, eventually producing the most extensive system of controls for a river of this size in the world. These interventions were motivated not by ecological implications but by the financial concerns of farmers, who depended on the availability of water for crops and livestock, and of citizens, who needed water for residential use.

In addition to creating both a reservoir of water and a source of hydro-electric energy, the Hoover Dam (1936) was built to help control flooding. Two years after its completion, the Army Corps of Engineers initiated a highly intrusive measure for flood control: three million barrels of concrete were used to channelize the Los Angeles riverbed (1938–60) for a hundred-year flood. The procedure turned the once dynamic waterway into what is essentially an open drainage channel, as depicted in numerous films such as *Chinatown* and *Grease*.

Land along the river, which had previously been prone to flooding, was now made developable and was quickly invaded by electric transformer substations, high tension wires, warehouses, factories, jails, sanitation truck parking lots, rail lines, and railyards, not to mention freeways. Because the river's water level is typically very low for much of its course, its use as an informal dumping ground was especially conspicuous. Occupation of the shoreline, together with the dangers of flooding, has made the river largely inaccessible, removing it until relatively recently from public awareness.

In an attempt to call attention to this eyesore, local poet Lewis MacAdams published in 1995 in *Whole Earth Review* an appeal to "restore the river to its original beauty and health." He concluded by calling the rehabilitation "an artwork, an ongoing performance." MacAdams's well-intentioned appeal ignores the fact that the river's revitalization is anything but an artwork. It is, in fact, a $1.4 billion project that involves politics, sociology, ecology, and finance; and also land acquisition, real estate values, probable gentrification, and the cooperation and coordination needed between professionals in many disciplines. Above all, the fiercely contentious restoration is about hydrology.

Countless master plans for the river have been created by such bodies as Los Angeles County (1986, 1996), various cities in the region, and agencies including the LA Metro and the Bureau of Sanitation. In 2018, the county called for proposals to update the master plan; the project was awarded to engineers Geosyntec (lead consultant), landscape architect OLIN, architect Gehry Partners, and non-profit River LA. Estimates of the project's duration extend well over fifty years.

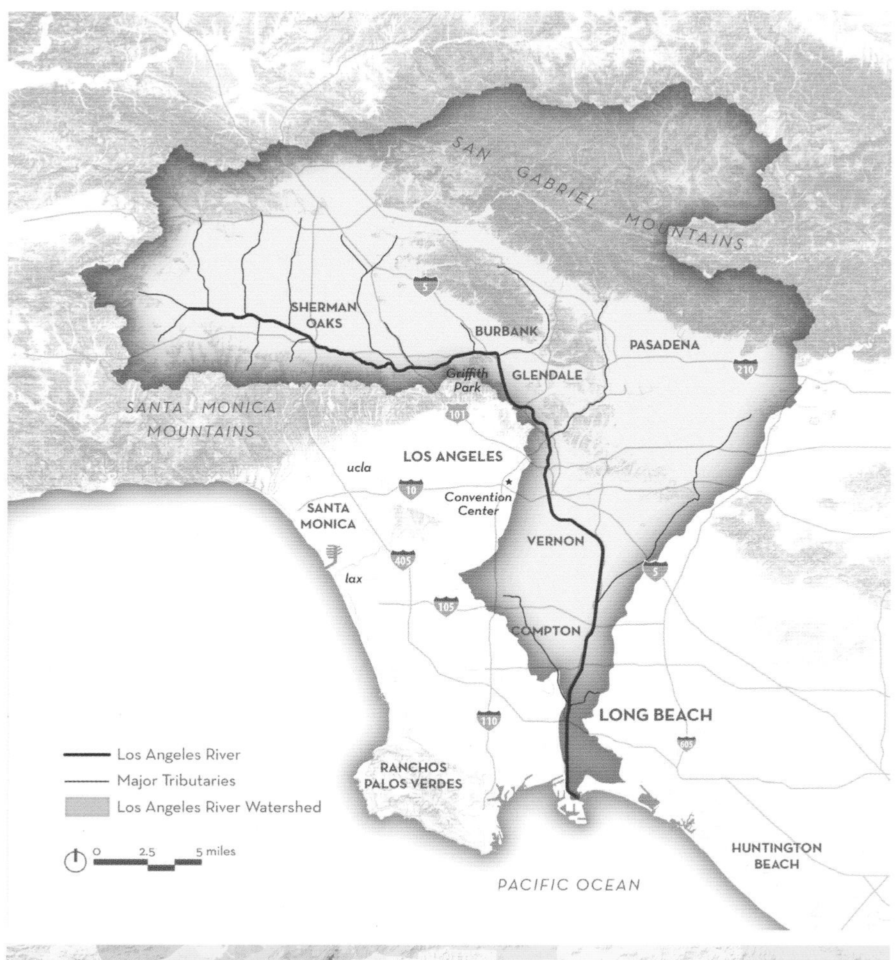

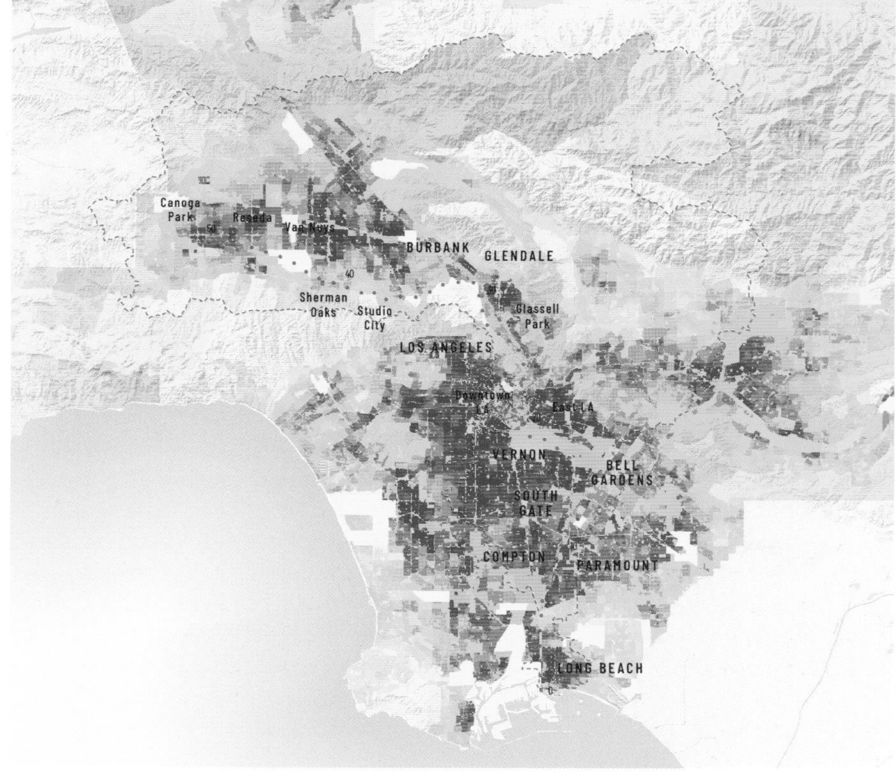

Watershed and tributaries of Los Angeles River, Studio-MLA

Analysis of access to green space, LA River Index, Gehry, OLIN et al.

In reality, Gehry's office has been working on the restoration of the Los Angeles River since 2014 as what the architect terms a conduit to other consultants. Gehry himself, local hero as well as internationally famous architect, acquainted Alex and me with the dangers of the Los Angeles River in December 2018. We stood on a protected shore in the Atwater Village neighborhood, where the effect of recent rainy days was evident: the river was a torrential flow that carried with it large tree limbs and other debris. During a hundred-year storm the river volume is 105,000 cubic feet per second and moves at a speed of 25–30 miles per hour.

Gehry is adamant that the river needs to satisfy flooding concerns first, with minimal or no alteration of the channel itself, and is instead focusing on discrete sites adjacent to the river. His office, along with River LA, OLIN, and Geosyntec, has synthesized years of data and a set of planning tools in the online LA River Index. The resource, which views the river as a connective open space for the nine million people who live near it, is intended to provide a "single, equitable framework for use in evaluating the river's possibilities." Additionally, the team has designed 130 plans for the project, adding material that was missing from previous plans, providing more robust data analysis, updating planting guidelines, inserting statistics about the various climates along the riverside given changes in elevation (780 feet), and studying issues of housing and social and environmental justice.

When Alex and I visited Los Angeles in mid-February 2020, we met again with Gehry and also with award-winning landscape architect Mia Lehrer, founder of Studio-MLA and co-author of the Los Angeles River Revitalization Master Plan in 2007, who since 2000 has devoted most of her career to improving the river. Her office has developed proposals for different riverside areas in the city, including Piggyback Yard, Ballona and Compton Creeks, and Baldwin Hills.

The two designers view the river from different perspectives. Lehrer sees it as a widespread system of water basins and hundreds of miles of tributaries; Gehry considers it as a single entity that should be preserved and also added to with such pieces as a park and a cultural center. Gehry's proposal could potentially be achieved more quickly but would not necessarily address flooding beyond the hundred-year flood mark; Lehrer's multiple projects are more complex and require policy changes but could help solve future flooding problems. In both cases, the concepts are tentative and may change over time. Each city has jurisdiction over its own land adjacent to the river, but only Los Angeles County and the Army Corps of Engineers can approve a project affecting changes in the actual channel, as Lehrer's do.

It is not by chance that the Studio-MLA office, an industrial shed that Lehrer renovated for herself and her team, is located beside rail lines that overlook the river. Upon entering the shed, we were struck by a line drawing of the Los Angeles River that dominates the floor of the reception area. The designer began our visit with a thirty-minute film about conditions in the river's watershed, which includes eighty-four cities and four counties in an 870-square-mile area. The presentation also touched on some of the studio's projects alongside the river.

A feasibility plan for Piggyback Yard (2013) was an early vision for rehabilitating the river. The project repurposes a railroad facility in the neighborhood of Boyle Heights as a mixed-use development with eighty acres of parkland and habitat. The river would be able to invade portions of the park during storms and then recede once flood waters subsided. Lehrer has suggested buying from private owners land parcels subject to flooding and therefore not suitable for development. The unrealized plan is similar in concept to Kongjian Yu's Sponge City, used in Tianjin's Qiaoyuan Wetland Park (page 290) and elsewhere, in which wetlands store rainwater that can recharge aquifers and be used when needed.

In 2017, the city's Bureau of Engineering selected Lehrer and engineers WSP, working in collaboration with non-profit environmental equity group Mujeres de la Tierra, for the transformation of Taylor Yard. The former Southern Pacific classification yard, which runs beside the Cypress Park and Glassell Park neighborhoods and across the river from Elysian Valley, is a particularly interesting part of the waterway, one of the few areas that has retained trees and vegetation. The soft (concrete-free) bottom allowed the formation of small islands and subsequently the growth of vegetation.

The heavily contaminated forty-two-acre parcel, which was vacated by the railroad in the mid-1980s, was purchased by the city for $60 million. In 2019, the MLA team proposed three alternative schemes—Island, Soft Edge, and the Yards—to re-create the site as habitat and green space; in 2020, Island was selected for further development. Once remediation of the polluted soil is completed, gentle hills will be planted with oaks and sycamores. A viewing platform that will give views of the river and the site is planned by the Spanish architecture firm SelgasCano prior to the 2028 opening.

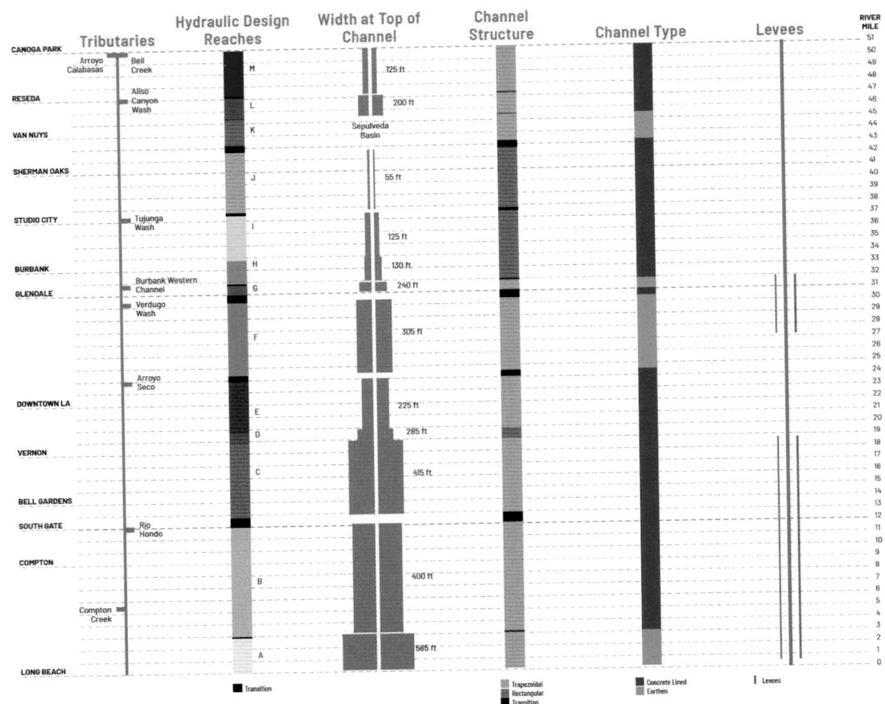

Analysis of Los Angeles River, LA River Index, Gehry, OLIN et al.

Alex and I visited the river's shore north of Taylor Yard with Lehrer on a dazzling, typically Southern California morning. The designer told us that cyclists have been using the asphalt trail along the riverside since 2010, and we noted that it has remained popular for bikers, joggers, and pedestrians. It is one of several such trails that have developed beside the waterway. The numerous small cafés that inhabit the former industrial buildings beside the trail in this area were crowded with lively young people.

Los Angeles's historically low-density residential areas are one reason why parks and public green space have never been a priority. However, continued growth and greater density (along with demands for increased environmental responsibility) have encouraged the city to seek ways in which green infrastructure can replace gray. Excitement about the Taylor Yard park is therefore understandable, and plans to improve the surrounding area have created a land rush and soaring real-estate prices, as similar plans have in other cities and countries.

When we saw Gehry during our February 2020 trip, he called our attention to a statement from the Army Corps of Engineers: that planting in the riverbed, to renaturalize it as advocated by the Friends of the LA River, could cause the river to overflow its banks to an area of two to seven times its current width in a flood. To follow through on this type of planting would occasion the displacement of a hundred thousand people and vastly increase the amount of land at risk of flooding, currently at 3,300 parcels in a hundred-year flood—not to mention hike the cost of flood damage insurance. The OLIN/Gehry team agrees with the Army Corps' assertions for much of their proposal yet is amenable to keeping the native Western sycamore, cottonwood, and willow trees that are currently growing in the river (provided that invasive species can be removed).

Rather than tamper with the volatile conditions of the water's flow, OLIN and Gehry have suggested "platform parks," or landscaped bridges, that would accommodate sports, social, and entertainment facilities. A pilot project shows a platform one to two hundred feet wide over a part of the river that is about 450 feet across; the resulting expanse would be between one and two acres. Similar to highway caps, these structures are in harmony with the pre–World War II concrete bridges built by the local engineer Merrill Butler that span the river at regular intervals. Mark Hanna, senior principal water resources engineer at Geosyntec, explains that the bridge decks would be supported by long walls parallel to the course of the river rather than by columns, which would create turbulence. OLIN has suggested slight modifications to the channel, including terraces and stairs down to the water.

As important for Gehry as improving the river's appearance, ecological condition, and accessibility is addressing the pollution, health hazards, and shortages of housing and cultural resources in underserved communities within the more southerly twenty-three neighborhoods that line the waterway. Hanna notes that gentrification pushes out the residents most in need of a park. He explained that the 2018 LA River Master Plan provides a toolkit for stabilized housing that incorporates tax increment financing and low-income housing, as well as consideration of land banking. The plan demonstrates that at least 25 percent of housing stock can remain low-income or subsidized. The Gehry team has identified a property in downtown Los Angeles where new high-income residential projects could be constructed to help subsidize low-income housing.

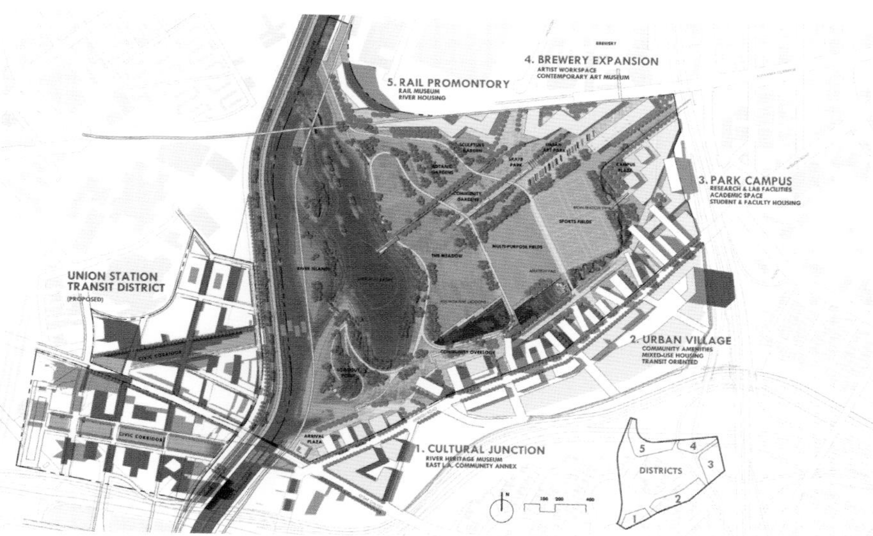

Piggyback Yard, plan, Studio-MLA

Aerial rendering, Studio-MLA

The architect drove us to the confluence of the Los Angeles River and one of its tributaries, Rio Hondo, in the South Gate area, where his firm has designed the new SELA Cultural Center. Programming for the building, which will have a quasi-industrial aesthetic, will include representatives of Gustavo Dudamel's Youth Orchestra, Benjamin Millepied's L.A. Dance Project, and art exhibitions curated by the Los Angeles County Museum of Art.

The remarkable improvements contemplated by the OLIN/Gehry team depend on water conditions, the many complexities of which we only began to understand during our meetings with Hanna and with Jessica Henson, an associate at OLIN. The essential difficulty of restoring the Los Angeles River, says Hanna, is that its course has shifted and been altered many times. Sometimes the river turned west near downtown, emptying into the sea at Playa del Rey; at other times it flowed south, joined the San Gabriel River, and reached the oceans as it does today at Wilmington Lagoon.

Hanna explained that each type of storm, depending on its severity, requires different measures that don't always overlap. For example, storm water gardens can handle twenty-five- and fifty-year floods, but not hundred-year floods. The goal is to have the river hold water back, clean it, and then release it, but in a hundred-year event there is just too much water flowing during too short a period of time.

SITE FEATURE
1 SYCAMORE GROVE
2 DISCOVERY PLAY
3 MEADOW
4 WILLOW UPLAND
5 LOW FLOW WALKWAY
6 ISLAND ECO RESERVE/LAB
7 RIVER EXHIBITION PAVILION
8 FLOATING ISLANDS
9 RIVER DECK
10 NATIVE COLLECTIONS
11 THE CROSSING
12 SCULPTURE GARDEN
13 AMPHITHEATER
14 ARBORETUM
15 VIEWING DECK
16 PARKING
17 TAYLOR YARD PEDESTRIAN BRIDGE

4.5 ACRES OF PROPOSED BUILDING FOOTPRINT
*2 STORY BUILDING
**3 STORY BUILDING

1 PARK OFFICE/ RANGER STATION*
2 KAYAK LAUNCH/ CAFE
3 RECREATIONAL CAMPING + RESTROOM
4 YOUTH ENRICHMENT CENTER
5 CAFE
6 RESEARCH BUILDING*
7 MUSEUM/CULTURAL CENTER*
8 PUBLIC FACILITY (PARKING BELOW)**
9 RESTAURANT
10 KAYAK LANDING / CAFE / KIOSK

SAN FERNANDO ROAD
RIVER PARK APARTMENTS
SOTOMAYOR LEARNING ACADEMIES
RIO DE LOS ANGELES
G1 BOWTIE PARCEL
LOS ANGELES RIVER GREENWAY TRAIL
5 ACRES
BLAKE AVE.
RIVERSIDE DRIVE
0 300 600 ft

Taylor Yard, Island scheme, plan, Studio-MLA

Current view from First Street

Proposed view from First Street, Studio-MLA

Proposed platform park, plan, OLIN/Gehry

Proposed platform park, rendering, OLIN/Gehry

Surface water is another problem. Measure W, a motion passed by the voters of Los Angeles County in 2018, allocated about $285 million to provide safe, clean water and will involve construction of green streets, pocket parks, and infiltration fields. As we saw with Gehry, at the turbulent flow in the Atwater Village area, the aftermath of rainstorms can bring about huge volumes of water at high speeds. Annually, the river carries 90 billion tons of water into the Pacific Ocean, 28 billion gallons of which could be captured and stored. Henson described one of the options the team is considering: a bypass tunnel under Griffith Park (along the watercourse in the eastern Santa Monica Mountains) that could move twenty thousand cubic feet of water per second. This strategy is similar to that implemented to relieve flooding along Austin's Waller Creek (page 90).

The Los Angeles River has not, in fact, flooded since the 1980s. Nevertheless, Henson was surprised, in her study of the watershed hydrology, to find reports from 1991–92 indicating that some sections of the river had not been addressed since the 1950s. Additionally, the Army Corps of Engineers stopped monitoring conditions in the upper part of the river in the 1990s, furthering its neglect.

Everyone with whom we discussed the renewal of the river referred to earlier reports and studies. Hanna has reviewed 140 master plans, including "Parks, Playgrounds, and Beaches for the Los Angeles Region," a plan devised in 1927 by Olmsted Brothers (Frederick Law Olmsted's successor firm) in collaboration with Harland Bartholomew & Associates. The thoughtful proposal, though endorsed by such Hollywood notables as Mary Pickford and Cecil B. DeMille, failed to find political champions.

Henson goes so far as to reject the idea of a deterministic master plan. She calls her work a "long-term adaptation framework that looks eighty years into the future to see what the channel will need to be." The most encouraging aspect of this Herculean effort is the coordination of disciplines and teamwork it has inspired in the face of two different concepts.

Aerial rendering

Freshkills Park

Staten Island, New York
2012, ongoing

James Corner Field Operations

2,315 acres
cost: undisclosed

Freshkills Park is the ultimate rehabilitation and the ultimate memorialization of what James Corner, its designer, calls the "ruins of engineering history." Most of the parks presented here remediate assaults on nature, but the one at Freshkills was a more troubling assault than most. First, at over 2,300 acres, or four square miles, in western Staten Island (and then known as Fresh Kills), it was designated as the largest landfill in the world beginning in 1986. The 150 million tons of waste was allegedly one of the few constructions on Earth visible from space besides the Great Wall of China. Second, the impact this huge dump had on the reputation of Staten Island for fifty-three years was unforgiving.

Staten Island's homogeneous, politically conservative population is unique in New York City. Shopping malls and housing complexes constitute much of the built environment. From 1847 to 1866, Frederick Law Olmsted lived on the island on 125-acre Tosomock Farm. He carried out experiments with agriculture as well as with fruit trees, cedars of Lebanon, black walnut, and other species of trees, and it was here that he completed, with the architect Calvert Vaux, Greensward, the competition-winning design for Central Park.

The name Fresh Kills comes from the Dutch word *kille*, or "channel," and indeed, the area consisted originally of tidal creeks and coastal marshes. The refuse heap opened in 1948 near a residential area in what was then considered useless swamp. Easy access to waterways allowed enormous barges to ship in garbage, which was loaded onto trucks and deposited on one of the landfill's four huge mounds. With development, people moved closer to the dump; those within proximity suffered from its stench as well as from the sight of prison-like fencing the Department of Sanitation installed around the site, the invasion of plastic garbage bags into nearby trees and open space, and the swarms of scavenging seagulls. Staten Islanders were also concerned, as they continued to be for several years after the landfill was closed, by the possible health hazards produced by methane gas emitted from the waste as well as by other pollutants.

Staten Island has been called the "forgotten borough," in part because of its historic lack of connectivity to the other four boroughs of New York City. The first bridges to Staten Island were built only in 1928—the Goethals Bridge and the Outerbridge Crossing, both over Arthur Kill Strait—and 1931—the Bayonne Bridge over Kill Van Kull Strait. The Verrazano-Narrows Bridge, a direct connection with Brooklyn, did not open until 1964. By contrast, the King's Bridge (connecting Manhattan and the Bronx, now demolished) was built in 1693, the Brooklyn Bridge (Manhattan and Brooklyn) in 1883, and the Queensboro Bridge (Manhattan and Queens) in 1909.

Protests about Fresh Kills—including three unsuccessful actions for Staten Island to secede from New York City—were equally forgotten, or at least ineffective, over more than half a century. It took the intervention of Mayor Rudolph Giuliani, Governor Michael Pataki, and Borough President Guy Molinari in 1996 to finally rid the borough of this disgrace.

After the pols succeeded in closing the dump, a new cast of characters introduced the unexpected idea of replacing Fresh Kills with a park, and it soon became clear that a public green space on the former landfill would be a boon to the borough and to the city. Ellen Ryan, at the time the director of planning issues for the Municipal Arts Society, admits that for that group Staten Island was "foreign territory, the hinterlands." Despite this earlier attitude, the MAS became what Ryan describes as "the glue" between several of the city's agencies in an effort to fundraise for and organize a competition to choose a designer for the project. The biggest hurdle was conveying the constraints, complexity, and scope of the site. Considering the daunting problem of making the area toxin-free, there was a pressing need for technical and design expertise "to make people see the opportunity."

In 1996, the Sanitation Department, which controls Fresh Kills, received permission from the New York State Department of Environmental Conservation to study remediation of the heavily contaminated site. The study paved the way for a complex process of decontamination that seals the landfill and also collects and treats methane, the combustible gas produced by the decomposition of organic matter. A multilayer capping system covers the waste, ensuring that it cannot pollute groundwater. Methane is captured by an apparatus that incorporates gas well heads, pumps, three flare stations, and pipes for gas transport. The collected gas is used to heat twenty-two thousand Staten Island residences. A leachate treatment plant at the southwest edge of the site manages any runoff from the landfill, separating liquids from solids and discharging cleansed liquid into the Arthur Kill. Storm water is captured in large retention ponds, which function as wetlands. During 2012's Hurricane Sandy, the four mounds and the wetlands protected Staten Island's commercial corridor.

The design competition for Fresh Kills was initiated on September 5, 2001, just six days before the 9/11 terrorist attacks. Three finalists were announced that December, and eighteen months later, in June 2003, James Corner Field Operations was announced as the winner. The firm would receive the commission for its best-known project, the High Line in Manhattan, a year later. Field Operations' scheme for Staten Island showed bands of woodlands, which provide wind shelter, surrounding the mounds and wet and dry prairies along the mound's steep slopes.

To demonstrate that change was in store for the borough, and to stimulate interest in plans for a green space, New York's Department of Parks and Recreation chose three sites peripheral to Fresh Kills to show the potential scope of transformation. The first, Schmul Park (2012), to the northwest of the landfill area, was built on farmland deeded to the city by the Schmul family. Within the park are sports fields and an exceptionally creative playground—a renovation by Field Operations of a 1939 park. Artificial mounds with brightly colored rubber-clad play surfaces (unfortunately, badly deteriorating) are favorites with small children; dancing water jets add to the park's gaiety. Close at hand is a neat, modern comfort station designed by BKSK Architects; its curving form mimics the graceful arcs in the park's design. An elegant, long pedestrian avenue planted with alternating oak and sweet gum trees is paved in permeable concrete pavers. When the park opened, the wide walkway, lined with sturdy wood and metal benches, was nestled among a mix of native grasses, but the community felt the meadow aesthetic was too messy, and the plantings have since been removed in favor of mown strips of lawn.

A second project, the New Springville Greenway, was commissioned in 2014 by the Department of Sanitation and designed by the city's in-house designers. The three-mile-long stretch runs parallel to the eight-lane Richmond Avenue, the island's main commercial corridor, and connects with the Staten Island Greenbelt. The greenbelt, which is adjacent to Freshkills, consists of 2,800 acres of open land in the center of the borough with thirty-five miles of trails. These trails will connect with new ones at Freshkills, adding to the network of paths for walkers, joggers, and cyclists. The 2,800 acres of the greenbelt combined with the 2,315 acres of Freshkills add up to a park system nearly six times the size of Central Park.

Owl Hollow soccer fields, the third project, was also originated by designers working for the city. Twenty acres in size, Owl Hollow sits just inside the southwestern boundary of Freshkills Park and provides sports fields, landscaped areas, and a surrounding footpath.

Designed by Field Operations, the $34 million, 233-acre North Park will occupy a tiny sliver of land within the vast Freshkills landscape. Organized as a large arc, the park's main path will allow visitors to move through a seed nursery, which will grow material to be used later throughout Freshkills, before finally arriving at a tall observation tower. A twenty-one-acre portion of the green space is scheduled to open in 2021.

Eloise Hirsh, administrator of Freshkills for the Parks Department and president of the Freshkills Park Alliance, says that 70 percent of the cost for the first section of North Park was for a hundred thousand cubic yards of clean soil—soil that is free of, or contains low levels of, heavy metals, pesticides, and other contaminants that could harm users. Of the four mounds (as high as 220 feet at the west), only the East Mound was covered with approved soil from Queens, New Jersey, and Pennsylvania. Soil on the North Mound was tested by the Freshkills Park Alliance working with the state Department of Environmental Conservation and, except for limited areas, was approved for public access. Even so, Corner says the compacted clay soil is "atrocious" and proposes an alternative: building soil organically. The process, which requires eight years and avoids the need for import, consists of growing plants for six months, plowing them under, and repeating.

There are other challenging aspects of the site. The landforms sink constantly. Corner likens them to "deflated balloons"; the engineers have had to fill them in with clay and regrade. Steep slopes make it difficult to build accessible paths.

The decontamination and reconstruction of Freshkills is subject to intense regulation by an endless number of state and city agencies, which insist on innumerable tests. Official approval is required to simply walk on the site. The park affords an interesting comparison with those in China. In both places,

Fresh Kills landfill when active

Main Creek

Landfill cap, diagram

Plan

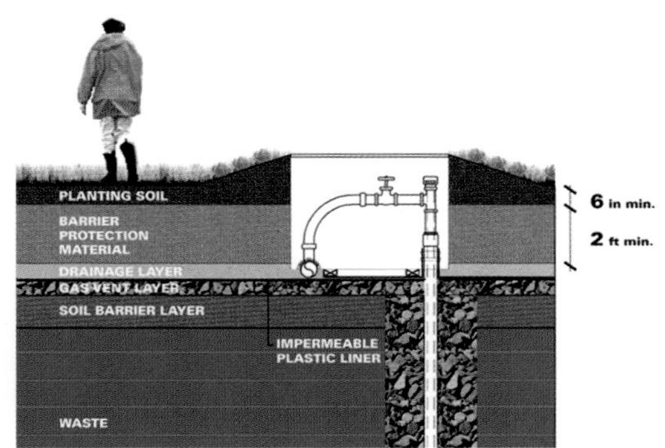

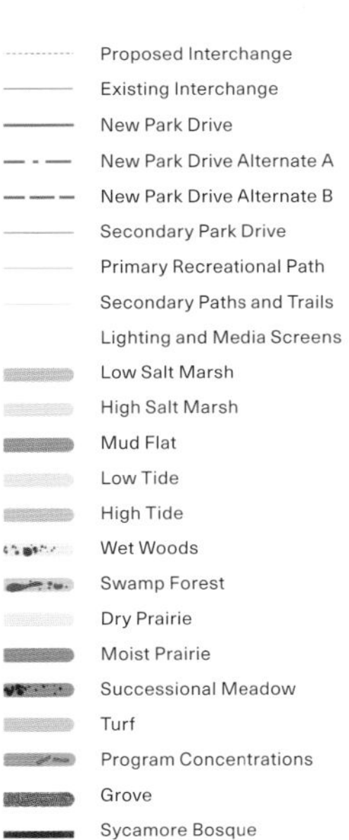

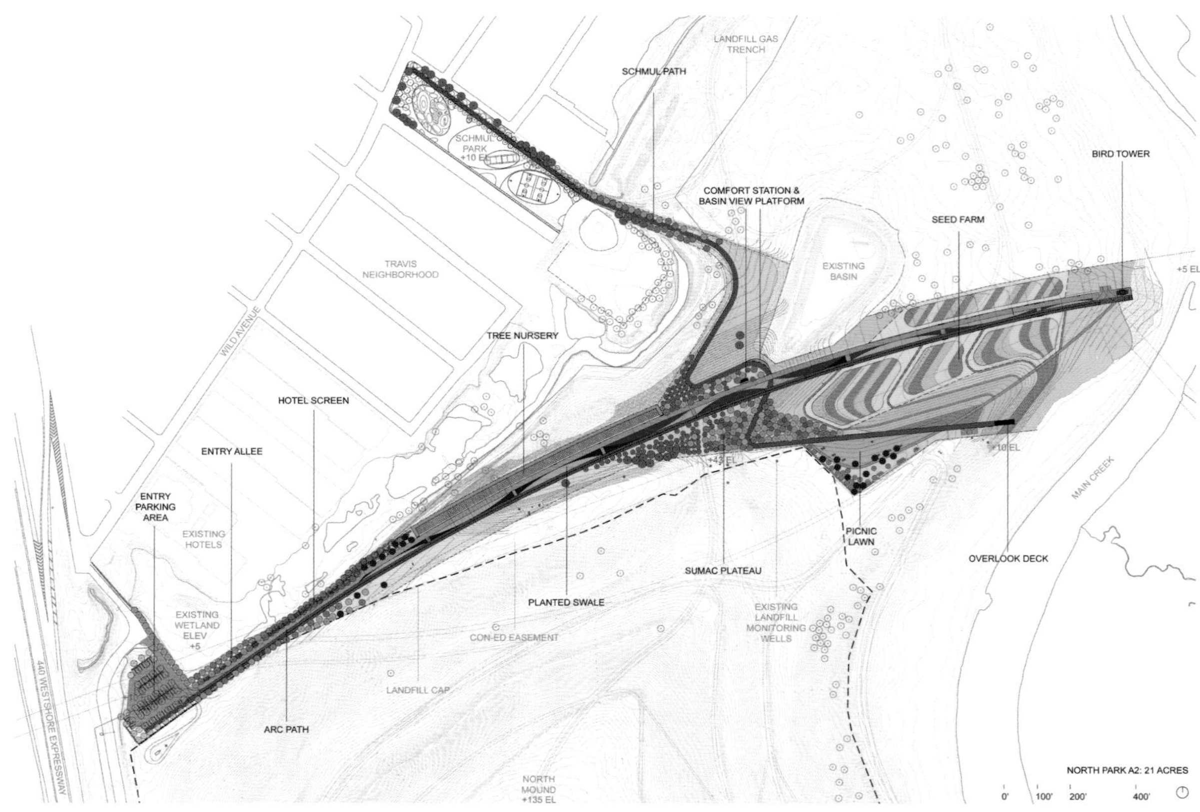

North Park, plan

Bird tower, North Park, rendering

officials want to show achievement at the end of their terms. Because the Staten Island open space will take years to complete, local authorities will receive no credit and are therefore reluctant to commit to it.

Alex and I met with Corner (and his associate Yan Shuo, who guided us around China) via Zoom in June 2020. Corner mentioned the unusual ongoing nature of the project: "It is not a design project. It is not about a conclusion, but about adaptive management." His work will last another fifteen years, he estimates. He maintains that there will not be significant differences in appearance between "completed" areas, such as North Park, and the rest of Freshkills. Work on the open space is "more like a farmer cultivating land" than like traditional landscape architecture, and he concluded early on that what was needed was a strategy derived from engagement, akin to America's historic pragmatism about working the land, and not a definitive plan.

The French landscape architect Gilles Clément, in his *Manifeste du Tiers paysage* (Manifesto of the Third Landscape), proposes a similar approach to abandoned urban and rural sites, transitional spaces, shores, and comparable landscapes. Clément, who in 1992 designed Parc André Citroën in Paris on the grounds of a former automobile factory, sees these sites as entrusted to nature alone:

> In an ecosystem that is outside human control, all these energies are generated only by plants and animals, of course, and also by the climate, the soil. In the end, everything, absolutely everything, interacts, with the aim of creating a balance . . . Human intervention often creates traumas, interruptions of the predatory chain, of the relations between beings, and this creates an imbalance in the systems.

GTL Landschaftsarchitektur adopted a parallel tactic for Alter Flugplatz in Bonames (page 62).

Of the vegetation at Freshkills, Corner said in 2020:

> Around the year 2000, before any work started on the park, there was very little biodiversity—mostly *Phragmites australis*, a very aggressive, invasive, tall weed grass that grows in wet soils, typically in swales and around wetlands. On the mounds, there was a grass mix of fescues, rye, and Kentucky bluegrass, good for stabilizing slopes and protecting them from erosion, but fairly aggressive and offering little habitat for other species. There were a few stray species of more native plants, originating from birds mainly, including poplar, locust, birch, sumac, tree of heaven, and red cedar. But these were few and far between, and they were threatened by cutback from the engineers as part of the landfill maintenance program.
>
> Today, many species occupy the site, including species proposed for North Park for grasslands and wetlands, as well as shrubs and trees including various oaks, willows, sycamores, sumacs, red cedars, white pines, dogwoods, serviceberries, and sassafras. Birds and other animals continue to bring in seeds, which leads to further biodiversity through natural succession.

Corner addressed the profusion of *Phragmites* by bringing in a herd of goats to feed on it, among other efforts. Also in regard to invasive species—the abundant mugwort, Chinese bush clover, and Japanese knotweed we noticed on the site—Hirsh told us that there was as yet no comprehensive plan to control them.

I visited Freshkills in May 2017 with Robin Geller from the Sanitation Department and Megan Moriarty from the Parks Department, and I returned in April 2019 and July 2020 with Alex and Eloise Hirsh. Each of these visits renewed my amazement at finding myself in an immense expanse of grass-covered hills and trees. Only twelve miles from the southern tip of Manhattan, the park feels like it could be hundreds of miles away. It was equally surprising to learn that most of the vegetation was self-propagating. Natural creeks are clean enough to use for boating and catch-and-release fishing, unlike the polluted Arthur Kill, the channel between Staten Island and New Jersey.

Each mound has a distinctive character: North has views over wetlands to the distant Bayonne Bridge, Goethals Bridge, and the Manhattan skyline; South overlooks Arthur Kill; West contains materials collected from the 9/11 terrorist attacks on the World Trade Center; and East offers a prospect over scenic Richmond Creek and the million-plus-square-foot Staten Island Mall.

The huge passenger jets taking off from Newark Liberty International Airport are one with the massive scale of the landscape. The innumerable gas head wells poking up amid wildflowers in the fields, the silo-like flare stations (expected to be retired) for gas treatment, and the leachate treatment plant are ubiquitous reminders of the former occupant of the site. But upstaging this past history are vast grasslands, stands of trees,

woodland edges, wetlands, and natural tidal creeks. The habitat diversity has attracted a large number of animal species. The grasslands are particularly valuable for birds, including rarely seen grasshopper sparrows, which have unexpectedly flocked to the area, and ospreys.

Freshkills will have an extensive programming plan, including art. The first permanent piece in the park will be *Landing* by Mierle Laderman Ukeles, since 1977 the unsalaried artist-in-residence of the Department of Sanitation. Collaborating with architect WXY Studio and engineer URS Corporation, Ukeles devised a soaring concrete and metal viewing platform (*Overlook*) and two earthworks (*Earth Bench* and *Earth Triangle*). Connecting the three components will be a 500-foot-long, 32-foot-high bridge.

Regrettably, there are no plans to implement Corner's own elegant earthwork, a memorial to the 9/11 attacks. Although the Fresh Kills landfill was closed in 2001, it reopened briefly to receive debris from the collapse of the World Trade Center, which may have contained human remains. To honor this possibility, and to commemorate those who survived the assault, Corner proposed a sculptural landform that matches the dimensions of the two towers. He envisioned visitors walking through this remembrance, ultimately reaching a view back to the original site in Manhattan. The landscape architect remarks that the cost of the memorial, along with the twenty-year time lag and the political and social implications, makes it unlikely that the tribute will be realized.

Two magnificent parks, both on former landfills—and therefore both subject to the same costly (approximately $250 million for each one) and time-consuming remediation as Freshkills Park—offer useful comparisons. Brookfield Park (2017), also on Staten Island, is downstream from Freshkills, so close that much of its wetland water flows into Richmond Creek. Shirley Chisholm Park (2019) overlooks Jamaica Bay in Brooklyn.

When these refuse dumps were being shut down in the early 1980s, the land they occupied was the subject of complex negotiations among city, state, and federal ownership. John McLaughlin, now a managing director at New York City's Department of Environmental Protection, worked on a design for the 258-acre Brookfield Park (which he calls "the baby Freshkills") for seventeen years. He created rolling hills and wetlands; imported seventeen thousand trees, which will develop into forests; and sowed native grasses.

Phragmites

Kayak tours on Main Creek

Landing, rendering, Mierle Laderman Ukeles

View over North Mound with
South Mound in distance

McLaughlin was also involved with the slightly later, state-owned Chisholm Park, named for the New York representative, the first Black woman elected to Congress. Of the five boroughs of New York City, Brooklyn has the least open space per capita, and McLaughlin saw an opportunity to introduce a natural setting to the dense urban environment.

The Brooklyn green space was designed by Michael Van Valkenburgh Associates; the budget—$30 million for 407 acres—was minimal in comparison to that for most parks. Matt Urbanski, the lead designer, remarked "It's like Kansas" as he guided us around the stunning public green space. Although panoramic views over Jamaica Bay may be the park's most valuable asset, the park itself is impressive. Among its offerings are a welcoming main entrance overseen by a large mural of Chisholm; destinations such as snappy new prefabricated metal piers and the Skybowl lookout; spots outfitted with colorful picnic tables, benches, and parasols; and ample parking. Gravel paths wind through expansive grasslands sprinkled with wildflowers and woody trees and shrubs.

The three former landfills share a natural, even messy look. McLaughlin notes that the driving force for the new aesthetic is ecology; human considerations are secondary. Yet despite their resemblance to a midwestern prairie, all three parks were created artificially. Hirsh describes Freshkills as "engineered gorgeousness," a phrase that might also characterize Brookfield and Shirley Chisholm Parks.

Freshkills is a "demonstration of our capacity to fix things; to restore nature if you partner with it," says Hirsh. Certainly our vertiginously changing world will provide ever more obsolete infrastructures in need of fixing. It is heartening to imagine that nature might be the fixer.

Brookfield Park

Shirley Chisholm State Park, Skybowl lookout, Michael Van Valkenburgh Associates

Entrance to Shirley Chisholm State Park

Overleaf: Freshkills Park, grass-lands with view to Manhattan

Drawings and selected plant palettes are included to provide further information regarding design intent and landscape character.

DEQUINDRE CUT

Detroit, Michigan

Section at Lafayette Street

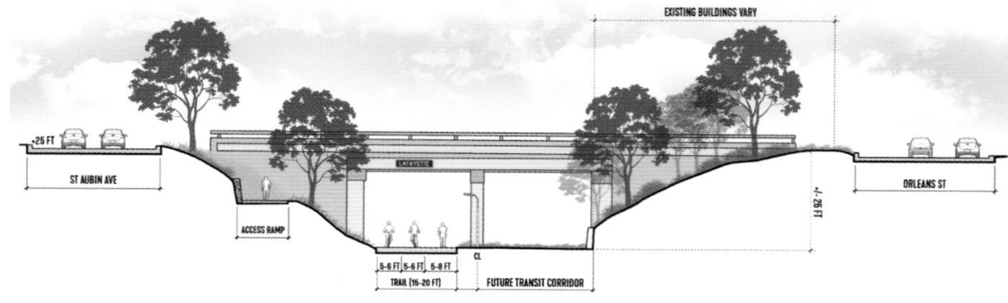

KLYDE WARREN PARK

Dallas, Texas

TREES
Betula nigra 'Dura-Heat'
Pistacia chinensis
Quercus macrocarpa
Quercus shumardii
Quercus virginiana 'Cathedral'
Taxodium ascendens
Ulmus parvifolia 'Allee'

SHRUBS
Agave havardiana
Agave lophantha
Agave 'Mr. Ripple'
Agave toumeyana var. *bella*
Hesperaloe parviflora
Leucophyllum frutescens
Morella cerifera
Salvia leucantha
Yucca arkansana

PERENNIALS
Achillea millefolium
Conoclinium greggii
Dietes iridioides
Equisetum hyemale
Glandularia bipinnatifida
Lantana montevidensis
Liatris spicata
Melampodium leucanthum
Perovskia atriplicifolia
Phlox pilosa
Physostegia virginiana
Salvia farinacea
Salvia greggii
Scutellaria suffrutescens
Symphyotrichum oblongifolium

GRASSES
Andropogon virginicus
Eragrostis curvula
Miscanthus sinensis 'Adagio'
Muhlenbergia capillaris
Muhlenbergia lindheimeri
Muhlenbergia reverchonii
Nassella tenuissima
Poa arachnifera
Setaria scheelei
Sorghastrum nutans

PARK OVER-BOS

Breda, Netherlands

Shrubs and vines, concept diagram

Trees, concept diagram

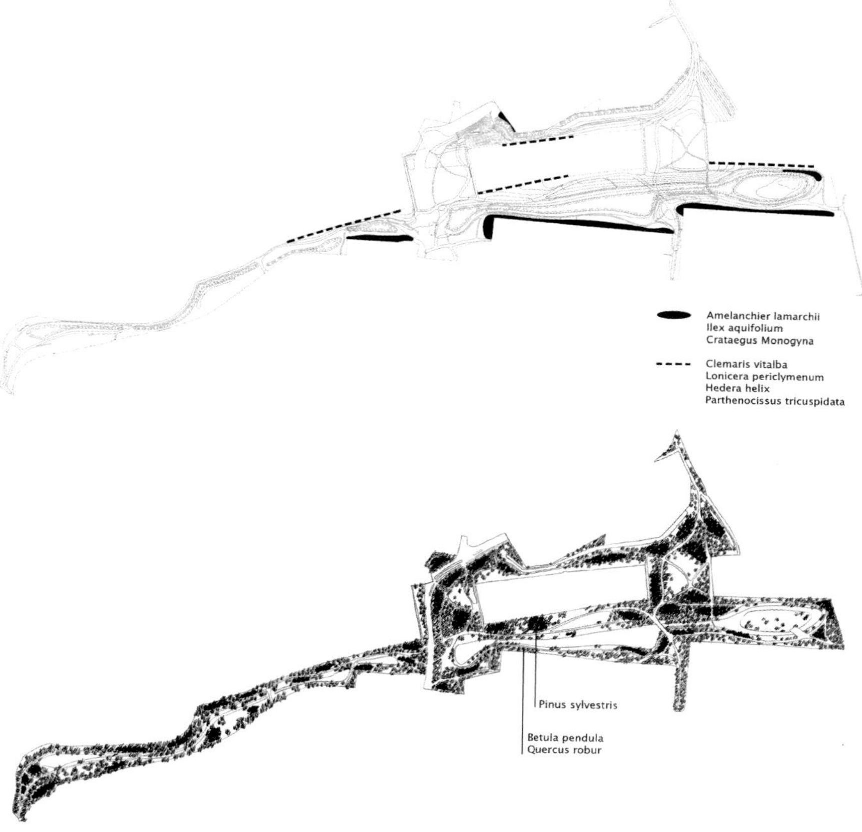

XUHUI RUNWAY PARK

Shanghai, China

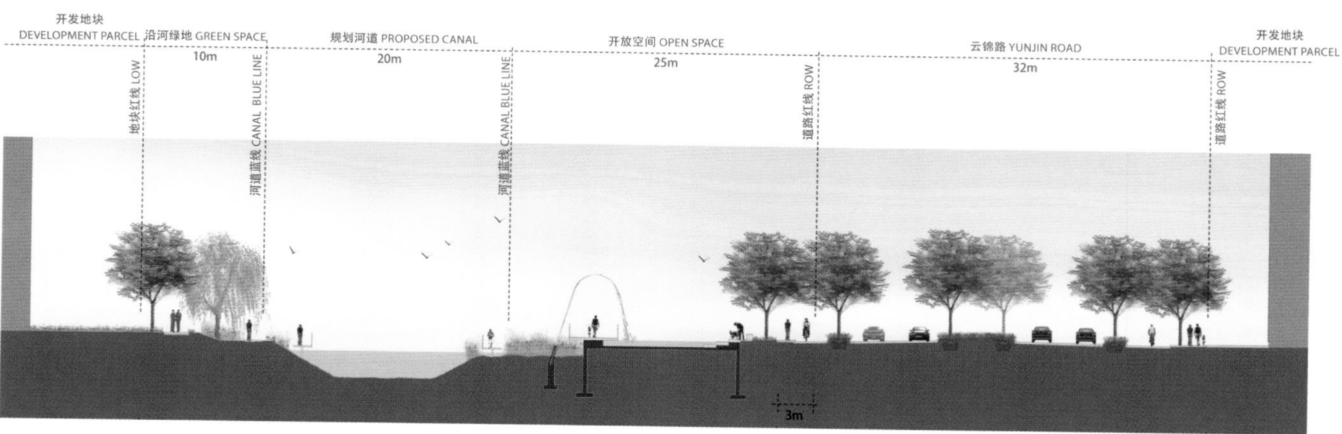

Section

TREES

Acer buergerianum
Albizia julibrissin
Cinnamomum camphora
Eriobotrya japonica
Firmiana simplex
Koelreuteria bipinnata var. *Integrifolia*
Liquidambar formosana
Liriodendron chinense
Melia azedarach
Platanus orientalis
Pterocarya stenoptera
Salix babylonica
Sapindus mukorossi
Sapium sebiferum

RAIN GARDEN

Acorus gramineus
Hemerocallis fulva var. *aurantiaca*
Hosta plantaginea
Iris ensata
Iris tectorum
Juncus effuses
Lythrum salicaria
Mentha canadensis
Pollia japonica
Reineckea carnea
Saururus chinensis
Scirpus triqueter

NANSEN PARK

Oslo, Norway

TREES
Acer platanoides
Acer tataricum subsp. *Ginnala*
Aesculus hippocastanum
Betula pendula
Betula utilis var. *jacquemontii*
Carpinus betulus
Cercidiphyllum japonicum
Fraxinus excelsior
Magnolia × *loebneri* 'Merrill'
Pinus sylvestris
Prunus avium 'Vestby'
Quercus petraea
Quercus robur
Sorbus aucuparia
Tilia cordata

SHRUBS
Aronia melanocarpa
Buddleja davidii
Ribes alpinum 'Schmidt'
Ribes aureum
Rosa 'Alba Suaveolens'
Rosa rubiginosa 'Magnifica'
Spiraea × *vanhouttei*
Syringa × *hyacinthiflora* 'California Rose'
Syringa meyeri 'Palibin'
Syringa vulgaris 'Katherine Havemeyer'

WATERLOO GREENWAY

Austin, Texas

Riparian restoration, flood benches, and aquatic habitat, section

RENAISSANCE PARK

Chattanooga, Tennessee

Plan

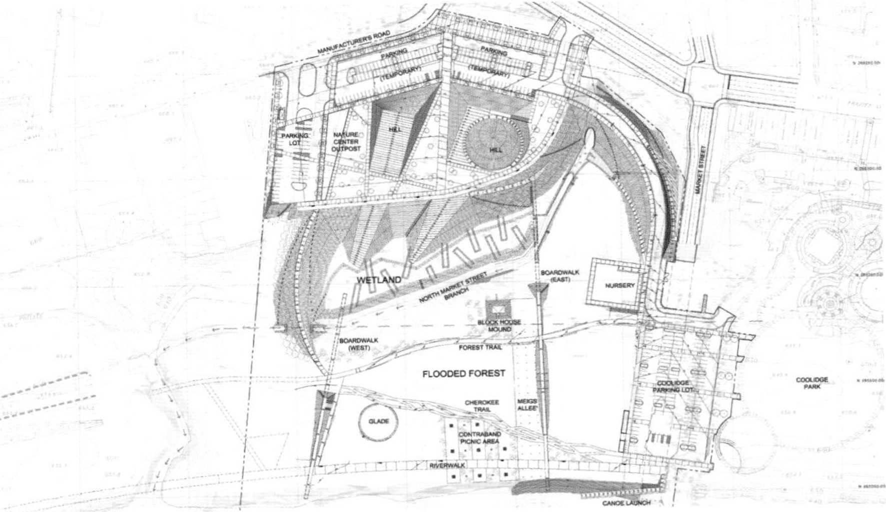

TREES
Carpinus caroliniana 'Palisade'
Carya aquatica
Catalpa bignonioides
Diospyros virginiana
Liquidambar styraciflua 'Rotundiloba'
Nyssa aquatica
Pinus taeda
Quercus alba
Quercus bicolor
Quercus macrocarpa
Taxodium distichum

WETLAND
Amorpha fruticose
Cephalanthus occidentalis
Cornus amomum
Juncus effuses
Justicia americana
Peltandra virginica
Sagittaria latifolia
Scirpus atrovirens
Scirpus cyperinus
Scirpus validus

THE BEACH AT EXPEDIA GROUP

Seattle, Washington

Section showing overlook and gravel beach

Trees, planting diagram

Meadow, beach, and bioretention, planting diagram

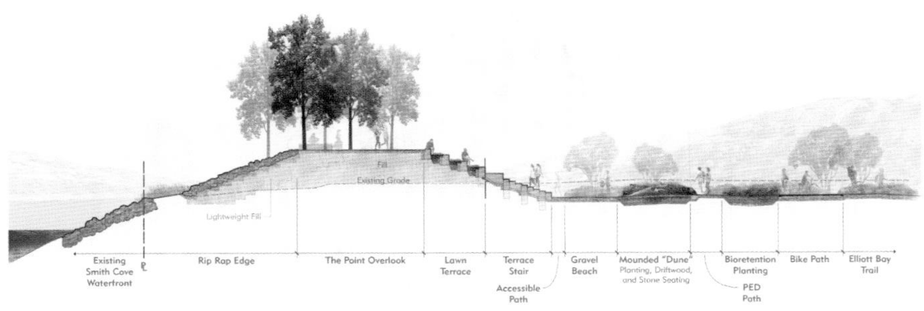

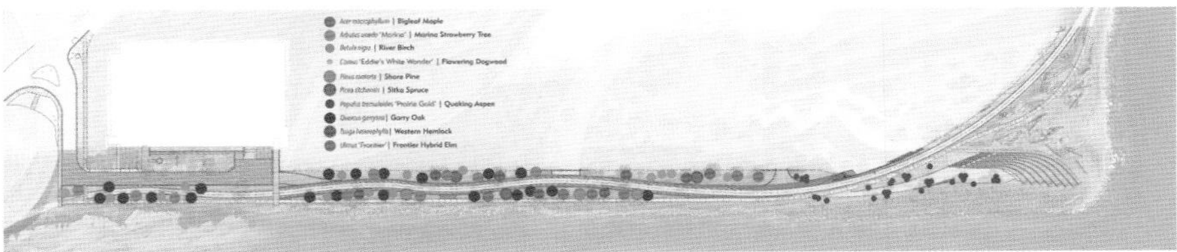

BROOKLYN BRIDGE PARK

Brooklyn, New York

Pier 1 salt marsh, section

TREES, PIER 1
Aesculus flava
Aesculus pavia
Catalpa speciosa
Gymnocladus dioica
Koelreuteria paniculate
Magno-lia acuminata
Platanus × acerifolia 'Bloodgood'
Populus acuminata × sargentii 'Highland'
Quercus bicolor
Quercus montana
Quercus phellos
Sassafras albidum

SHRUBS, PIER 1
Amelanchier arborea
Baccharis halimifolia
Cephalanthus occidentalis
Clethra alnifolia 'Hummingbird'
Cornus racemosa 'Muszam'
Cornus sericea
Hamamelis × intermedia 'Jelena'
Hydrangea quercifolia
Ilex glabra
Ilex verticillata 'Red Sprite'
Kalmia latifolia
Lindera benzoin
Physocarpus opulifolius 'Nanus'
Prunus laurocerasus 'Otto Luyken'
Rhododendron maximum
Rhus aromatica
Rhus copallinum
Rhus typhina
Rosa palustris
Spiraea tomentosa
Symphoricarpos × chenaultii 'Hancock'
Viburnum dentatum 'Blue Muffin'
Viburnum prunifolium
Xanthorhiza simplicissima

GRASSES, RUSHES, AND SEDGES, PIER 1
Carex laevigata
Carex lurida
Carex stricta
Carex vulpinoidea
Distichlis spicata
Equisetum hyemale
Eriophorum angustifolium
Panicum virgatum
Scirpus cyperinus
Spartina alterniflora
Spartina pectinata

SHANGHAI SHIPYARD RIVERSIDE PARK

Shanghai, China

Tripartite terrace concept for flood protection, diagram

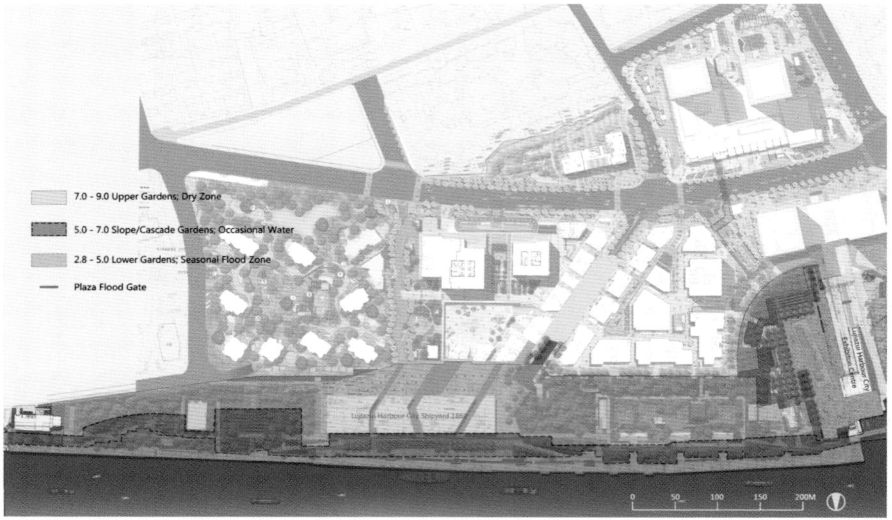

CULTURE OF WATER ECOLOGY PARK

Changchun, China

TREES
Abies holophylla
Acer negundo 'Aurea'
Betula platyphylla
Fraxinus mandshurica
Maackia amurensis
Malus baccata
Phellodendron amurense
Picea meyeri
Pinus sylvestris var. *mongolica*
Quercus mongolica
Tilia mandshurica
Ulmus pumila

SHRUBS
Deutzia parviflora var. *amurensis*
Ligustrum obtusifolium
Lonicera caerulea
Lonicera ruprechtiana
Physocarpus amurensis
Rhododendron dauricum
Sorbaria sorbifolia
Spiraea japonica
Spiraea thunbergii
Syringa oblata
Weigela 'Red Prince'

PERENNIALS
Aster tataricus
Astilbe chinensis
Chelidonium majus
Hemerocallis middendorffii
Hosta plantaginea
Hylotelephium erythrostictum
Iris domestica
Iris ensata
Leucanthemum maximum
Nelumbo nucifera
Paeonia lactiflora
Phlox paniculate
Salvia farinacea

MASCHINENFABRIK OERLIKON PARK

Zurich, Switzerland

VINES AND CLIMBING SHRUBS
Actinidia arguta 'Weiki'
Ampelopsis aconitifolia
Campsis radicans
Clematis alpina 'Frances Rivis'
Clematis flammula
Clematis 'Fujimusume'
Clematis 'General Sikorski'
Clematis 'Lady Betty Balfour'
Clematis macropetala 'Jan Lindmark'
Clematis montana 'Mayleen'
Fallopia baldschuanica
Hedera helix 'Plattensee'
Humulus lupulus
Lonicera caprifolium 'Inga'
Lonicera japonica 'Hall's Prolific'
Parthenocissus quinquefolia
Passiflora caerulea
Periploca graeca
Rosa 'Albertine'
Rosa 'Blush Rambler'
Rosa 'Bobbie James'
Rose filipes 'Kiftsgate'
Rosa 'Warm Welcome'
Schizophragma hydrangeoides 'Roseum'
Vitis aestivalis
Vitis coignetiae
Wisteria floribunda 'Macrobotrys'
Wisteria sinensis 'Alba'

CULTUURPARK WESTERGASFABRIEK

Amsterdam, Netherlands

TREES
Acer griseum
Acer palmatum 'Sango-kaku'
Cladrastis kentukea
Fagus sylvatica
Fraxinus angustifolia
Liriodendron tulipifera
Magnolia kobus
Nothofagus antarctica
Nyssa sylvatica
Robinia pseudoacacia 'Frisia'
Salix alba 'Serica'
Sophora japonica
Stewartia pseudocamellia
Taxodium distichum

SHRUBS
Buddleja davidii 'Empire Blue'
Caryopteris × clandonensis 'Arthur'
Daphne laureola subsp. *Philippi*
Euonymus europaeus
Fuchsia magellanica var. *molinae*
Hippophae rhamnoides
Ilex glabra 'Nigra'
Osmanthus × burkwoodii
Potentilla fruticosa 'Tilford Cream'
Rhododendron campanulatum
Salix elaeagnos
Salix purpurea 'Nana'
Sarcococca hookeriana var. *humilis*
Viburnum opulus

PERENNIALS AND AQUATIC PLANTS
Ajuga reptans
Alchemilla mollis
Anemone nemorosa
Aponogeton distachyos
Asarum europaeum
Aster divaricatus
Brunnera macrophylla
Calla palustris
Epimedium pubigerum
Euphorbia amygdaloides var. *robbiae*
Galium odoratum
Iris ensata
Nymphaea 'Marliacea Albida'
Pontederia cordata
Pulmonaria saccharate
Symphytum caucasicum
Vancouveria hexandra

PARQUE BICENTENARIO

Mexico City, Mexico

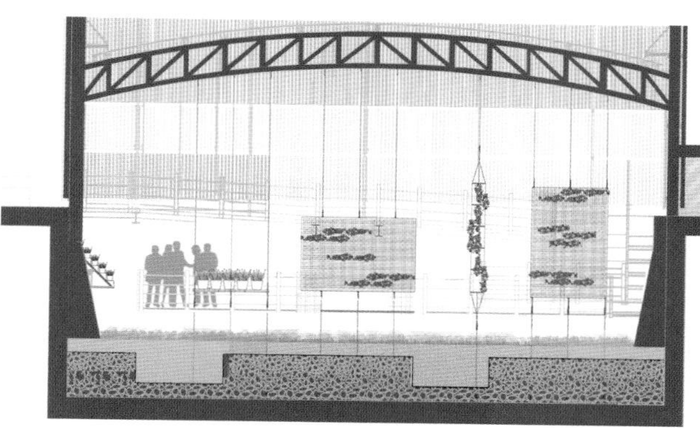

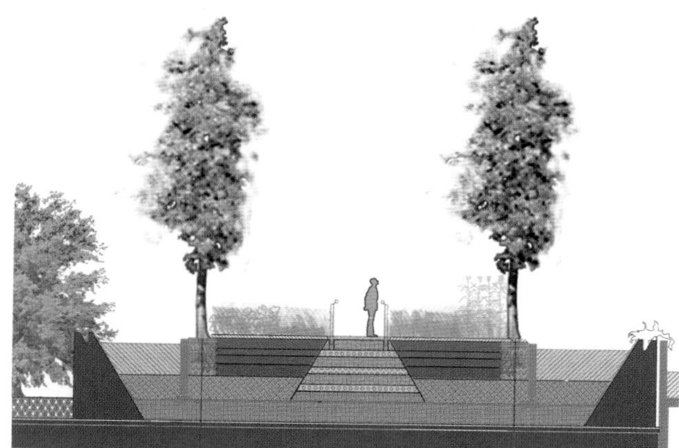

Orchidarium, section

Chinampa, section

Natura, section

MESOPHYLL MOUNTAIN FOREST BIOME
Carpinus caroliniana
Chiranthodendron pentadactylon
Cyathea divergens
Liquidambar styraciflua
Magnolia schiedeana
Platanus mexicana
Ulmus mexicana

TROPICAL EVERGREEN FOREST BIOME
Acaciella angustissima
Amphipterygium adstringens
Bocconia frutescens
Bursera copallifera
Ceiba aesculifolia
Erythrina americana
Eysenhardtia polystachya
Ficus petiolaris
Leucaena esculenta
Lysiloma divaricata
Plumeria rubra
Pseudobombax ellipticum
Thevetia thevetioides

DESERT BIOME
Cercidium microphyllum
Echinocactus grusonii
Fouquieria splendens
Lemaireocereus thurberi
Opuntia fulgida
Senegalia berlandieri
Vachellia farnesiana

PARC DU PEUPLE DE L'HERBE

Carrières-sous-Poissy, France

PERENNIALS, MEADOW
Achillea millefolium
Anthyllis vulneraria
Centaurea scabiosa
Daucus carota
Knautia arvensis
Leucanthemum vulgare
Lotus corniculatus
Origanum vulgare
Papaver rhoeas
Primula veris
Ranunculus acris
Salvia pratensis
Sanguisorba minor
Saponaria officinalis
Sedum album
Scabiosa columbaria
Tragopogon pratensis
Verbascum thapsus

GRASSES, MEADOW
Agrostis capillaris
Dactylis glomerate
Festuca pratensis
Festuca rubra
Phleum pratense
Poa pratensis
Poa trivialis

ZHENSHAN PARK

Suzhou, China

Pond cypress islands, plan

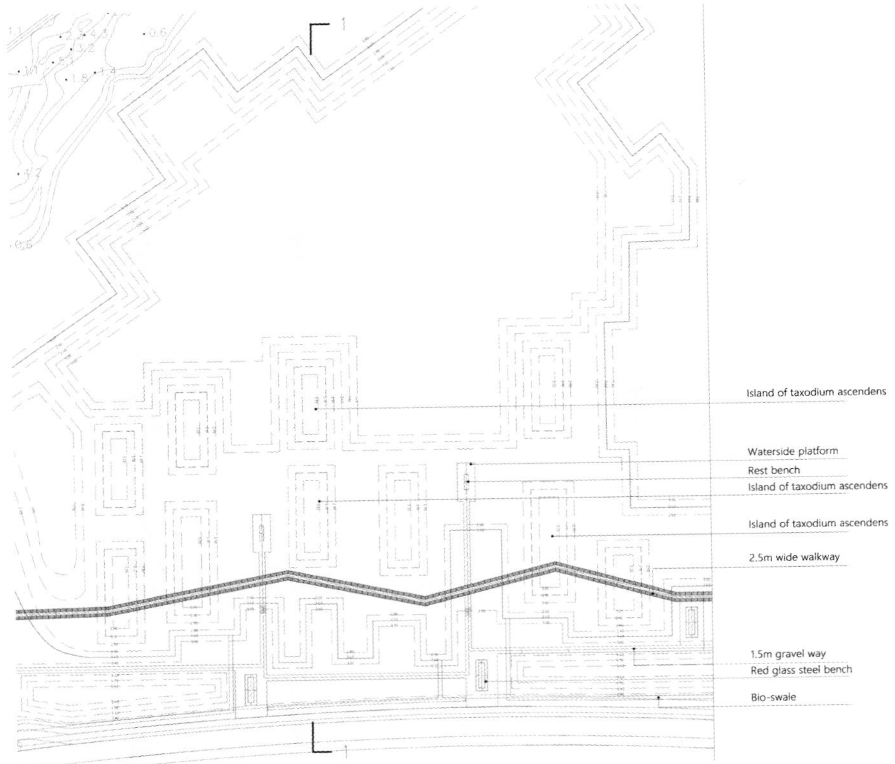

TREES
Cinnamomum camphora
Ginkgo biloba
Koelreuteria bipinnata var. *Integrifolia*
Metasequoia glyptostroboides
Populus × *canadensis*
Taxodium ascendens
Zelkova serrata

PERENNIALS
Canna glauca
Centella asiatica
Iris pseudacorus
Lythrum salicaria
Nuphar pumila
Nymphaea tetragona
Orychophragmus violaceus
Pontederia cordata
Thalia dealbata

GRASSES
Miscanthus floridulus
Miscanthus sinensis
Nassella tenuissima
Pennisetum alopecuroides 'Rubrum'

MEI GARDEN

Jinhua, China

Constructed wetland, diagram

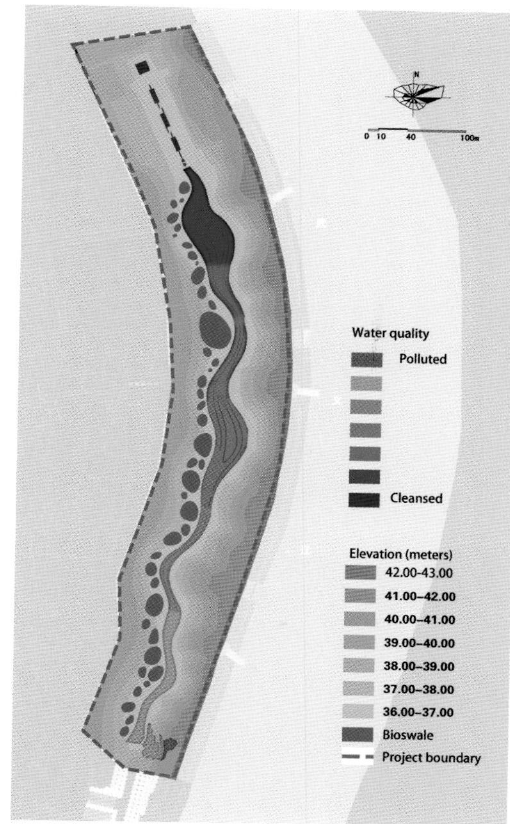

THOMAS C. WALES PARK

Seattle, Washington

Section

SHRUBS, WETLAND
Acer circinatum
Cornus sericea
Gaultheria shallon
Lonicera involucrata
Mahonia aquifolium
Physocarpus capitatus
Ribes sanguineum
Rosa nutkana
Rosa pisocarpa
Rubus spectabilis
Sorbus sitchensis
Spiraea douglasii
Symphoricarpos albus

PERENNIALS, WETLAND
Argentina egedii
Mentha arvensis
Stachys chamissonis var. *cooleyae*

RUSHES AND SEDGES, WETLAND
Carex obnupta
Juncus tenuis
Scirpus cyperinus
Scirpus microcarpus

LORSCH ABBEY

Lorsch, Germany

Inclement weather gear, concept drawings

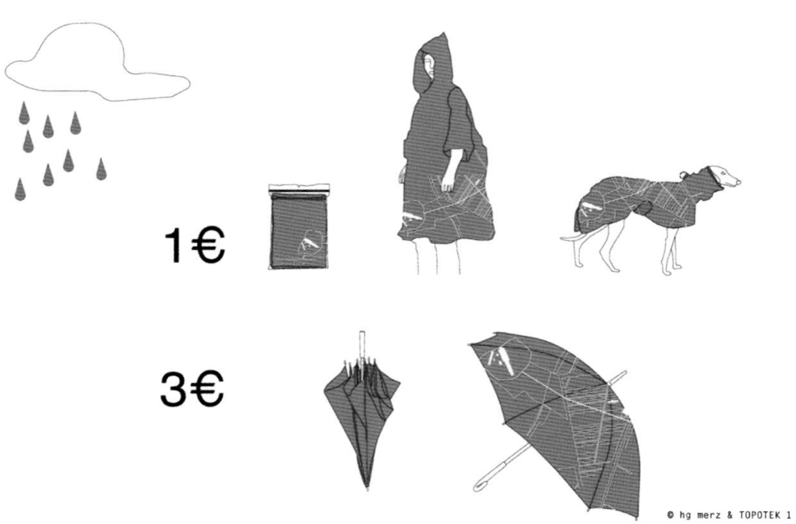

PARC DRÄI EECHELEN

Luxembourg City, Grand Duchy of Luxembourg

Paving detail, plan, section

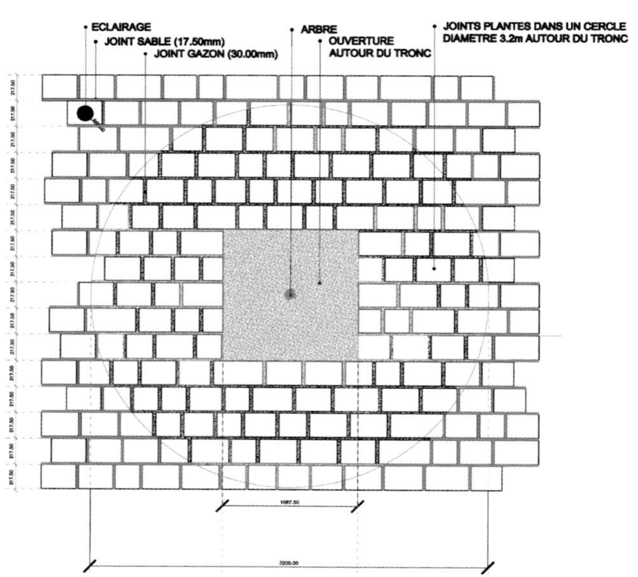

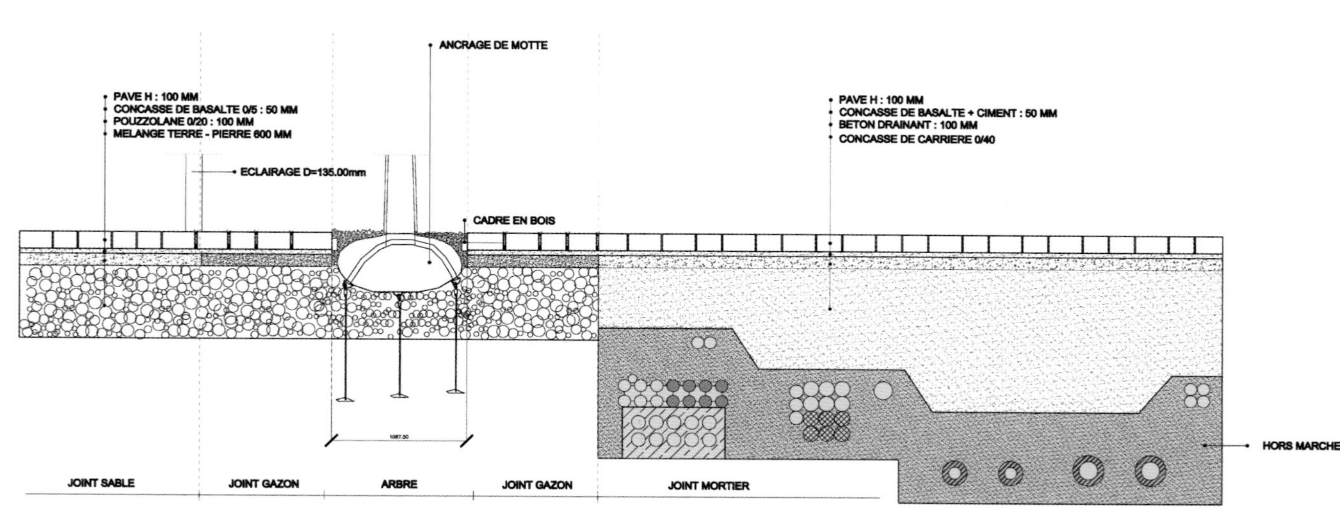

FORT BIJ VECHTEN

Utrecht, Netherlands

Restoration strip, plan

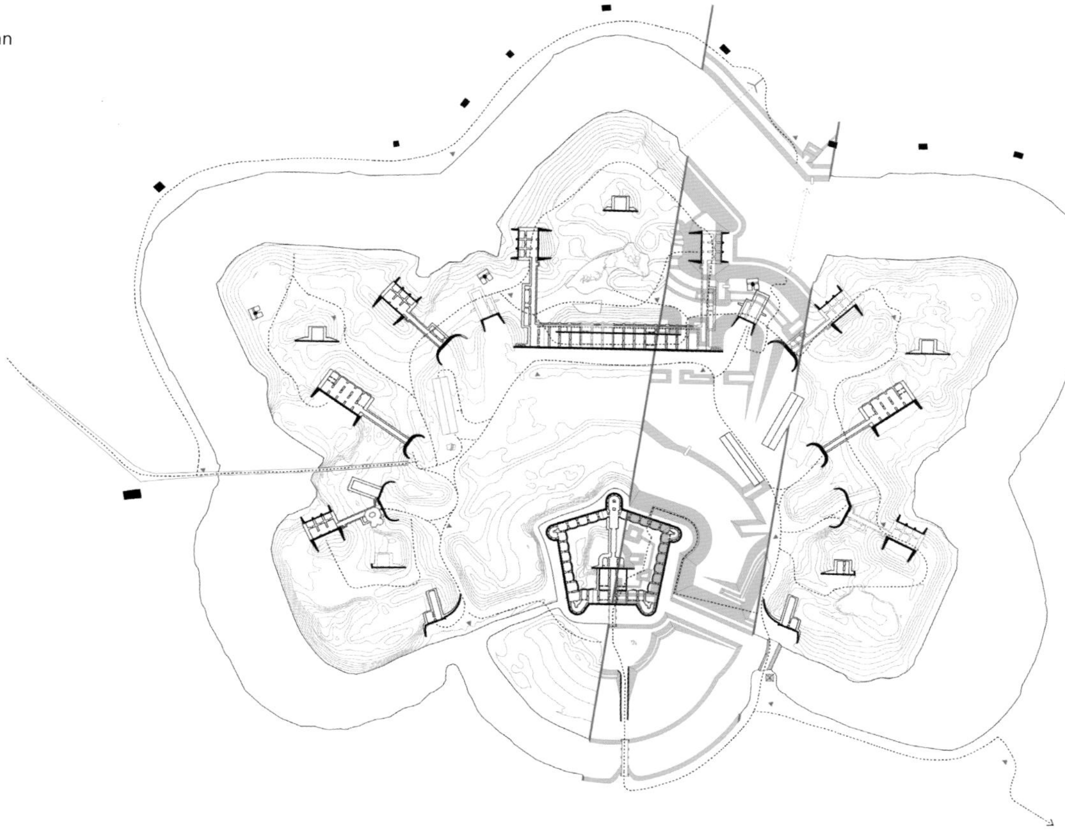

QIAOYUAN WETLAND PARK

Tianjin, China

Wetland pods and plant palette, plan, section diagram

GRAFFITI PIER PARK

Philadelphia, Pennsylvania

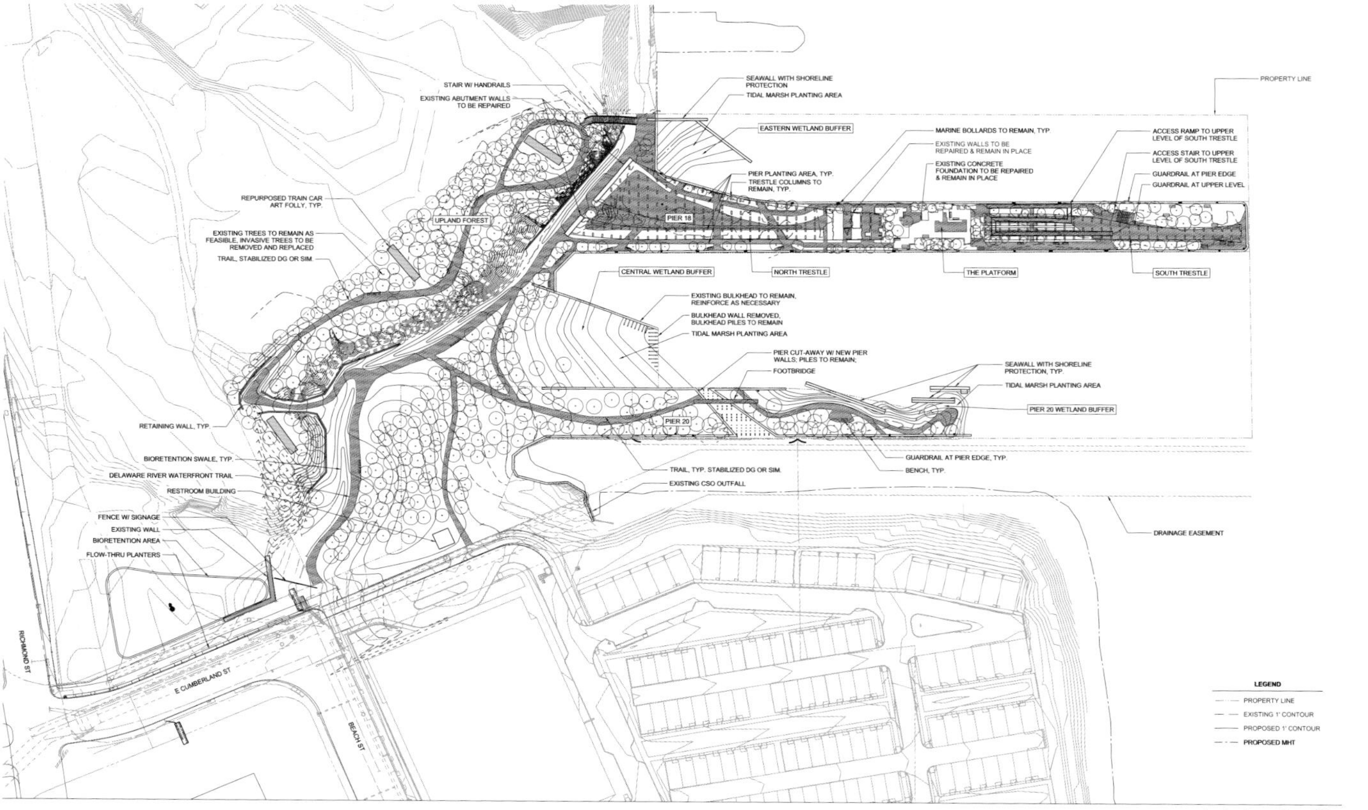

STAIR W/ HANDRAILS
EXISTING ABUTMENT WALLS TO BE REPAIRED
SEAWALL WITH SHORELINE PROTECTION
TIDAL MARSH PLANTING AREA
PROPERTY LINE
EASTERN WETLAND BUFFER
MARINE BOLLARDS TO REMAIN, TYP.
EXISTING WALLS TO BE REPAIRED & REMAIN IN PLACE
EXISTING CONCRETE FOUNDATION TO BE REPAIRED & REMAIN IN PLACE
ACCESS RAMP TO UPPER LEVEL OF SOUTH TRESTLE
ACCESS STAIR TO UPPER LEVEL OF SOUTH TRESTLE
GUARDRAIL AT PIER EDGE
GUARDRAIL AT UPPER LEVEL
PIER PLANTING AREA, TYP.
TRESTLE COLUMNS TO REMAIN, TYP.
REPURPOSED TRAIN CAR ART FOLLY, TYP.
UPLAND FOREST
PIER 18
EXISTING TREES TO REMAIN AS FEASIBLE, INVASIVE TREES TO BE REMOVED AND REPLACED
TRAIL, STABILIZED DG OR SIM.
CENTRAL WETLAND BUFFER
NORTH TRESTLE
THE PLATFORM
SOUTH TRESTLE
EXISTING BULKHEAD TO REMAIN, REINFORCE AS NECESSARY
BULKHEAD WALL REMOVED, BULKHEAD PILES TO REMAIN
TIDAL MARSH PLANTING AREA
PIER CUT-AWAY W/ NEW PIER WALLS; PILES TO REMAIN;
FOOTBRIDGE
SEAWALL WITH SHORELINE PROTECTION, TYP.
TIDAL MARSH PLANTING AREA
PIER 20 WETLAND BUFFER
RETAINING WALL, TYP.
PIER 20
BIORETENTION SWALE, TYP.
DELAWARE RIVER WATERFRONT TRAIL
RESTROOM BUILDING
GUARDRAIL AT PIER EDGE, TYP.
BENCH, TYP.
TRAIL, TYP. STABILIZED DG OR SIM.
EXISTING CSO OUTFALL
FENCE W/ SIGNAGE
EXISTING WALL
BIORETENTION AREA
FLOW-THRU PLANTERS
DRAINAGE EASEMENT
RICHMOND ST
E CUMBERLAND ST
BEACH ST

LEGEND
PROPERTY LINE
EXISTING 1' CONTOUR
PROPOSED 1' CONTOUR
PROPOSED MHT

1" = 50'-0"
0 25 50 100FT

Site plan

SANLIN ECO VALLEY

Shanghai, China

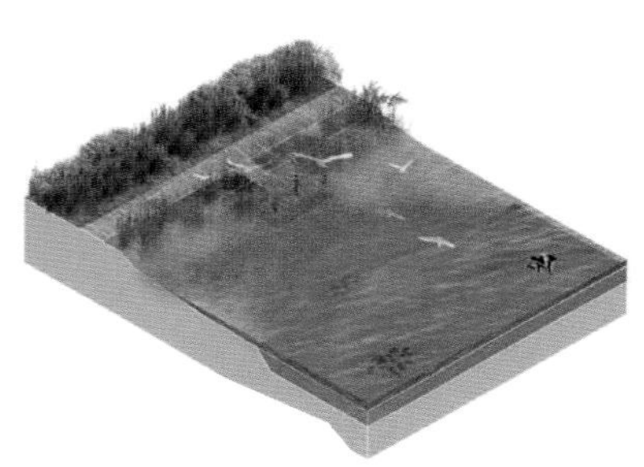

Rain Garden and Emergent Wetlands

Oxygenation of Canal

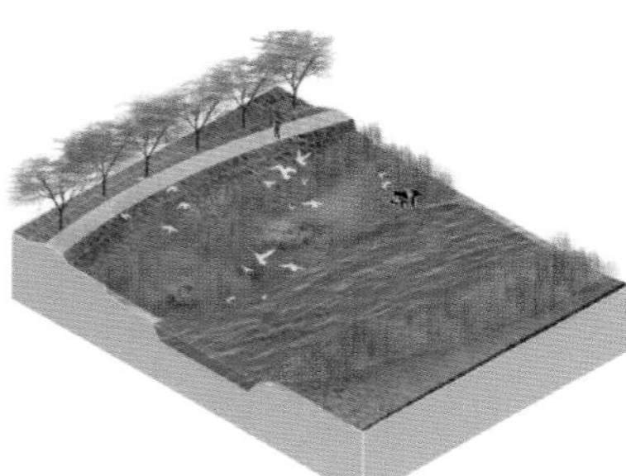

Reed Marsh Wetland

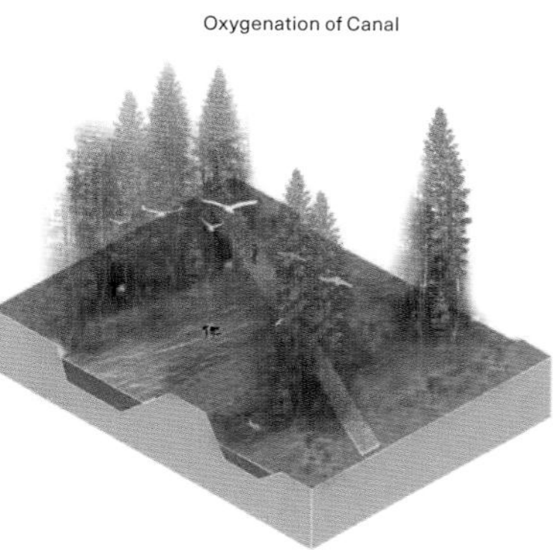

Cypress Swamp Wetland

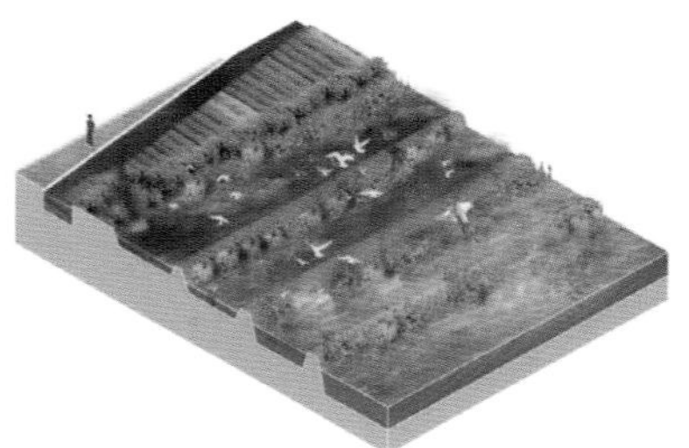

Terraced Wetland

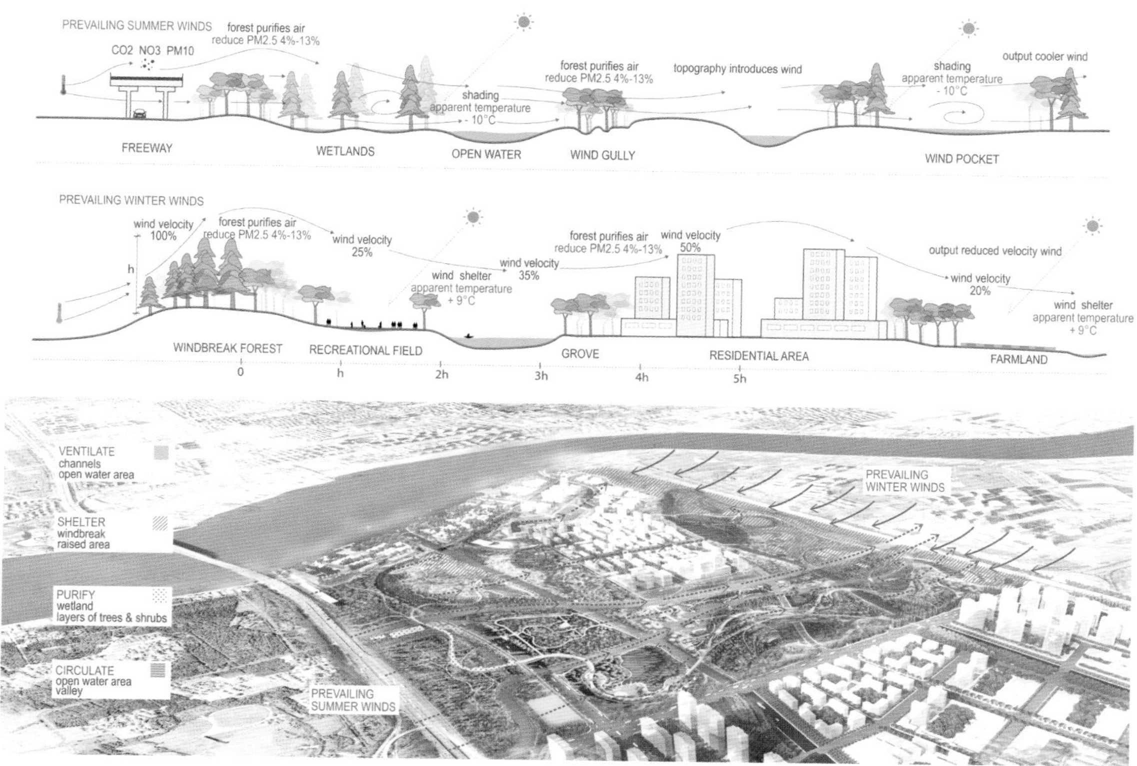

Windflow diagrams, section perspective

FRESHKILLS PARK

Staten Island, New York

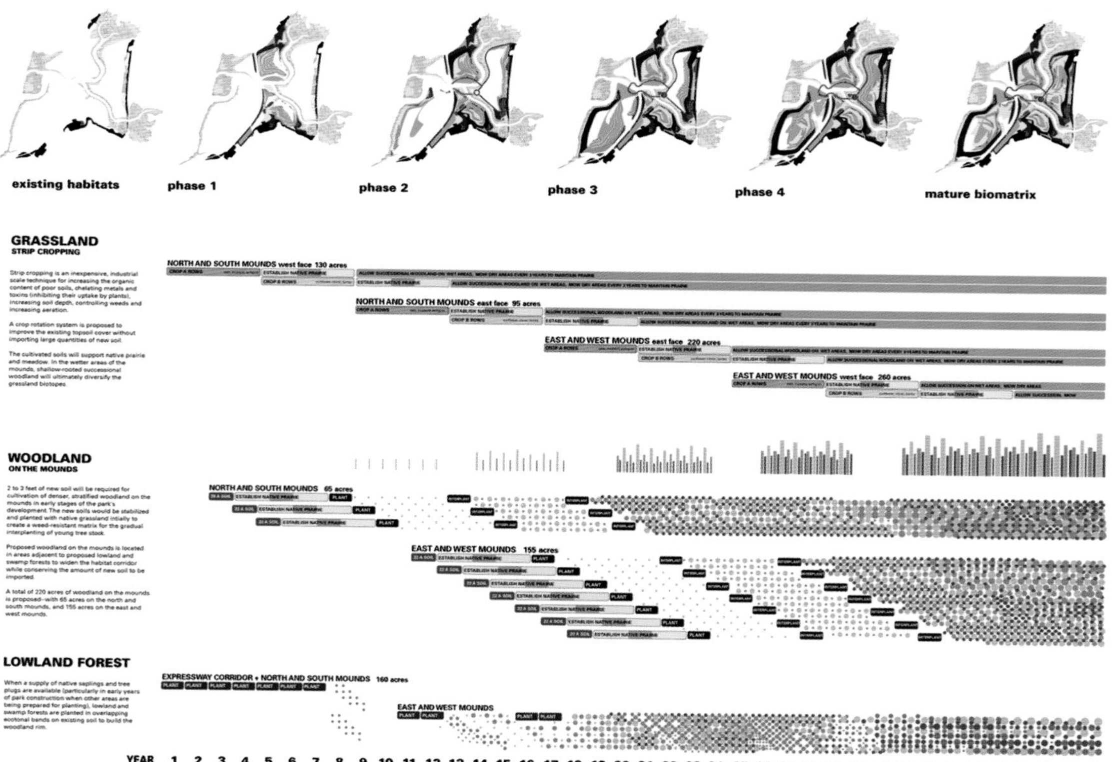

Planting and habitat phasing

acknowledgments

We first thank Dorothée Imbert, director of the Knowlton School of Architecture at Ohio State University. An early conversation with her inspired us to direct our research toward parks that rehabilitate damaged sites.

We are immensely grateful to the many landscape architects whose work is included here. They accompanied us, often on weekends and holidays, to the parks and also provided essential background and details, along with the images of their designs that are so important for a full understanding of the work.

We are likewise deeply indebted to the New York City Department of Sanitation and the New York City Department of Parks and Recreation, and especially to Eloise Hirsh, administrator of Freshkills Park, for access to and information about Fresh Kills/Freshkills.

Françoise Ged, director of l'Observatoire de l'architecture de la Chine contemporaine, Cité de l'architecture & du patrimoine, Paris, provided invaluable information about park projects in Shanghai.

Without the help of cultural consultant Joanna Lee, we could never have taken our two frantically wide-ranging trips to China (and we would never have known the world's greatest cuisine!).

As usual, I relied on Robert Gottlieb's advice in structuring the material.

Many others made valuable contributions: Sophia Ma for her contextual studies, photo research, and astute observations. Suzanne Stephens, deputy editor, *Architectural Record*, for her helpful comments on several chapters. Jon McMillan, senior vice president and director of planning at TF Cornerstone, for his timely updates on New York City real estate development. Sarah Rafson and her collaborators, Ilana Curtis and Avocet Greenwell, for their expert contextual photo research. Sarah Coleman for her diligent fact checking. Julia van den Hout for her meticulous proofreading. Andrea Monfried for her unparalleled, and always patient, text editing. Luke Bulman for his elegant design. Douglas Curran for his charming, never-failing guidance through the labyrinth of book production. And finally, Charles Miers for his many years of faith in me.

WHY NOW?

7 "this worldwide burst": Adrian Benepe, president, Brooklyn Botanic Garden, called it a "new golden age of park creation" in discussion with author, Mar. 19, 2019, and elsewhere.

10 "By the mid-1990s": Charles Waldheim, "Landscape Urbanism," *The Landscape Urbanism Reader* (New York: Princeton Architectural Press, 2006), 37.

10 "His concepts have been embraced": Mohsen Mostafavi and Ciro Najle, eds., *Landscape Urbanism: A Manual for the Machinic Landscape* (London: Architectural Association, 2010). Waldheim, *Landscape Urbanism Reader*. Charles Waldheim, *Landscape as Urbanism: A General Theory* (Princeton, NJ: Princeton University Press, 2016).

10 "Social media may be": Beatriz Colomina, "Privacy and Publicity in the Age of Social Media," in *Public Space? Lost and Found,* ed. Gediminas Urbonas, Ann Lui, and Lucas Freeman (Cambridge, MA: MIT Press, 2017), 253–61.

10 "President Donald Trump's": Mikaela Lefrak, "The White House and Lafayette Park Went From 'Public Square' to 'Veritable Fortress,'" *NPR-WAMU*, June 5, 2020, https://www.npr.org/local/305/2020/06/05/870877297/the-white-house-and-lafayette-park-went-from-public-square-to-veritable-fortress.

10 "by 2015, its designers": James Corner Field Operation and Diller Scofidio + Renfro, *The High Line* (London: Phaidon, 2015), 444. One High Line imitator is especially promising: the elevated Reading Viaduct by Studio Bryan Hanes, under construction in 2020 in the Callowhill neighborhood of Philadelphia.

11 "The Sumerian *Epic of Gilgamesh*": This brief history of parks is based on Karen R. Jones and John Wills, *The Invention of the Park: Recreational Landscapes from the Garden of Eden to Disney's Magic Kingdom* (Cambridge, UK: Polity Press, 2005), 9–24.

11 "In China, and later in Europe": The description of hunting parks is based on Edward H. Schafer, "Hunting Parks and Animal Enclosures in Ancient China," *Journal of the Economic and Social History of the Orient* 11, no. 3 (Oct. 1968): 318–43.

15 "As the most manipulated": Blake Gumprecht, *The Los Angeles River: Its Life, Death, and Possible Rebirth* (Baltimore: Johns Hopkins University Press, 1999), 173.

18 "Urban planning in China": Xiaolong Luo, Jianfa Shen, and Wen Chen, "Urban Networks and Governance in City-Region Planning: State-Led Region Building in Nanjing City-Region, China," *Geografiska Annaler*, ser. B, Human Geography 92, no. 4 (Dec. 2010): 311–26.

18 "Because the local official": Rémi Curien, "Chinese Urban Planning: Environmentalising a Hyper-Functionalist Machine?," trans. Will Thornely, *China Perspectives* 2014, no. 3: 23–31.

18 "landscape architecture has existed": Kongjian Yu and Mary Padua, eds., *The Art of Survival: Recovering Landscape Architecture* (Victoria, AUS: Images Publishing, 2006), 54.

18 "Despite the tremendous recent growth": Daniel Jost, "The Great Exchange," *Landscape Architecture*, Feb. 2013, https://landscapearchitecturemagazine.org/2013/02/08/the-great-exchange/.

18 "Sponge City, a system that protects": Kongjian Yu, "Editorial: Sponge Philosophy," *Landscape Architecture Frontiers* 3, no. 2 (2015), https://journal.hep.com.cn/laf/EN/article/downloadArticleFile.do?attachType=PDF&id=13105.

18 "Turenscape's Houtan Wetland Park": The description of Houtan Park relies on Peter G. Rowe, "China's Water Resources and Houtan Park," in *Designed Ecologies: The Landscape Architecture of Kongjian Yu*, ed. William S. Saunders (Basel, CH: Birkhäuser, 2012), 187–88.

18 "Houston, Texas": Christopher Ingraham, "Houston Is Experiencing Its Third '500-Year' Flood in 3 Years. How Is That Possible?," *Washington Post*, Aug. 29, 2017, https://www.washingtonpost.com/news/wonk/wp/2017/08/29/houston-is-experiencing-its-third-500-year-flood-in-3-years-how-is-that-possible/.

18 "Yu has lobbied": Xianming Tu and Tina Tian, "Six Questions Towards a Sponge City—Report on Power of Public Policy: Sponge City and the Trend of Landscape Architecture," *Landscape Architecture Frontiers* 3, no. 2 (June 2015): 22–31.

19 "Dutch hydrological engineers": Dirk Sijmons et al., *Room for the River: Safe and Attractive Landscapes* (Wageningen, NL: Blauwdruk, 2017).

19 "For centuries": Gary Austin and Kongjian Yu, *Constructed Wetlands and Sustainable Development* (Abington: Routledge, 2016), 17. A similar issue is the disappearance of wetlands in the United States: 50 percent of the nation's wetlands no longer exist.

19 "The celebrated American": The description of Olmsted's work in Boston relies on Alex Marks et al., *Boston "Emerald Necklace" Case Study* (Ramboll Foundation, 2015), https://ramboll.com/-/media/files/rgr/lcl/bgi_final-report_mit_boston_20160403.pdf?la=en.

19 "In New York": Oliver Milman, "Hudson River Shows Signs of Rebound after Decades as New York's Sewer," *Guardian*, Mar. 28, 2019, https://www.theguardian.com/us-news/2019/mar/28/hudson-river-pollution-cleanup-new-york.

19 "increased interest": Xiangrong Wang et al., "Ecological Restoration for River Ecosystems: Comparing the Huangpu River in Shanghai and the Hudson River in New York," *Ecosystem Health and Sustainability* 1, no. 7 (2015): 1–14, https://www.tandfonline.com/doi/full/10.1890/EHS15-0009.1.

19 "H. W. S. Cleveland": August Heckscher with Phyllis Robinson, *Open Spaces: The Life of American Cities* (New York: Harper and Row, 1977), 192–97.

19 "Olmsted was impressed": Sarah Faiks, Jarrett Kest, Amanda Szot, and Molly Vendura, "England and Birkenhead Park: Influencing the Design of Riverside," in "Revisiting Riverside: A Frederick Law Olmsted Community" (master's project, University of Michigan, Apr. 2001), http://seas.umich.edu/ecomgt/pubs/riverside/RSchapter3.pdf.

19 "It is a well-known fact": John L. Crompton, "The Role of the Proximate Principle in the Emergence of Urban Parks in the United Kingdom and in the United States," *Leisure Studies* 26, no. 2 (April 2007): 213–34, quoted in Terence Young, *Building San Francisco's Parks 1850–1930* (Baltimore: John Hopkins University Press, 2004), 122.

19 "in the five years": Joshua K. Leon. "Who Really Benefits from Central Park?," *Metropolis* (online), Dec. 6, 2013, https://www.metropolismag.com/architecture/landscape/who-really-benefits-from-central-park/.

22 "New York City forcibly removed": "Seneca Village, New York City," National Park Service, last updated Jan. 28, 2019, https://www.nps.gov/articles/seneca-village-new-york-city.htm.

22 "Seeking to address": Michael Friedrich, "How 'Landscape Urbanism' Is Making Gentrification Look Like Fun," *Washington Post*, Nov. 19, 2019, https://www.washingtonpost.com/outlook/2019/11/19/how-landscape-urbanism-is-making-gentrification-look-like-fun/.

22 "This 'green gentrification'": Kenneth A. Gould and Tammy L. Lewis, "The Environmental Injustice of Green Gentrification: The Case of Brooklyn's Prospect Park," in *The World in Brooklyn: Gentrification, Immigration, and Ethnic Politics in a Global City*, ed. Judith N. DeSena and Timothy Shortell (Lanham, MD: Lexington Books, 2012), 113–46.

22 "Michael Van Valkenburgh has written": Michael Van Valkenburgh with William S. Saunders, "Landscapes over Time," *Landscape Architecture*, March 2013, https://landscapearchitecturemagazine.org/2013/03/14/landscapes-over-time/.

22 "Pittsburgh was reported": Diana Nelson Jones, "Pittsburgh's Parks Are $400 Million Behind in Repairs, $13 Million Short for Maintenance," *Pittsburgh Post-Gazette,* July 15, 2019, https://www.post-gazette.com/local/city/2019/07/15/Pittsburgh-Parks-Conservancy-400-million-behind-repairs-165-parks/stories/201907150087.

23 "Another area where parks": Intergovernmental Panel on Climate Change, *Climate Change and Land* (2020), https://www.ipcc.ch/site/assets/uploads/sites/4/2020/02/SPM_Updated-Jan20.pdf.

23 "Less well-known": Angela Licata and Alan Cohn, "Finding the Balance in New York City: Developing Resilient, Sustainable Water and Wastewater Systems," in *The Water Problem: Climate Change and Water Policy in the United States,* ed. Pat Mulroy (Washington, DC: Brookings Institution Press, 2017), 167–85.

23 "After several starts and stops": Caroline Spivack, "Plan to Extend Lower Manhattan into East River to Be Studied by Experts," *Curbed New York*, Oct. 1, 2019, https://ny.curbed.com/2019/10/1/20893221/lower-manhattan-expansion-plan-planning-process.

23 "In France in 2016": Angelique Chrisafis, "Paris Floods: 'There's Something Terrifying About It,'" *Guardian*, June 4, 2016, https://www.theguardian.com/world/2016/jun/03/paris-river-seine-floods.

23 "Climate change is a water story": Eric Holthaus, "Gigantic Water Tunnels Won't Save Houston from the Next Harvey," *Grist*, Apr. 10, 2018, https://grist.org/article/gigantic-water-tunnels-wont-save-houston-from-the-next-harvey/.

RAILWAYS

27 “symbol of landscape design”: Maurice Cox, in discussion with author, Sept. 24, 2017.

27 “Within a few years”: Detroit Future City Implementation Office, “Background,” *Achieving an Integrated Open Space Network in Detroit*, February 17, 2016, https://detroitfuturecity.com/wp-content/uploads/2016/02/Final_DFC_open_space-_02_17_16-2.pdf, 15, 25, 58.

27 “The use of landscape architecture”: Charles Waldheim, *Landscape as Urbanism: A General Theory* (Princeton and Oxford: Princeton University Press, 2016), 21.

27 “Ludwig Hilberseimer”: Caroline Constant, “Hilberseimer and Caldwell: Merging Ideologies in the Lafayette Park Landscape,” in Charles Waldheim, ed., *CASE: Hilberseimer/Mies van der Rohe Lafayette Park Detroit* (New York: Prestel Publishing, 2004), 108.

30 “The idea of creating”: Brian Charlton, principal, SmithGroupJJR, in discussion with author, May 2, 2019.

30 “The Cut was funded”: Improvements and specific parts of the Cut, such as the Campbell Terrace, were financed by a wide variety of sources.

32 “Projects like the revitalization”: Joe Guillen, “Detroit's Showcase Neighborhood Project Falls a Year Behind Schedule,” July 6, 2018, *Detroit Free Press*; University of Vermont, “Study Explains Why Thousands of Detroit Residents Rejected City's Tree Planting Efforts,” Jan. 7, 2019.

32 “Stunted lending”: See Jodie Adams Kirshner, *Broke* (New York: St. Martin's Press, 2019).

32 “On the positive side”: Corey Williams, “Detroit Released From State Financial Oversight Three Years after Exiting Bankruptcy,” *Detroit Free Press*, April 30, 2018, https://www.freep.com/story/news/local/michigan/detroit/2018/04/30/detroit-released-state-financial-oversight-3-years-after-exiting-bankruptcy/565500002/.

35 “Equally impressive”: “Nearly $7 billion in construction value” generated by the Chicago Riverwalk, since 2009: “2018 AIA Awards: Regional and Urban Design,” *American Institute of Architects*, https://www.aia.org/showcases/169351-chicago-riverwalk.

35 “Emanuel wanted to make”: Matt Urbanski, chief landscape architect for the 606, Michael Van Valkenburgh Associates, in discussion with author, Nov. 30, 2017.

37 “Bikers and joggers”: Ben Helphand, in discussion with author, Oct. 19, 2017.

37 “Tall evergreens”: Whet Moser, “The 606 Shows How to Design a Park in the 21st Century (and Beyond),” *Chicago Magazine,* June 5, 2015, https://www.chicagomag.com/city-life/June-2015/The-606-Park-Design/.

38 “Galvanized steel fences”: Urbanski, discussion.

38 “Planting on the 606”: Francis Whitehead, in discussion with author, July 8 and July 29, 2019.

38 “Despite the efforts”: Juanita Irizarry, in discussion with author, Nov. 1, 2017. Amita Sinha makes the same criticism in her article “Slow Landscapes of Elevated Linear Parks: Bloomingdale Trail in Chicago,” *Studies in the History of Gardens and Designed Landscapes* 34, no. 2 (2014): 113–22.

38 “tremendous (50 percent) spike”: Fran Spielman, “Aldermen Propose Hefty Fees to Stop 606 Gentrification,” *Chicago Sun-Times*, May 23, 2017, https://chicago.suntimes.com/2017/5/23/18358212/aldermen-propose-hefty-fees-to-stop-606-gentrification.

38 “Gentrification is also an issue”: John Bynorth, “Turning Derelict Land into Parks Proves Mixed Blessing in the US,” *Herald* (Scotland), June 26, 2017, 14.

42 “There is no visible threshold”: Carol Kekez and Mauricio Villarreal, in discussion with author, Feb. 18, 2020.

42 “Mauricio Villarreal asserts”: Mauricio Villarreal, in discussion with author, May 1, 2020.

HIGHWAY CAPS

45 “Lawrence Halprin”: Angela Danadjieva, “Seattle's Freeway Park II: Danadjieva on the Creative Process,” *Landscape Architecture* 67, no. 5 (Sept. 1977): 404–6.

45 “The Freeway Park Association”: Joel Moreno, “Night Walk Highlights Potential Danger Zones in Freeway Park,” *KomoNews.com*, Sept. 1, 2017, https://komonews.com/news/local/night-walk-highlights-potential-danger-zones-in-freeway-park.

47 “The year 2019”: Bill Hethcock, “Governor: DFW Engine Drives Powerful Texas Economy,” *Dallas Business Journal*, Dec. 13, 2019, https://www.bizjournals.com/dallas/news/2019/12/13/governor-dfw-engine-drives-powerful-texas-economy.html.

47 “Dallas and Houston”: Scott Beyer, “Dallas and Houston: Centers for Economic Development,” *Forbes.com*, July 26, 2016, https://www.forbes.com/sites/scottbeyer/2016/07/26/dallas-and-houston-centers-for-economic-development/#50c8b4086bea.

47 “At the time of the Winspear”: Amanda G. Johnson, “Developing Urban Arts Districts: An Analysis of Mobilization in Dallas, Denver, Philadelphia, Pittsburgh, and Seattle” (PhD diss., University of Pennsylvania, 2011).

47 “absence of a ‘town square’”: Sheila Grant, in discussion with author, July 20, 2019.

47 “glue and leader”: James Burnett, in discussion with author, Apr. 29, 2019.

51 “the villagers of Prinsenbeek”: Wim Hupperetz, “The Cultural Biography of a Street: Memory, Cultural Heritage and Historical Notion of the Visserstraat in Breda, the Netherlands (1200–2000),” in *Landscape Biographies: Geographical, Historical, and Archaeological Perspectives on the Production and Transmission of Landscapes*, Landscape and Heritage Research, ed. Jan Kolen, Hans Renes, and Rita Hermans (Amsterdam: Amsterdam University Press, 2015), 313.

52 “The dirt paths here”: Cor Geluk, in discussion with author, June 15, 2019.

AIRPORTS

57 “For air travel”: Sonja Dümpelmann, *Flights of Imagination: Aviation, Landscape, Design* (Charlottesville: University of Virginia Press, 2014), 81, 126, 144.

63 “A self-propagating ruderal landscape”: Jens Lachmund has argued that what we today call “urban ecology” originated in the 1950s in studies of ruderal growth in urban rubble: “Exploring the City of Rubble: Botanical Fieldwork in Bombed Cities in Germany after World War II,” *Osiris*, 2nd series, vol. 18, Science and the City (2003): 234–54.

65 “What we see in Bonames”: Michael Triebeswetter, email to author, Oct. 16, 2018.

69 “There is no dense urban”: Andrea S. B. Forsberg, “The Impact of Growth on Urban Form in the Oslo Region” (master's thesis, Graduate School of Architecture, Preservation, and Planning, Columbia University, 2016), 59.

75 “In fact, Tempelhofer Feld”: For the history of Tempelhof Airport and the effort to create a park in its place, I am indebted to Dr. Michael Krebs, then the director of Grün-Berlin, who guided Alex and me through the park on March 1, 2019.

WATERSIDE INDUSTRY: PARKS

83 “world's fourth most expensive”: Ainsley Smith, “Vancouver Ranked 4th Most-Expensive Housing Market in the World,” *Daily Hive*, Apr. 16, 2019, https://dailyhive.com/vancouver/vancouver-4-most-expensive-housing-market-cbre-2019.

91 “In 2011, the Waller Creek Conservancy”: “Timeline,” Waterloo Greenway, https://waterloogreenway.org/overview/timeline/.

94 “The project is a pushback”: John Rigdon, in discussion with author, Apr. 28, 2018.

103 “rugged”: Gary Hilderbrand, in discussion with author, Aug. 14, 2019.

111 “Desvigne compares the method”: Dorothée Imbert, ed., *A Landscape Inventory: Michel Desvigne Paysagiste*, Source Books in Landscape Architecture (Columbus: Knowlton School of Architecture/Novato, CA: Applied Research and Design Publishing, 2018), 58–60.

111 “We have to be vigilant”: Imbert, ed., *A Landscape Inventory*, 47.

112 “The landscape architect thinks”: Gilles Davoine, “Interview with Michel Desvigne,” in Portrait d'agence AMC (*AMC Le Moniteur architecture*, Nov. 2017), 16.

112 “my own [Bilbao] Guggenheim”: Alain Juppé, “Les quais sont mon Guggenheim,” interview by Bertrand Escolin, *Le Moniteur*, Sept. 7, 2012, https://www.lemoniteur.fr/article-les-quais-sont-mon-guggenheim.1400264.

117 “Landscape architect Margot Long”: Margot Long, in discussion with author, Feb. 16, 2020.

121 “The city's growth”: “Olmsted Park Study,” *Seattle Parks and Recreation*, Summer 2018, http://www.seattle.gov/Documents/Departments/ParksAndRecreation/Projects/Olmsted/OlmstedParksStudyFinalReport_October2018.pdf, 12.

WATERSIDE INDUSTRY: PARK SYSTEMS

126 “Transportation and communication”: Thaïsa Way, ed., *River Cities, City Rivers* (Washington, DC: Dumbarton Oaks Research Library and Collection, 2018), 3.

126 “Seventy percent”: R. Timothy Sieber, “Waterfront Revitalization in Postindustrial Port Cities of North America,” *City and Society* 5, no. 2 (Dec. 1991): 120–36.

126 "new cities": Sarah Moser, "New Cities," lecture, Morgan Library and Museum, New York, Oct. 7, 2019.
126 "since 1978, Shanghai": Jacob Dreyer, "Shanghai and the 2010 Expo: Staging the City," in *Aspects of Urbanization in China: Shanghai, Hong Kong, Guangzhou,* IIAS Publications Series, ed. Gregory Bracken (Amsterdam: Amsterdam University Press, 2012).
127 "then-mayor of Shanghai": Zhu Rongji, "We Must Be Determined to Treat the Upstream Pollution of the Huangpu River, July 26, 1989," *Zhu Rongji on the Record: The Shanghai Years, 1987–1991* (Washington, DC: Brookings Institution Press, 2018), 344–50.
127 "Sightings of sturgeon": Oliver Milman, "Hudson River Shows Signs of Rebound after Decades as New York's Sewer," *Guardian*, Mar. 28, 2019, https://www.theguardian.com/us-news/2019/mar/28/hudson-river-pollution-cleanup-new-york. Katie Rogers, "A Whale Takes Up Residence in the Hudson River," *New York Times,* Nov. 22, 2016, https://www.nytimes.com/2016/11/22/nyregion/humpback-whale-hudson-river-manhattan.html.
127 "such efforts have been": Shanghai Urban Sculptures Committee, 2017 Urban Space Art Season Main Exhibition (Shanghai: Tongji University Press, 2018), 282.
127 "By the same token": Shanghai Urban Sculptures Committee, 287; Emmanuelle Blondeau, in discussion with author, May 23, 2018.
131 "Once he had readjusted his focus": Herbert Muschamp, "Where Iron Gives Way to Beauty and Games," *New York Times*, Dec. 13, 1998, 2:35.
133 "Balsley compared them": Thomas Balsley, in discussion with author, July 16, 2018.
133 "The next decades will see": Sydney Franklin, "At Hunters Point South, a Popular Park Paves the Way for Housing" *New York Times,* Oct. 6, 2020, https://www.nytimes.com/2020/10/06/realestate/hunterspointsouth.html.
139 "The inception of Brooklyn Bridge Park": Joanne Witty and Henrik Krogius, *Brooklyn Bridge Park: A Dying Waterfront Transformed* (New York: Fordham University Press, 2016), muse.jhu.edu/book/46478.
139 "While the local community": Eric Landau, president, Brooklyn Bridge Park Corporation, in discussion with author, July 31, 2018.
139 "the groups reached a compromise": Laura Kusisto, "New York City's Parks Grow with Private Funds, But Some Question Wisdom of Such Funding for Long Term," *Wall Street Journal*, July 8, 2013, https://www.wsj.com/articles/SB10001424127887324507404578591893956006764.
139 "The well-to-do, predominantly white": Jake Offenhartz, "An Interview with the New President of Brooklyn's Most Controversial Park," *Gothamist*, Sept. 12, 2017, https://gothamist.com/arts-entertainment/an-interview-with-the-new-president-of-brooklyns-most-controversial-park.
141 "excessively wide": Michael Van Valkenburgh attributes the extreme width of this main roadway to Fred Kent, founder and former president of Project for Public Spaces, who insisted during the design phase that the road should link piers that he considered too distant from one another.
141 "Van Valkenburgh pointed out": The Squibb Bridge was designed by Ted Zoli to cross over the road opposite the salt marsh to connect the park with Brooklyn Heights; after recurring structural problems, it finally reopened in 2020.
142 "To create the marsh": These details are based on Anne Raver, "Here Comes Everybody," *Landscape Architecture*, Dec. 2018, 73–131, which also includes a description of the financial negotiations for the park and residential buildings, and the park's construction.
142 "the park received": Landau, discussion; Raver, "Here Comes."
142 "Making a park": Michael Van Valkenburgh, in discussion with author, July 19, 2018.
145 "undisputed candidate": David Koren, "Shanghai: The Biography of a City," in *Landscape Biographies*, ed. Jan Kolen, Johannes Renes, Rita Hermans, eds. (Amsterdam: Amsterdam University Press, 2015), 267.
145 "the US firms": Richard Marshall, "Shanghai's Waterfront: Presenting a New Face to the World," *Shanghai: Architecture and Urbanism for Modern China*, Seng Kuan and Peter G. Rowe, eds. (Munich, Berlin, London, New York: Prestel Publishing, 2004), 160–72.
145 "the master plan for the east": Blondeau, discussion.
153 "moving target": Adriaan Geuze, in discussion with author, Nov. 26, 2018. In fact, the two firms were given three years to complete the project.
157 "cradle of China's modern industry": Wang Ying, "Yangpu: A Transformation to Emulate," *China Daily,* Dec. 10, 2018, http://europe.chinadaily.com.cn/a/201812/10/WS5c0dd694a310eff30329010e.html.
157 "the industrial landscape": Wang Ying, "Yangpu."
157 "the aim was": M. Zhang et al., "The Prosperity of Cleaning the Shore: The Renaissance of the Waterfront Public Space in the South Section of Shanghai Yangpu Riverside," *Architectural Journal,* Aug. 2019, https://mp.weixin.qq.com/s/waQ488qOu8VicxMfivBC-A.

INLAND INDUSTRY

167 "To save on the costs": Dwight Law, email to author, Dec. 24, 2019.
169 "The Japanese colonization": Louise Young, *Japan's Total Empire: Manchuria and the Culture of Wartime Imperialism* (Berkeley: University of California Press, 1998), 248.
169 "Gotō Shinpei": Xiaofan Wu and Songjie Zhao, "Creating a Colonial Landscape: Park Construction in the Capital of Manchukuo (1932–1945)," *Studies in the History of Gardens and Designed Landscapes* 39, no. 4 (2019).
169 "Japan implemented": Young, *Japan's Total Empire,* 249.
169 "Sano Toshikata": Qinghua Guo, "Changchun: Unfinished Capital Planning of Manzhonghou, 1932–42," *Urban History* 31, no. 1 (2004): 100–117.
169 "SHUISHI, based in Shanghai": Principals of SHUISHI, presentation to author, Sept. 16, 2019.
169 "When the landscape architects": SHUISHI, *Breathing Landscape* (Shanghai: Tongji University Press, 2019), 25.
185 "Novartis is one of the world's": The history of Novartis and its site in Basel are described in *Novartis Campus: A Contemporary Work Environment; Premises, Elements, Perspectives* (Ostfildern, DE: HatjeCantz, 2009).
190 "Imbert states that the project": Dorothée Imbert, in discussion with author, July 12, 2019.
195 "Jiading is typical": Wade Shepard, *Ghost Cities of China: The Story of Cities without People in the World's Most Populated Country,* Asian Arguments (London: Zed Books, 2015), 5, 33.
195 "In 2017, over 56 percent": Benjamin Haas, "More than 100 Chinese Cities Now above 1 Million People," *Guardian*, Mar. 20, 2017, https://www.theguardian.com/cities/2017/mar/20/china-100-cities-populations-bigger-liverpool.
195 "residential ownership is expected": Youqin Huang, "Housing and Migration" (lecture, University of Pennsylvania, Philadelphia, Feb. 7, 2020).
195 "because there is no property tax": Alexandra Stevenson and Cao Li, "Empty Homes and Protests: China's Property Market Strains the World," *New York Times*, Dec. 30, 2018, https://www.nytimes.com/2018/12/30/business/china-economy-property.html.
195 "Owners do not rent": Shepard, *Ghost Cities,* 58.
205 "there is considerable scholarly opinion": Paul Avilés, "Seven Ways of Looking at a Mountain: Tetzcotzingo and the Aztec Garden Tradition," *Landscape Journal* 25, no. 2 (Jan. 2006): 143–53; Patrizia Granziera, "Concept of the Garden in Pre-Hispanic Mexico," *Garden History* 29, no. 2 (Winter 2001): 185–213.
205 "former industries located in the area": Mario Schjetnan G., "The Post-Industrial City: Growing Inward," in Felipe Correa and Carlos Garciavelez Alfaro, *Mexico City: Between Geometry and Geography* (Cambridge, MA: Harvard Graduate School of Design/Novato, CA: Applied Research and Design, 2014), 149–55.
205 "Our ignorance": Mario Schjetnan, email to author, Mar. 29, 2019.
206 "To avoid the expense": Mario Schjetnan, in discussion with author, Feb. 13, 2019.
206 "it was also the site": Michael Kimmelman, "Mexico City, Parched and Sinking, Faces a Water Crisis," *New York Times*, Feb. 17, 2017, https://www.nytimes.com/interactive/2017/02/17/world/americas/mexico-city-sinking.html.
211 "Mosbach proposed demonstrating": Unless otherwise indicated, all quotations from Catherine Mosbach are from her discussion with author, June 14, 2019.
213 "the basis of humanity": Mosbach and Agnès Daval, "De sol, d'air, d'eau sous photons/Of Soil, Air and Water Under Photons," *Projets de Paysage* 14 (July 2016).
223 "A master plan maintained": Wang Wenjing and Yuan Fang, "Detailed Regulations of the North District of Shougang Industrial Park Receives Official Approval," *Shougang News Center*, Nov. 17, 2017, https://www.wxwenku.com/d/103763782.
223 "much of the machinery": Zhu Yufan, in discussion with author, Sept. 15, 2019.

QUARRIES

228 "Hundreds of thousands of quarries": Urban planner Catherine McCandless estimates that there are approximately 25,000 mines for industrial minerals and 100,000 quarries for construction aggregates throughout the world. "No Longer Just a Hole in the Ground: The Adaptive Re-Use of Resource Depleted Quarries" (paper, Massachusetts Institute of Technology, 2013), http://www.mit.edu/people/spirn/Public/Ulises-11-308/Quarrying.pdf.

229 "Scholars believe": G. S. P. Freeman-Grenville, "The Basilica of the Holy Sepulchre, Jerusalem: History and Future," *Journal of the Royal Asiatic Society of Great Britain and Ireland* 2 (1987): 189.

231 "The tale is an apt source": Zhu Yufan, in discussion with author, May 20, 2018.

235 "The year 2014": Brooke Jarvis, "The Insect Apocalypse Is Here," *New York Times Magazine*, Dec. 2, 2018, 40–45.

243 "plans of Gothic cathedrals": Maggie Keswick, *The Chinese Garden: History, Art and Architecture* (Cambridge, MA: Harvard University Press, 2003), 9.

243 "A noteworthy difference": John Dixon Hunt, "Chinese Gardens at First Hand," *Historic Gardens Review* 26 (Dec. 2011–Jan. 2012): 12–16.

243 "traditional Chinese gardens": Charles Jencks, "Meanings of the Chinese Garden," in Keswick, 217.

249 "Yu's declared merging": Kongjian Yu, in discussion with author, Sept. 15, 2019.

249 "Urban runoff and polluted water": Thanks to the technicians in charge of test plots at the Shanghai Botanical Garden, who explained the process to us.

249 "The form is based": Alfred Schine, *The Magic Square in Chinese Cities in Ancient China* (Stuttgart-Fellbach: Axel Menges, 1996).

255 "Guangzhou is the manufacturing hub": "Greater Bay Area: China's Ambitious but Vague Economic Plan," *BBC News,* Feb. 26, 2019, https://www.bbc.com/news/business-47287387.

255 "The government's plan to link": Jiang Xu and Yanyan Chen, "Planning Intercity Railways in China's Mega-City Regions: Insights from the Pearl River Delta," *China Review* 14, no. 1 (Spring 2014): 11–36.

255 "long-held Chinese belief": Keswick, *Chinese Garden,* 181.

255 "this course avoids evil spirits": Keswick, *Chinese Garden,* 154.

257 "this look was favored": Yingyin Lu, principal, Palm Design, in discussion with author, Oct. 21, 2019.

267 "like a jungle": All quotations from Clayton Beaudoin are from his discussion with author, Feb. 17, 2020.

STRONGHOLDS

275 "It may have served": W. Jacobsen, "Lorsch Abbey," Grove Art Online, 2003, https://www.oxfordartonline.com/groveart/view/10.1093/gao/9781884446054.001.0001/oao-9781884446054-e-7000052014.

275 "likens the imprints": Barbara Steiner, ed., *Creative Infidelities: On the Landscape Architecture of Topotek 1* (Berlin: JOVIS, 2016), 180.

278 "The most 'dramatic situation' ": Steiner, *Creative Infidelities,* 173.

278 "convinced that the perception": Steiner, *Creative Infidelities*, 409.

282 "he professes to hate": Dorothée Imbert, ed., *A Landscape Inventory: Michel Desvigne Paysagiste,* Source Books in Landscape Architecture (Columbus: Knowlton School of Architecture/Novato, CA: Applied Research & Design, 2018), 48.

285 "The new park": Gerdy Verschuure-Stuip, *New Dutch Waterline and Arcadian Landscape; Guidelines for New Spatial Development Based on Heritage,* 2014, 2020, https://www.researchgate.net/publication/269776271_project_new_dutch_waterline_and_project_arcadian_landscape_guidelines_for_new_spatial_development_based_on_heritage.

285 "environmental Taliban": Adriaan Geuze and Christian Dobrick, in discussion with author, June 15, 2019.

FUTURE

303 "Michel Desvigne has said": Michel Desvigne, in discussion with author, Apr. 17, 2016.

305 "the project demonstrated": Karen Thompson, in discussion with author, Aug. 5, 2020.

309 "Sanlin Eco Valley will join": Wade Shepard, "No Joke: China Is Building 285 Eco-Cities, Here's Why," *Forbes*, Sep. 1, 2017, https://www.forbes.com/sites/wadeshepard/2017/09/01/no-joke-china-is-building-285-eco-cities-heres-why/. Jonathan Kaiman, "China's 'Eco-Cities': Empty of Hospitals, Shopping Centres and People," *The Guardian,* Apr. 14, 2014, https://www.theguardian.com/cities/2014/apr/14/china-tianjin-eco-city-empty-hospitals-people.

309 "The park . . . is energized": "Shanghai Sanlin Eco Valley," Tom Leader Studio Landscape Architecture, https://tlslandarch.com/portfolio_page/shanghai-sanlin-eco-valley/.

313 "The fifty-one-mile-long Los Angeles River": Blake Gumprecht, *The Los Angeles River: Its Life, Death, and Possible Rebirth* (Baltimore: Johns Hopkins University Press, 1999), 22.

313 "the city's burgeoning population": Background on the water supply to Los Angeles is based on William Deverell and Tom Sitton, *Water and Los Angeles: A Tale of Three Rivers 1900–1941* (Oakland: University of California Press, 2017), chapter 2.

313 "the question of how to control": Gumprecht, *Los Angeles River,* 173.

313 "Land along the river": Joseph Giovannino, "Just Subtract Water: The Los Angeles River and a Robert Moses with the Soul of a Jane Jacobs," *Los Angeles Review of Books*, Dec. 18, 2015, 6.

313 "the river's water level": Gumprecht, *Los Angeles River*, 18–22.

313 "an appeal to 'restore'": Lewis MacAdams, "Restoring the Los Angeles River: A Forty-Year Art Project," *Whole Earth Review* 85 (Spring 1995): 62.

313 "fiercely contentious restoration": Louis Sahagún, "Frank Gehry's Bold Plan to Upgrade the L.A. River Seeks to Atone for Past Injustices," *Los Angeles Times,* Jan. 11, 2021, https://www.latimes.com/environment/story/2021-01-11/frank-gehry-plan-los-angeles-river.

315 "conduit to other consultants": Frank Gehry, interview with Cathleen McGuigan (*Architectural Record* Innovation conference), Oct. 28, 2020.

315 "the river needs to satisfy": Tensho Takemori, Gehry partner, in discussion with author, Feb. 19, 2020.

315 "the MLA team proposed": Mimi Zeiger, "L.A. River Planners Float Three Design Proposals for a Major New Park," *Los Angeles Times,* July 17, 2019, https://www.latimes.com/entertainment/arts/la-et-cm-river-taylor-yard-park-design-proposals-20190708-story.html.

316 "as similar plans have": Tracy Jan, "A New Gentrification Crisis," *Washington Post*, July 31, 2020, https://www.washingtonpost.com/business/2020/07/31/ethnic-enclaves-gentrification-coronavirus/?arc404=true.

316 "planting in the riverbed": Army Corp of Engineers, Los Angeles District, *Los Angeles River Ecosystem Restoration Integrated Feasibility Report*, Sept. 2013, https://www.spl.usace.army.mil/Portals/17/docs/publicnotices/DraftIntegratedReport.pdf.

316 "vastly increase the amount": Ben Poston, "New Warnings about Risk of Major Flooding on L.A. River amid New Development, Revitalization," *Los Angeles Times*, October 17, 2016, https://www.latimes.com/local/lanow/la-me-ln-los-angeles-river-flood-zone-20161017-snap-story.html.

316 "bridge decks would be supported": All information and quotations from Mark Hanna are from his discussion with author, Mar. 3, 2020.

317 "Sometimes the river turned west": Vittoria di Palma and Alexander Robinson, "Willful Waters: Los Angeles and Its River Have Long Been Enmeshed in an Epic Struggle for Control," *Places Journal*, May 2018, https://placesjournal.org/article/willful-waters-los-angeles-river/?cn-reloaded=1.

319 "28 billion gallons": Hanna, discussion.

319 "reject the idea": Jessica Henson, in discussion with author, Feb. 19, 2020.

321 "ruins of engineering history": All quotations from Corner and additional information about Freshkills are from Corner's discussion with author, June 12, 2020.

321 "for that group": Ellen Ryan, in discussion with author, July 9, 2020.

322 "Field Operations' scheme": Anita Berrizbeitia, "Re-Placing Process," in *Large Parks,* ed. Julia Czerniak and George Hargreaves (New York: Princeton Architectural Press, 2007).

322 "70 percent of the cost": All quotations and information from Eloise Hirsh are from her discussion with author, July 15, 2020.

325 "a similar approach": Gilles Clément, *Manifeste du Tiers paysage* (Montreuil, FR: Sujet Objet, 2005).

325 "In an ecosystem": *The Third Landscape*, video, Canadian Centre for Architecture. https://www.cca.qc.ca/en/articles/issues/19/the-planet-is-the-client/32771/the-third-landscape.

326 "design for the 258-acre Brookfield Park": John McLaughlin, in discussion with author, July 27, 2020.

328 "It's like Kansas": Matt Urbanski, in discussion with author, July 1, 2020.

image credits

COVER
©Xiu Wang/SHUISHI

ENDPAPERS
Yan Shuo

FRONTISPIECE
Hai Zhang

WHY NOW?
8–9: ©Alex MacLean/Landslides Aerial Photography; 12–13: John Gollings; 16–17: Francisco Gomez Sosa, courtesy Grupo de Diseño Urbano SC; 20–21: MDP Michel Desvigne Paysagiste

DEQUINDRE CUT
26: Mark Wallace; 28 top: City of Detroit; 28 center, 31 top, 33 top: SmithGroup; 28 bottom: PixieMe, pisaphotography; 29 top: Julio Alberto Cedano; 31 bottom: Pravin Sitaraman; 33 center: Tod Hardin; 33 bottom: Michael Van Valkenburgh Associates

THE 606
34: Adam Alexander Photography; 36 top: ©Tom Harris; 36 center left: Cathyrose Melloan/Alamy Stock Photo; 36 center right: Daniel Hudson Burnham (Architect), Plate 111 from *The Plan of Chicago, 1909: Chicago, Plan of the Center of the City, Showing the Present Street and Boulevard System, 1909*; CC0 Public Domain Designation, on permanent loan to The Art Institute of Chicago from the City of Chicago; 36 bottom: ©Christian Phillips Photography; 37: Michael Van Valkenburgh Associates; 39 top: Soaring Badger Productions, courtesy The Trust for Public Land; 39 bottom left: Dr. Jorge Pinto, School of Math and Science at Chicago Public Schools; 39 bottom right: ©Alex MacLean/Landslides Aerial Photography

PRAIRIE LINE TRAIL
40, 42 top, 43 center, 43 bottom: Jeff Caven/ University of Washington Tacoma; 42 bottom: PLACE; 43 top: Cody Char/University of Washington Tacoma

KLYDE WARREN PARK
46, 49 top: Liane Rochelle; 48 top: Payne M. Wingate; 48 bottom, 49 bottom: courtesy OJB Landscape Architecture

PARK OVER-BOS
50, 53, 54–55: Juurlink en Geluk Urbanism and Landscape

XUHUI RUNWAY PARK
All images courtesy Sasaki; 58, 60 center, 61 bottom: ©INSAW Photography; 60 top, 60 bottom, 61 center: ©Sasaki; 61 top: ©Zhang Fan

ALTER FLUGPLATZ
62: ©Florian Machner, courtesy GTL Landschaftsarchitektur; 64 top: Friedrich, Caspar David (1774–1840), *The Polar Sea [Das Eismeer]*, 1823–1824, oil on canvas, 96.7 x 126.9 cm, Inv. 1051, Photo: Elke Walford, Hamburger Kunsthalle; 64 bottom, 65 top, 66, 67: courtesy GTL Michael Triebswetter Landschaftsarchitektur; 65 bottom: ©Kai Spurling, courtesy GTL Michael Triebswetter Landschaftsarchitektur

NANSEN PARK
68, 70, 71, 72, 73: ©Bjørbekk & Lindheim

TEMPELHOFER FELD
74, 80–81: Manuel Frauendorf, ©manuel frauendorf fotografie, courtesy Grün Berlin GmbH; 76–77 top: Holger Koppatsch, ©Holger Koppatsch, courtesy Grün Berlin GmbH; 77 bottom: Nürnberg Luftbild, Hajo Dietz; 78: ©GROSS.MAX. Landscape Architects/Sutherland Hussey Architects; 79: ©Hanns Joosten

RACE STREET PIER
84: ©Cooper Robertson/Delaware River Waterfront Corporation; 87 top, 89 top: ©Matt Stanley; 88 top: courtesy Edward Savaria Jr., New Communications, for Delaware River Waterfront Corporation; 88 bottom: ©James Corner Field Operations; 89 bottom, R. Kennedy for Visit Philadelphia

WATERLOO GREENWAY
90: Waterloo Greenway Conservancy/DPR Construction; 92, 93 top, 94–95: Michael Van Valkenburgh Associates; 93 bottom: Kyle Grist, dwg.

RENAISSANCE PARK
96, 98 bottom, 99, 100 top: John Gollings; 100 bottom, 101: Charles Mayer

LONG DOCK PARK
102, 108–9: James Ewing/JBSA; 104 top, 104 bottom, 105: courtesy Reed Hilderbrand; 104 center: ©Barrett Doherty; 106–7: ©Sahar Coston-Hardy

PARC AUX ANGÉLIQUES
All images courtesy MDP Michel Desvigne Paysagiste; 110: ©Mairie de Bordeaux and Thomas Sanson; 113 bottom, 114 top: ©Guillaume Leuregans; 115 top: Alex Pisha

HINGE PARK
116, 118, 119: PWL Partnership Landscape Architects Inc.

THE BEACH AT EXPEDIA GROUP
All images courtesy Surfacedesign, Inc.; 120, 122 bottom, 123, 124–25: Marion Brenner

MAPS
128, 144: Molly O'Halloran, mollyohalloran.com

HUNTER'S POINT SOUTH WATERFRONT PARK
All images courtesy SWA/Balsley and Weiss/ Manfredi; 130, 132 bottom: ©Singleton/SWA; 132 top, 136–37: ©Albert Vecerka/Esto; 132 center right, 134: ©Lloyd/SWA; 135 top: ©Wade Zimmerman

BROOKLYN BRIDGE PARK
138: ©Alex MacLean/Landslides Aerial Photography; 140 top left: Port Authority of New York and New Jersey; 140 top right, 140 bottom: Michael Van Valkenburgh Associates; 141 top: ©Etienne Frossard; 141 center: ©Scott Shigley; 141 bottom: Elizabeth Felicella; 143 top, 143 center: ©Julienne Schaer; 143 bottom: Lexi Van Valkenburgh

RIVERSIDE PARKS, PUDONG (EAST)
146, 148: ©Agence Ter; 149: YIYU Design; 150, 151: Design Land Collaborative; 152 top: courtesy Henderson Land Development; 152 bottom left: Alex Pisha; 152 bottom right: Zilu Wang; 154, 155: courtesy Atelier Liu Yuyang Architects

RIVERSIDE PARKS, PUXI (WEST)
156, 158, 159: Original Design Studio, TJAD; 160 top, 160 center: da landscape 大观景观; 160 bottom: Yan Shuo; 161: courtesy Atelier Liu Yuyang Architects; 162, 163, 164–65: Zhangyujianzhu, courtesy Original Design Studio

CULTURE OF WATER ECOLOGY PARK
All images courtesy SHUISHI; 168, 170 top right, 171 bottom, 175 top: ©Shuang Pan; 170 top left: courtesy International Center for Japanese Studies (Nichibunken); 172 top, 173 bottom, 175 bottom, 176: ©Xiu Wang

MASCHINENFABRIK OERLIKON PARK
178: Jacob Rope Systems, jakob.com; 180 top: NeuOerlikon, Marcin Ganczarski, 2012; 180 bottom, 181 top left, 181 top right: raderschallpartner ag landschaftsarchitekten; 181 bottom, 182–83: Michael Freisager, Switzerland

THE SQUARE
184: aerial view of the Basel Campus, Novartis HQ, Novartis AG; 186 top, 187 top: PWP Landscape Architecture; 186 bottom left: Novartis; 186 bottom right, 192–93: ©Christian Vogt; 187 bottom: Jan Raeber; 188–89, 191: Biondopictures

JIADING CENTRAL PARK
All images courtesy Sasaki; 194, 196 right: ©Sasaki; 196 left, 197 top: ©Xiaotao Gao; 197 bottom left, 197 bottom right: Yan Shuo

CULTUURPARK WESTERGASFABRIEK
198: Delphine Gidoin; 200: Gustafson Porter + Bowman; 201 top: C. van Eesteren and Th.K. van Lohuizen, General Extension Plan for Amsterdam, 1934, NAI Collection, EEST 1-84; 201 bottom, 202 bottom, 203 top: Thomas Schlijper; 202 top: Ben Bender; 203 bottom: Dilip Lakhani

PARQUE BICENTENARIO
204: Sergio Medellin, courtesy Grupo de Diseño Urbano SC; 207 left: courtesy Grupo de Diseño Urbano SC; 207 top right: Paul Aviles; 207 bottom right: courtesy Städel Museum, Frankfurt; 208, 209: Francisco Gomez Sosa, courtesy Grupo de Diseño Urbano SC

JARDIN BOTANIQUE
210, 212, 214, 215, 216–17: Mosbach Paysagistes

TAOPU CENTRAL PARK
218, 221 top: ©INSAW Photography; 220: ©James Corner Field Operations; 221 bottom: ©Holi Photography

CAPITAL STEEL WORKS PARK
222: Cai Guo-Qiang, Fireworks Project for the Opening Ceremony of the 2008 Beijing Olympic Games, 2008, realized in Beijing, August 8, 2008, 8:00pm, fireworks, commissioned by The International Olympic Committee and The Beijing Organizing Committee for the Games of the XXIX Olympiad [Ephemeral], photos courtesy Xinhua News Agency, https://caiguoqiang.com/projects/projects-2008/beijing-olympics/; 224, 225, 226, 227: All images courtesy THUPDI, Zhu Yufan Studio; 224 top: Li Bin and Lyu Hui; 224 bottom, 226 top left, 227: Chen Yao; 225: Li Bin; 226 top right: Ma Ke; 226 bottom: Siyu Zhu

QUARRY GARDEN
230, 232 top, 232 bottom, 233: courtesy THUPDI, Zhu Yufan Studio; 232 center: Hertha Hurnaus (architecture: AllesWirdGut); 233: Chen Yao

PARC DU PEUPLE DE L'HERBE
234, 237, 238 top, 239: ©Agence Ter; 238 bottom, 240–41: ©S. Parc, courtesy Agence Ter

ZHENSHAN PARK
242, 244 center, 244 bottom, 245, 246, 247: Kongjian Yu, Turenscape; 244 top: photo credit: Wiki Common user Peripitus

MEI GARDEN
248, 250, 251, 252: Kongjian Yu, Turenscape; 253: Alex Pisha

HUADU LAKE PARK
254: Qingjun Zheng; 256 bottom, 257, 258: Palm Design, provided by Yingyin Lu; 259: Zhenlun Guan

TANGSHAN QUARRY PARK
260, 262, 264, 265: Hai Zhang; 263: Z+T Studio

THOMAS C. WALES PARK
266, 268 bottom, 269, 270–71: Stuart Isett/www.isett.com; 268 top left: courtesy Seattle Municipal Archives, map #2333; 268 top right: Site Workshop Landscape Architecture

LORSCH ABBEY
274, 276 bottom, 277, 278, 279: ©Hanns Joosten; 276 top: ©Topotek 1

PARC DRÄI EECHELEN
280, 282 bottom, 283: MDP Michel Desvigne Paysagiste; 282 top: Univesitäts- und Landesbibliothek Darmstadt

FORT BIJ VECHTEN
284: Ossip van Duivenbode; 286: Dutch National Archives; 287 top: West 8; 287 bottom, 288, 289: Jeroen Musch

QIAOYUAN WETLAND PARK
290, 292, 293 bottom, 294: Kongjian Yu, Turenscape; 293 top, 295 bottom: Yan Shuo

FUZHOU FOREST TRAIL
296, 298, 299 top, 300, 301: LOOK Architects; 299 bottom: Elizabeth Joss, The Museum Times (www.themuseumtimes.com)

GRAFFITI PIER PARK
304, 306, 307: Studio Zewde, courtesy Delaware River Waterfront Corporation

SANLIN ECO VALLEY
308, 310, 311: TLS Landscape Architecture

LOS ANGELES RIVER REVITALIZATION PLAN;
LOS ANGELES RIVER MASTER PLAN
312: Citizen of the Planet/Alamy Stock Photo; 314 top, 317, 318: Studio-MLA; 314 bottom, 316, 319: LA River Master Plan 2020, LA County Public Works, OLIN, Gehry Partners, Geosyntec

FRESHKILLS PARK
320, 323 center right, 323 bottom, 324: ©James Corner Field Operations; 323 top: Andy Levin/Science Source; 323 center left, 326 top, 326 center, 330–31: City of New York, Department of Parks and Recreation; 326 bottom: Mierle Laderman Ukeles, courtesy the artist and Ronald Feldman Gallery, New York; 327: City of New York, Department of Parks and Recreation, courtesy James Corner Field Operations/©Alex Maclean/Landslides Aerial Photography; 328: Nathan Kensinger; 329: courtesy Michael Van Valkenburgh Associates

APPENDIX
332: SmithGroup; 333 top, 333 center: Juurlink en Geluk Urbanism and Landscape; 333 bottom: image courtesy Sasaki, ©Sasaki; 334 top, 335 bottom: Michael Van Valkenburgh Associates; 334 bottom: Hargreaves Jones Associates; 335 top three images: courtesy Surfacedesign, Inc.; 336: Design Land Collaborative; 337: courtesy Grupo de Diseño Urbano SC; 338, 339 top, 341 bottom: Kongjian Yu, Turenscape; 339 bottom: Site Workshop Landscape Architecture; 340 top: hg merz and Topotek 1; 340 center, 340 bottom: MDP Michel Desvigne Paysagiste; 341 top: ©Jonathan Penne Architecten/Rapp + Rapp, courtesy West 8; 342 top: Studio Zewde, courtesy Delaware River Waterfront Corporation; 342 bottom five images, 343 top: TLS Architecture; 343 bottom: ©James Corner Field Operations

Architectural historian VICTORIA NEWHOUSE has written extensively on the architecture of cultural facilities. She is the author of *Chaos and Culture: Renzo Piano Building Workshop and the Stavros Niarchos Foundation Cultural Center in Athens*, *Site and Sound: The Architecture and Acoustics of New Opera Houses and Concert Halls*, *Art and the Power of Placement*, *Towards a New Museum*, and *Wallace K. Harrison, Architect*.

ALEX PISHA is a landscape and architectural designer for cultural, academic, and civic projects. He has worked in design offices in the United States and Germany and has conducted research and fieldwork in China, Poland, Italy, and throughout Scandinavia.

First published in the United States of America in 2021 by
RIZZOLI INTERNATIONAL PUBLICATIONS, INC.
300 Park Avenue South
New York, NY 10010
www.rizzoliusa.com

Photography is credited on page 350.

Publisher: Charles Miers
Acquiring Editor: Douglas Curran
Production Manager: Colin Hough Trapp
Managing Editor: Lynn Scrabis

Editor: Andrea Monfried

Design: Office of Luke Bulman

Printed and bound in Singapore

2021 2022 2023 2024 2025
10 9 8 7 6 5 4 3 2 1

ISBN-13: 978-0-8478-7062-2

Library of Congress Cataloging-in-Publication Control Number: 2021017256

Visit us online:
Facebook.com/RizzoliNewYork
Twitter: @Rizzoli_Books
Instagram.com/RizzoliBooks
Pinterest.com/RizzoliBooks
Youtube.com/user/RizzoliNY
Issuu.com/Rizzoli